William Scully

Brazil

Its Provinces and Chief Cities: the Manners and Customs of the People

William Scully

Brazil
Its Provinces and Chief Cities: the Manners and Customs of the People

ISBN/EAN: 9783337425685

Printed in Europe, USA, Canada, Australia, Japan

Cover: Foto ©Andreas Hilbeck / pixelio.de

More available books at **www.hansebooks.com**

BRAZIL;

ITS PROVINCES AND CHIEF CITIES;

THE

Manners & Customs of the People;

AGRICULTURAL,
COMMERCIAL, AND OTHER STATISTICS,

Taken from the Latest Official Documents;

WITH A VARIETY OF

USEFUL AND ENTERTAINING KNOWLEDGE,

BOTH FOR THE MERCHANT AND THE EMIGRANT.

BY

WILLIAM SCULLY,

Editor of the "Anglo-Brazilian Times."

LONDON:
MURRAY & CO., 13, PATERNOSTER ROW.
1866.

The Right of Translation and Reproduction is reserved by the Author.

TO

HIS EXCELLENCY

SR JOÃO LINS VIEIRA CANSANÇÃO DE SINIMBÚ,

TO WHOM

BRAZIL IS SO LARGELY INDEBTED FOR HER

ADVANCEMENT,

THIS

Short Compendium of Brazil

IS DEDICATED BY

THE AUTHOR.

PREFACE.

BRAZIL has been visited at sundry times by many distinguished naturalists and writers, whose researches, published to the world, have become "household words" among all classes, and thus most readers of the present day are familiar with her flora, her fauna, her entomology, and her diamonds. Still these works, though most interesting and instructive, and enlivened by the most varied charms of style and eloquent description, do not in all things meet the requirements of the age, as they do not usually condescend to those details which, in these commercial days, are looked upon by many as a *sine quâ non* in a descriptive work. It is for this reason that the author, encouraged by the good wishes of many experienced literary friends, and possessing at his hand peculiar and valuable facilities for the undertaking, has ventured to fill up, in part, the void, and thus to make the public better acquainted with a country which has of late years made extraordinary strides in political and commercial progress, but which still remains to most a demi-savage, forest-covered wild, producing coffee, sugar, insects, gums, gold, snakes, and precious stones.

Therefore, avoiding ground already so ably occupied, and rarely indulging himself in divergence from the strict limits of his purpose, the author has condensed, systematised, and arranged the mass of private and official matter at his command into such a suitable form and size as he hopes may render this work, in the eyes of the statesman, the merchant, the seaman, and the agriculturist, a true and convenient guide-book to Brazil.

INTRODUCTORY CHAPTER.

A TRAVELLER without a guide-book is like a ship at sea without a compass, and must resign himself to being dragged about in the wake of a courier who, though perhaps long a resident, may yet remain perfectly ignorant of the manners and customs of the people, and of the points of interest in the country. The author, therefore, designs to give a succinct account, and a clear outline, of the different provinces, and of their capabilities, together with a skeleton tour through their capitals.

A man must carry knowledge with him if he desire to bring more home; but it is a lamentable fact that many persons leave Brazil, after a long residence in it, as ignorant of its grand sights, and of the laws, institutions, and habits of the people, as when they came; remaining, as is too often the case, prejudiced against what they had not even tried to understand.

One great requisite in a traveller is coolness of temper. Contrarieties will arise even in the best organised countries; and, in Brazil, where *espere um pouco* (wait a little), *ámantiã* (tomorrow), and *paciencia* (patience), are words in everyone's mouth, an easy-tempered man makes the best traveller. Therefore let your motto be "keep cool," and if circumstances absolutely require the *fortiter in re*, at least let it be tempered with the *suaviter in modo;* for the Brazilian is innately courteous, and, appreciating in a high degree the quality in others, will yield much more to the politeness and suavity of the stranger than could be extorted by the menaces of the Foreign Office.

Next to conformity with the manners and customs comes a knowledge of the simple coinage, and of the easy, terse, and beautiful language of the Lusiad and Brazil. Better than a thrice-filled purse will the traveller find this knowledge, and he should at least become familiar with his vocabulary, and with *vintens, pataques, testoēs,* and *milreis.*

Money offers but little difficulty, for sovereigns are legal tender at nearly nine *milreis* each (8$890), but the safest and most convenient mode of carrying money is by a letter of credit on some bank, whose credit stands so high as to be known and respected in every part of the empire.

Passports are necessary, and may be procured either from the Brazilian consuls, or from the authorities of your own country, but we recommend the latter in every case. The different members and the servants of a family can travel with the one passport if they be included in it. On arrival, it will be viséd at once by the police officer, and handed back to you on board. On wishing to leave Brazil you will have to advertise your intention for three preceding days, or procure some respectable person to become responsible for your debts and liabilities.

We advise all British subjects to call and pay their respects to the representatives of their country, whom they will find in general obliging and gentlemanly ; and, if in Rio de Janeiro, most valuable information may be obtained from the English consul there, Mr. Hunt, who is a perfect encyclopedia of useful and entertaining knowledge, and whose dicta may be strictly relied on, while, in case of any occurrence requiring his official intervention as a British consul, there is no man whose reclamations for redress are better attended to by the authorities of Brazil.

Could the intelligent English, Irish, and Scotch agriculturists, possessed of small capital, be induced to scale the confining walls of home-ties and prepossessions to come here to judge for themselves of the climate, the resources, and the capabilities of this vast and fertile empire, on which nature, in the collocation and accumulation of its mineral and agricultural wealth, seems to have smiled benignantly, and to have lavished with a munificent hand her choicest treasures, we think that few would be willing to leave the prospects which it offers to the enterprising and industrious farmer, whether in the pursuit of agriculture or of grazing—prospects far superior to those offered by Australia, New Zealand, or the United States.

It is too much the fashion with foreigners to make "odious comparisons" between Brazil and their own country. They may be perfectly conscientious in their belief, but, with the superficial knowledge they acquire without mingling with the natives, they become discontented, knowing nothing of the real kindness, courtesy, and hospitality of the people among whom they may be mere " birds of passage," and in their writings and conversation the temptation of a well-rounded period, or pointed sarcasm, often carries the day against their better sense of justice.

To no citizen of any country is it becoming to play the Pharisee, for in no country are the institutions and customs beyond improvement, or beyond criticism and detraction. There are many things in Brazil susceptible of alteration for the better, but strike a fair balance, and there are few countries freer and more prosperous.

The constitution and the laws are a reflex of the English. The Emperor is a highly educated gentleman, speaking most European languages; and as a monarch, is a pattern to those of Europe. The Empress is a lady, and a Christian, and she and her illustrious husband are easy of access alike to rich and poor.

The court and aristocracy of Brazil have learnt to carry their pride without offence, and there is a rising class which is rearing imperishable monuments of their zeal and patriotism in the promotion of just and salutary laws. Religious opinions of all kinds are respected, and though a Roman Catholic country, the Government pays Protestant clergymen for the benefit of the German emigrants.

The River Plate is a nest of petty republics constantly at cross purposes, and without any combined plan of material progress; Monte Vidéo, a state bankrupt in everything but oppression; and the other republics of South America, smouldering volcanoes, ready at any moment to vomit forth anarchy and bloodshed.

The laws of Brazil are far from perfection, but its constitution is upheld in its integrity, and gives a sufficient guarantee to every one of life and property. Foreigners are welcomed, and the people and Government endeavour by every means to encourage emigration; and, with the great facilities afforded, and the immense field for enterprise for industrious agriculturists, it is surprising that Scotch and Irish emigrants do not seek this country, where a life of more prosperity and of greater ease awaits them than can be realised in the United States, where the foreigner is despised, and where the frightful winter of an arctic clime exacts from the panting farmer excessive labour in a summer heat that is never experienced even in the hottest equatorial regions of Brazil.

Brazil, in truth, enjoys the finest, the most equable, and the healthiest climate that is found in any country in similar latitudes. Her soil yields everything that tropical and temperate climes produce; and, if there were but sufficient labour, she could easily become the source from which Europe would obtain, not only her luxuries and her comforts, not only the staples which feed her manufactures, the dyewoods, the indigo and the cochineal of her dyers, the drugs, gums, balsams, and resins of her druggists, but even the grain and cattle with which she nourishes her population.

BRAZIL.

THE IMPERIAL FAMILY.

THE present Emperor, Dom Pedro II., ascended the throne of Brazil while only five years old, his father, Dom Pedro I., having abdicated in his favour on April 7, 1831.

The ceremony of his coronation took place on July 18, 1841, and on September 4, 1843, he espoused the present Empress, Donna Theresa Christina Maria, aunt of the ex-king of Naples.

It is not too much to say that it is to the wise and vigorous administration of the present Emperor that Brazil owes her present rank among civilised nations, and the prosperity and tranquillity she has enjoyed for so many years in the midst of the continuous outbreaks against law and order which have desolated and ruined the unhappy republics that surround her. In achieving this great result the personal character and acquirements of the Emperor have been of incalculable service, as displaying a high standard of excellence, in manners, education, and morality, to which his courtiers and his people might aspire. Foremost and indefatigable in every project likely to advance the interests of his country, morally or materially, he has used the great powers entrusted to him by the Constitution, and the still greater acquired through the influence of his own character and talents, for the benefit of the people themselves, and not for the aggrandisement of himself or family, and it is no wonder that, imbibing his spirit and stimulated by his example, the public men of Brazil number among their ranks some of the most patriotic and large-minded statesmen to be found in the world.

His Majesty is accessible to all ranks of society, and ready to listen to any tale of distress. His annuity of 800,000 milreis scarcely enables him to obey the dictates of his heart in the distribution of his charity.

Nor in this beautiful characteristic is Her Majesty the Empress deficient, and the 96,000 milreis she receives annually is chiefly disbursed, not in the wasteful extravagance of fashion, but in the alleviation of poverty and sickness, she contenting herself in her dress with the elegant simplicity of taste without the ornamental jewellery and expensive modes of Paris.

The two princesses, one 18 years, the other 17 years old, have been very carefully educated by the most competent professors procurable, and under the personal superintendence of the Emperor, who, whatever his avocations, devoted an hour each day to their instruction in history and geography.

The eldest, Donna Isabel, is heiress to the throne, the Salic law not obtaining in Brazil, and great expectations are entertained from her well-known amiable disposition and natural talent. She was married on October 15, 1864, to Louis Gaston d'Orleans, Compte d'Eu, a grandson of Louis Philippe, who distinguished himself greatly while in the Spanish service during the last war between Spain and Morocco.

The younger sister, Donna Leopoldina, married Augustus, Duke of Saxe Coburg, a member of one of the richest and most illustrious families in Germany.

MANNERS AND CUSTOMS.

AMONG the various classes of which Brazilian society is composed, the nobility naturally claims the first attention. As the creation of a Brazilian aristocracy took place only after the declaration of independence in 1822, the length of their pedigrees is but short, and by a very wise and salutary law, all titles conferred on persons become extinct at their death, so that, in order that their heirs may obtain the same honours, they must render some public service which will merit the appreciation of the Emperor, whose selection is in conformity with all his public acts, and confers "honour only on those to whom honour is due." The nobility possess many amiable qualities. They are temperate, generous, charitable, attached to their sovereign, and courteous to their inferiors in society. Even when occupying the offices of Ministers of State, the affable manner in which they receive both foreigner and native, contrasts very agreeably with the assumed dignity and inaccessibility of the English placeman.

This is truly a pleasant characteristic of Brazilian officials, from the highest to the lowest; and even the Emperor, at his levees, denies access to none, receives petitions, and listens courteously to any requests or communications made to him by native or foreigner, usually speaking the language of the latter to him. At the office of a Minister of State, the applicant of any degree enters in his turn, is bowed to a chair, and is received as if he were conferring a favour rather than seeking one. If he is a foreigner, his native tongue is used in preference; his views are listened to and discussed, and when he takes his leave it is with a feeling that, even if not adopted, they will, at least, receive a full consideration.

The ladies, in their out-door life, usually attire themselves in the latest Paris fashions, and, on days of ceremony and celebrations, don their finest dresses and most brilliant jewellery. At home, however, they in general are seen in very plain apparel, employed industriously in some small domestic economy.

Many of the ladies are very attractive in their appearance and in their manners, but, as in all warm climates, their bloom is usually very evanescent, and after 25 they are apt to become very stout, a charm, however, which is not without the appreciation of their compatriots. Among them you cannot find the blue-stocking or the strong-minded lady, for in literary pursuits the Brazilian ladies take little interest, but they are in general skilful and devoted musicians of the Italian school.

The Brazilian gentlemen are remarkable for temperance and frugality, and for natural talent may compete with any other nation, but so much cannot be said of their industry. Some yield themselves up to the charms of literature and science, but most of the upper class are content with a monotonous daily round of existence, made up of many naps during the day, gapes over the balconies in the afternoon, and a réunion in the evening, with an occasional visit to the opera. In truth, the warm and mild climate predisposes to indolence, and the youth, after having passed through the ordinary course of a college education, or having loitered a few years with a private tutor, enters into public offices, or, sinking into domestic insignificance, fritters away his life in indolence, or in the endless frivolities of street perambulation.

In fact, a great want in Brazil is the out-door games, the debating clubs, the cheap concerts, the lectures, the periodicals, and all the various appliances which the European at home has at his command, to strengthen and improve both mind and body, and which would be of incalculable service to the youth of both sexes, in this delicious but somewhat enervating climate; and thus it is that the situation of the young Englishmen, sent out as clerks to the many English mercantile houses in Brazil, becomes most deplorable. Placed by their employers in a house with one or two negroes to attend them, and rigidly shut out from the society of their compatriots, by that snobbishness of English intercourse abroad (nowhere greater than in Brazil), which makes the tinker of kettles dread contaminating association with the tinker of saucepans, these, in many cases, gentlemanly young men, too often take refuge from the dreary monotony of their existence, and from their feelings of isolation in a foreign land, in all the excitement of immorality and dissipation.

The clergy, degraded by State patronage, and poorly supported by a scanty stipend, do not enjoy a lofty pre-eminence ; and are ill able to fulfil their sublime mission. Ecclesiastical preferments are often bestowed on worthless persons as rewards for services rendered not to God, but to Ministers of State, for exertions made, not in the cause of morality and religion, but in canvassing votes at elections ; and thus, the great weakness of the Brazilian Church is the thraldom in which it is held by the State, for the true Pope of Brazil is the Minister of the Empire. Still, though the religious feelings of the people have been in a great measure shocked and undermined, the attachment of many to the creed of their forefathers is undeniable. Unfortunately, also, the clergy, having no good seminary for their theological education, are generally ignorant, and their only mode of administering religious instruction is by the exhibition of gaudily dressed saints, paraded through the streets, and followed by a long procession of the priests and religious orders, and by every class of the laity, from the stately marquis to the humble negro. In the evening, the celebration terminates with a display of fireworks, and so ends a sublime religious ceremony, made ridiculous by its adjuncts.

Of course such a state of things should leave great room for the efforts of the missionaries, so freely furnished by the societies in England and the United States for the enlightenment of Roman Catholics; but, unfortunately, little benefit has been derived from the exertions of the missionaries, or from the tracts distributed to improve and direct the religious feelings of the Brazilians.

As regards the poorer classes of the Brazilians, the old saying that pride and poverty are first cousins is too true; for, rather than descend to certain menial and laborious occupations, they will beg, borrow, or live in starvation and filth ; while the less fastidious Portuguese, by habits of industry, lays up a provision for his family, and often rises to a respectable station in society.

The Brazilians show much courtesy and kindness to strangers who come among them ; and it is by no means a rare thing for them to voluntarily take a great deal of trouble to do them a service. In their intercourse with one another they are very sociable, but somewhat ceremonious. Even among the working-classes and the blacks, two acquaintances never meet in the street without an interchange of compliments. A negro, doffing his hat (if he has one), addresses his friend with—"Salveo Deos," or "Deos the dê bons dias;" then follows a full inquiry into the state of his health, and that of his family and relations; and on parting the compliments and protestations are regularly renewed. It is also the custom among Brazilians, when speaking to one another, to remove their hats, and to remain uncovered until desired to put them on.

In their receptions, whenever a stranger comes in, he is immediately saluted by every one present; and, if seated, they all rise to pay him respect. When receiving a visitor, the master of the house is not too proud to go to the door to meet him, with the most affable expression of—"Tenha a bondade d'entrar, a casa é sua," and ushers him into the room, himself following behind. On leaving the room, the order is reversed, and the host then precedes his guest. The parting ceremony usually begins at the top of the stairs, and consists ordinarily of an "Adeos" accompanied with a bow; the guest then descends a few steps, followed by the host; here take place a few more complimentary exchanges; and finally, at the door, the guest again turns round and salutes his friend, and a few more bows and polite expressions pass between them. On meetings, however, of more than ordinary interest—such as that of long absent friends—their mutual sympathy expresses itself in a warm and hearty embrace; one lifting the other fairly off the ground—a welcome rather embarrassing to an Englishman when first subjected to it. The salutations of ladies among themselves, both at meeting and parting, are not less ardent and affectionate; and are made on all occasions by a mutual profusion of kisses on both cheeks.

In personally addressing one another, the Brazilians pay great regard to distinction and rank, and, perhaps, in no other language are these so precisely determined. Every *fidalgo* must be addressed with *vossa excellencia*, and this term is extended to all persons holding high offices of Government. Bishops are similarly addressed; a simple clergyman is entitled to *vossa reverencia;* and all other persons of respectability to *vossa senhoria.* In speaking to ladies, *vossa excellencia* is the title given.

In epistolary correspondence, all persons entitled to *excellencia* are addressed *illustrissimo e excellentissimo senhor,* or, *illustrissima e excellentissima senhora donna,* if to a lady. All others receive *illustrissimo senhor.* In writing to a superior, etiquette requires you to sign your name at the very bottom of the page, and the superscription is generally placed at right angles with that on English letters. The name is preceded by the *illustrissimo e excellentissimo senhor,* or in accordance with the rank, and is followed by three etceteras, and, if occupying any high office, it is customary to put under the above, *dignissimo,* with his official title. If sent by hand, the name of the writer is placed at the bottom.

HISTORY.

BRAZIL was first discovered on April 22, 1500, by Pedro Alvares Cabral, who landing at Porto Seguro, took possession of the country in the name of the Portuguese king, Dom Manoel, in the reign of whose successor, Dom João III., the country was granted to twelve donatorios for the purpose of colonisation; they, however, being able to effect little, the grants finally reverted to the Crown, either by purchase or resumption. The Indian population, consisting of 160 tribes, offered great obstacles to the settlement, and during the absorption of Portugal by Spain, the Dutch possessed themselves, from 1624 to 1654, of the sea-coast provinces from the Maranhão to the S. Francisco. The immigration of the Portuguese Court, during the seizure of Portugal by Napoleon, gave a great impulse to the development of the country, but after the return of the King to Portugal, the dissatisfaction of the

Brazilians at their connexion with Portugal led, on September 7, 1822, to the proclamation of their independence, and Dom Pedro I., the son of the King of Portugal, was declared the first Emperor of Brazil; he granting the present Constitution enjoyed by the people. However, April 7, 1831, this monarch abdicated in favour of the now reigning Emperor, Dom Pedro II., under whom, after some outbreaks in various provinces, Brazil has settled down into its present state of peace and prosperity.

The *climate* of Brazil is remarkable for its general salubrity and mildness of temperature, though situated almost entirely in the torrid zone. This is due to the high elevation of the greater part of its surface, to the prevailing winds being from the sea, and in the south to the comparative narrowness of the continent. In the northern provinces the seasons are pretty regular, the winter being the rainy, and the summer the dry season; but in the southern and interior provinces much irregularity occurs, and the rains are sometimes more frequent in summer than in winter, while in some of the middle ones much injury is caused by frequent want of rain.

HISTORY.

Brazil lies between 4° 15' north latitude, and 33° 43' south latitude, and 34° 32' and 75° 3' west longitude. It is bounded on the north by the Atlantic Ocean, Guiana, and Venezuela; on the west by Equador, Peru, Bolivia, Paraguay, and Argentina; on the south by Argentina and Uruguay; and on the east by the ocean. It has a sea-coast of 1,200 leagues, is 765 leagues from north to south, 727 from east to west, and has an area of 280,460 square leagues.

The capital is the city of Rio de Janeiro.

The *surface*, with the exception of the provinces of Amazonas and Pará, and a strip of land along the sea-coast, is one vast, high, broken plateau, which, rising from the north and south, has its culmination in the provinces of Minas Geraes, Goyaz, and Mato Grosso, where are found plains and mountains from 2,000 to 5,800 feet above the level of the ocean.

From this ridge, excepting the Amazonas and its northern and more western tributaries, flow all the great rivers of Brazil, but all of which lying east of the Purús and south of the Amazonas have their navigation interrupted by the falls and rapids which occur in their courses, where they descend from the general plateau, into the lower lands of the north, east, and south.

The *mineral* wealth of Brazil is extraordinarily great, but remains undeveloped from want of capital, enterprise, and labour, almost the only receipts being from the gold and diamond washings, which, after yielding two tons of diamonds and eight hundred of gold, seem exhausted of their rich stores, and have been in a great measure abandoned. Most of the known metals and precious stones have been found, and iron, the most useful of all, is in great abundance throughout. Coal is in a degree deficient, for though immense deposits of lignite and valuable bituminous earth exist in the central provinces, true coal has been found only in those at the extreme south.

The *zoology* of the country is varied, though presenting nothing recent of great size. The principal animals are the jaguar, ounce, fox, tiger-cat, hyena, saratus, wolf, tapir, peccary, water-hog, porcupine, armadillo, sloth, ant-eater, monkeys, deer, and cutia. Among the great number of birds are the emu, or ostrich of the western continent, and many of note for their plumage, such as humming-birds of all sizes, parrots, ouira, aral, salian, and candidi. In the reptile class are many serpents, remarkable either for their poison, like the cobra and coral snakes, or for their size and strength, like the anaconda and boa; besides which are alligators, lizards, and turtles, great numbers of the latter existing in the rivers and sea, and giving, together with the abounding fisheries, employment to very many persons.

Insects are also very numerous, such as the herbivorous ant, sometimes an inch long, whose ravages in the plantations have caused the abandonment of districts in Espirito Santo, the timber-eating cupim or white ant, the visits of which are dreaded by every household, huge spiders living on birds, scorpions, centipedes, mosquitoes, and other minor plagues, bees of different kinds, some storing up sweet, and others sour honey, the silkworm, which feeds on orange and pines, the cochineal insect, fire-flies, and magnificent butterflies.

AGRICULTURE.

In Brazil, agricultural science is studied but by few, and by the few rather as an amusement than as a means, consequently no care is taken to preserve or renovate the ground. This may be deplored, but it is only natural. In Brazil, labour is dear and land of little value, and no manure can be as cheap as the soil of newly-cleared lands. Therefore, when a farm or plantation ceases to produce largely, a fresh attack is made upon the virgin forest, and with the aid of axe and fire a piece of new ground is made ready for the plant. Though ploughs and other farming implements have been introduced within the last six years, and are much used in some localities, in most places the preparation of the soil, planting, and cultivation of the crop are done solely with heavy hoes wielded by the labourers. Like the cultivation, the gathering and preparation of the crop are susceptible of great improvements, but the capital of most of the planters is sunk in the purchase of the needful slave labour, and many are obliged to hypothecate their crops long before maturity, in order to procure the sums requisite for their expenses. From these causes, and from the profits of planting being very great, the planters (with some honourable exceptions) are as a general rule content with their processes as they are, even though they may be aware of others by which not only the quantity but the quality of their products would be materially improved.

COFFEE.

This is the most important of the productions of Brazilian agriculture, as its export is equal to that of all the other articles united, and Brazil grows one-half of the coffee produced in the whole world. The profits of the culture of this plant have been so great as to have caused in some provinces an encroachment on that of sugar. The chief coffee raising provinces are

Rio de Janeiro, St. Paulo, Bahia, Ceará, and Minas Geraes.

The tree on which this valuable berry grows is an evergreen, commonly from 8 to 12 feet high, though oftentimes attaining a much greater altitude. When a plantation is to be formed the sunny slope of a hill is selected, the soil of which is not too retentive of the water falling on it. This, after being cleared and burnt off in the usual manner of treating timber lands, is planted over in rows, with year old plants, previously reared in a nursery. These receive little further care than to keep the weeds down, and to have the upward growth checked by pruning, so as to facilitate the gathering of the crop. In three years the trees are productive, and will in general continue so for upwards of twenty years. Its thick clusters of white flowers burst forth in abundance at certain seasons, but the dark green foliage is rarely seen unrelieved by them and by the fruit in all stages of maturity. This resembles a cherry, and the flesh that surrounds the bean is sweet and agreeable to the taste, but like the leaves, partakes of the flavour of the berry. The harvest is usually made twice in the year, at which time the fruit is collected and spread out to dry in the sun on a flagged floor, care being taken to frequently stir it up. When sufficiently desiccated it is passed through a rude machine, which separates the dried flesh from the bean, after which the tough membrane that encloses both parts of the bean is rubbed away by a similar machine, and the berries being winnowed are then ready for market.

From its strong flavour Brazilian coffee is improved by age, perhaps in a greater degree than any other coffee, and it is said if kept for ten or twelve years, would fully equal the best Mocha.

COFFEE.—Exports to Foreign Countries.

Years.	Arrobas.	Value in milreis.
1840–41	5,059,223	17,804,000
1841–42	5,565,325	18,396,000
1842–43	5,897,555	17,091,000
1843–44	6,294,282	17,986,000
1844–45	6,229,277	17,508,000
1845–46	7,034,582	21,307,000
1846–47	9,747,730	21,971,000
1847–48	9,558,141	25,159,000

BRAZIL.

Coffee.—Exports to Foreign Countries—*continued*.

Years.	Arrobas.	Value in milreis.
1848–49	8,600,032	21,513,000
1849–50	5,935,770	22,838,000
1850–51	10,148,268	32,604,000
1851–52	9,544,858	32,954,000
1852–53	9,923,983	33,897,000
1853–54	8,698,036	35,444,553
1854–55	13,027,524	48,491,003
1855–56	11,651,806	48,013,000
1856–57	13,026,299	54,107,000
1857–58	9,719,054	43,502,851
1858–59	11,169,241	50,138,253
1859–60	10,307,708	60,238,437
1860–61	14,585,908	79,663,552
1861–62	9,881,590	58,746,993
1862–63	8,724,142	56,574,935

SUGAR.

Sugar is one of the great articles of export from Brazil, forming about one sixth of the total value exported. It has not had the same rapid increase that, of late years, has been observed in coffee, and its culture has in some provinces even become stationary, owing to the preference given to the growth of coffee and cotton, which are, for many reasons, supposed to be more advantageous to the planter, as requiring less capital and labour. The cultivation of this plant is in general carried on in the most primitive manner, and, owing to the rudeness of the machinery, and the want of knowledge of the latest and most improved processes of manufacture, the quality of Brazilian sugar is, with some few exceptions of note, greatly inferior to that of other American countries. However, in this as in most other matters, the Brazilians are seeking to put themselves on an equality with other nations, and many enterprising planters are availing themselves of the latest improvements that machinists and scientific men have placed at their disposal. Sugar-cane can be grown in almost every part of Brazil, but is raised for export chiefly in the provinces of Rio Janeiro, St. Paulo, Bahia, Pernambuco, Parahyba, Ceará, Alagôas, and Rio Grande do Norte.

The larger planters usually manufacture only their molasses into rum, but many of the smaller planters use their cane for the production of a superior quality of rum and spirits, which are much prized and largely exported.

Sugar.—Exports to Foreign Countries.

Years.	Arrobas.	Value in milreis.
1840-41	6,698,392	11,892,000
1841-42	4,817,578	8,373,000
1842-43	5,209,721	9,998,000
1843-44	5,682,981	10,313,000
1844-45	7,476,287	14,325,000
1845-46	7,110,804	15,860,000
1846-47	7,098,843	14,782,000
1847-48	7,768,309	14,121,000
1848-49	8,305,659	15,879,000
1849-50	7,933,586	15,026,000
1850-51	8,907,852	15,779,000
1851-52	7,490,099	13,488,000
1852-53	10,681,344	18,232,000
1853-54	8,258,378	16,356,553
1854-55	8,193,137	16,679,191
1855-56	7,448,582	18,910,000
1856-57	7,670,430	25,845,000
1857-58	7,257,758	22,705,711
1858-59	10,664,245	27,656,863
1859-60	5,816,344	15,721,259
1860-61	4,528,756	11,055,679
1861-62	10.743,048	23,335,799
1862-63	10,121,719	19,281,027

Rum and Spirits.—Exports to Foreign Countries.

—	Years.	Canadas.	Value in milreis.
Average of the six years	1840-41 to 1845-46	2,526,200	507,650
Ditto ditto	1846-47 to 1851-52	2,503,373	588,080
Ditto ditto	1852-53 to 1857-58	2,709,501	1,006,260
Ditto of the four	1858-59 to 1861-62	2,143,431	752,711
	1862-63	2,995,186	819,231

COTTON.

Several varieties of this plant are indigenous to the tropical regions of Brazil, and it is supposed that the green seed cotton, so largely grown in the United States, was originally procured from Brazil. Cotton will grow, with little care, in every province; but its culture as an article of export was, until lately, almost confined to the provinces north of Bahia. At present it is grown in more or less quantities in every sea-coast province north of St. Pedro do Rio Grande do Sul.

The cotton of Brazil is good, and at one time the fine cotton of Pernambuco and its neighbouring provinces was the most highly-prized quality imported into England; but this reputation was quickly lost through the folly of the planters and exporters, who not only intermingled different qualities, but even mixed in damaged cotton. As far as soil and climate are concerned, Brazil possesses almost unlimited capacity for the production of cotton of all kinds, and, with the now increasing introduction of improved machines for ginning and packing it, it is probable that, instead of standing still as it had for some years previous to 1862, the production of this valuable staple will yearly increase until, perhaps, Brazil may become the greatest cotton growing country in the world.

Cotton.—Exports to Foreign Countries.

Years.	Arrobas.	Value.
1840–41	691,872	3,920$000
1841–42	639,580	3,224$000
1842–43	685,149	3,452$000
1843–44	814,255	3,650$000
1844–45	826,455	3,277$000
1845–46	645,346	2,912$000
1846–47	608,890	3,152$000
1847–48	639,288	3,588$000
1848–49	854,829	3,490$000
1849–50	1,109,313	5,679$000
1850–51	883,440	5,696$000
1851–52	898,249	4,288$000

Cotton.—Exports to Foreign Countries.

Whence Exported.	1852—1853.		1853—1854.		1854—1855.	
	Arrobas.	Value.	Arrobas.	Value.	Arrobas.	Value.
Rio de Janeiro	...	...	267	1,593$488	57	114$000
Bahia	69,211	386,809$287	14,636	80,720$831	23,792	131,280$169
Pernambuco	213,131	1,180,678$012	123,915	820,955$400	131,272	741,398$640
Maranhão	297,212	1,303,336$324	402,422	1,974,392$158	306,750	1,632,697$300
Pará	3,933	18,979$187	3,875	19,379$999	2,599	11,929$518
S. Pedro	317	1,106$200	35	63$000	340	612$900
Parahyba	185,266	962,997$604	133,879	766,425$609	193,665	1,019,154$992
Ceará	67,523	340,279$728	50,860	289,894$500	48,367	237,535$160
Alagôas	156,024	875,926$091	156,371	923,063$963	150,600	838,170$720
Sergipe	46	185$250	...	...	...	...
Rio Grande do Norte	5,244	24,034$273	1,875	9,843$642	10,517	49,514$479
Piauhy	...	...	4,137	15,758$620	6,217	24,176$372
Total	997,907	5,094,331$956	892,272	4,902,091$210	877,176	4,686,584$250

COTTON.—Exports to Foreign Countries—*continued*.

Whence Exported.	1855—1856.		1856—1857.	
	Arrobas.	Value.	Arrobas.	Value.
Rio de Janeiro...	...	...	32	315$188
Bahia	46,041	256,453$954	62,650	369,712$315
Pernambuco	111,607	633,273$980	153,708	1,082,907$629
Maranhao	292,020	1,618,887$775	267,823	1,710,806$511
Pará...	2,014	10,065$495	3,075	18,740$089
S. Pedro	...	...	...	...
Parahyba	256,495	1,338,887$917	289,593	1,845,323$130
Ceará	65,646	355,620$720	61,578	369,958$150
Alagôas	232,487	1,332,287$165	230,270	1,483,749$719
Sergipe	...	...	...	...
Rio Grande do Norte	11,451	60,100$994	11,229	66,974$909
Piauhy	7,040	29,374$840	8,067	41,915$873
Total	1,024,801	5,634,952$840	1,088,025	6,990,403$513

COTTON.—Exports to Foreign Countries—*continued.*

Whence Exported.	1857—1858.		1858—1859.		1859—1860.	
	Arrobas.	Value.	Arrobas.	Value.	Arrobas.	Value.
Rio de Janeiro	2	4$000	...	...	...	...
Bahia	18,671	149,372$925	9,361	67,356$324	9,279	70,137$171
Pernambuco	121,458	1,005,271$510	83,457	670,762$230	130,765	1,078,492$360
Maranhão	281,255	2,119,505$184	230,993	1,825,189$563	240,777	1,850,098$859
Pará	2,056	13,764$167	1,906	13,832$375	1,765	15,466$194
S. Pedro	...	...	...	...	...	...
Parahyba	188,741	1,458,270$832	156,151	1,193,443$736	221,557	1,654,107$000
Ceará	76,820	519,865$112	74,324	526,206$715	77,581	596,485$920
Alagôas	312,661	1,305,973$271	167,024	1,147,275$439	152,951	1,034,725$878
Rio Grande do Norte	6,970	50,776$559	12,008	80,609$975	12,094	76,347$061
Piauhy	5,916	32,517$443	16,124	99,420$360	7,855	56,711$500
Total	1,014,550	6,655,321$003	751,348	5,624,096$717	854,624	6,432,571$943

COTTON.—Exports to Foreign Countries—*continued.*

Whence Exported.	1860—1861.		1861—1862.	
	Arrobas.	Value.	Arrobas.	Value.
Rio de Janeiro...	...	...	...	...
Bahia	1,160	9,875$063	18,493	178,981$940
Pernambuco	79,586	624,825$626	116,718	1,207,864$057
Maranhão	207,954	1,440,827$967	210,259	2,062,360$057
Pará...	2,143	14,622$375	3,499	30,549$625
S. Pedro	...	...	4	7$200
Paralhyba	178,267	1,273,233$203	183,900	1,791,313$503
Ceará	58,728	419,810$372	50,785	470,479$800
Alagôas	130,443	823,251$281	273,397	1,914,947$821
Rio Grande do Norte	1,564	9,665$461	4,018	43,191$480
Piauhy	11,015	66,030$262	11,137	86,455$887
Total	670,860	4,682,141$610	872,210	7,786,151$370

COTTON.—Exports to Foreign Countries—continued.

Whence Exported.	1862—1863.		Average Prices.	
	Arrobas.	Value.	Years.	Value.
Rio de Janeiro	6,008	58,351$920	1852—1853	5$105
Bahia	45,814	729,730$204	1853—1854	5$494
Pernambuco	256,649	4,327,971$383	1854—1855	5$342
Maranhão	230,451	4,006,546$472	1855—1856	5$498
Paraltyba	201,899	3,021,124$036	1856—1857	6$424
Sergipe	31	372$000	1857—1858	6$559
Alagôas	283,200	3,738,808$389	1858—1859	7$485
Piauhy	6,436	87,611$159	1859—1860	7$526
Pará	4,886	79,333$937	1860—1861	6$979
Ceará	44,250	659,234$960	1861—1862	8$927
Rio Grande do Norte	5,514	105,694$520	1862—1863	15$495
Espirito Santo	490	3,026$200	1863—1864	21$693
S. Paulo	...	...	...	...
Total	1,085,628	16,817,808$180	...	...

No change in the Cotton. 1,971 bales, March 4, 1865.

TOBACCO.

Tobacco occupies the fourth place in the exports of Brazil. This plant was introduced in the beginning of the sixteenth century, and grows well in every part of the empire; but, as an article of export, is chiefly raised in Bahia, St. Paulo, Minas Geraes, and Rio de Janeiro. Brazilian tobacco is fine, but does not enjoy a reputation equal to that of the United States and Cuba; but this probably arises from want of care in the gathering and after-treatment of the crop. The growth of Minas Geraes is reputed the best in Brazil for all purposes, but is chiefly manufactured into twist, and exported through Rio de Janeiro to the South American Republics. The tobacco of Bahia is much esteemed in Europe; and the greater part of the leaf-tobacco exported from Brazil comes from that province.

Unfortunately many frauds have been committed in this article, and the Brazilian consuls have had to remonstrate frequently against the foolish practice of adulteration pursued. The Government has, however, interfered, and succeeded in considerably diminishing this practice by the regulations it has established. The cigars of Bahia are of good quality, and being looked upon as next to those of Havana, are in great request throughout the empire and the South American Republics.

Tobacco.—Exports to Foreign Countries.

Years.	Arrobas.	Value in milreis.
1711–12	220,000	344,650
1840–41	218,886	653,000
1841–42	342,310	907,000
1842–43	314,604	764,000
1843–44	292,844	772,000
1844–45	390,491	996,000
1845–46	290,339	968,000
1846–47	330,709	939,000
1847–48	323,841	747,000
1848–49	236,290	893,000
1849–50	346,522	1,051,000
1850–51	490,508	1,703,000
1851–52	566,113	1,794,000
1852–53	412,825	1,169,000
1853–54	680,151	2,101,370
1854–55	681,230	2,028,160
1855–56	526,366	2,075,000
1856–57	602,268	3,438,000
1857–58	302,278	2,372,000
1858–59	563,399	3,046,636
1859–60	685,414	4,022,455
1860–61	314,950	2,382,567
1861–62	777,922	4,878,619
1862–63	1,140,467	6,202,010

CAOUTCHOUC, OR GUM ELASTIC.

The Indian rubber of Brazil is procured from a tree indigenous in many parts of Brazil, but is found in especial abundance in the great forests of the valley of the Amazonas, where it forms large woods, and, consequently, from Amazonas and Pará is sent almost all the caoutchouc exported from Brazil. In those provinces the collection is mostly effected by the half-domesticated Indians, called Tapuios, who stipulate with the owners of the lands, giving them one-fourth of the gum elastic gathered.

The process is very simple. After procuring a large number of clay cups, which the Indians themselves manufacture and burn, one man goes along with a small hatchet chopping into the trees, while another, who follows with the cups, places one beneath each incision. Four hours afterwards they return to collect the juice, which, when first drawn, looks like milk both in colour and liquidity, but after a time the caoutchouc separates, and slowly solidifies into an opaque whitish substance.

The bottles and other small articles, which are sometimes exported, are formed on clay moulds, which are dipped repeatedly into the liquid until coated with a sufficient thickness, each layer being dried in the sun or over a gentle fire, the smoke in the latter case giving them a dark colour. When dry the mould is broken and the pieces extracted.

Within the last fifteen years this trade has become greatly developed, and gum elastic is now the fifth in rank among the exports of Brazil.

CAOUTCHOUC.—Exports to Foreign Countries.

Years.	Arrobas.	Value in milreis.
1840-41	25,344	198,200
1841-42	35,986	296,200
1842-43	19,805	104,300
1843-44	24,320	136,400
1844-45	24,988	149,600
1845-46	26,833	153,700
1846-47	35,469	178,000
1847-48	48,701	220,900
1848-49	51,547	257,400
1849-50	59,878	375,000
1850-51	94,998	1,046,600

CACAO, OR COCOA. 37

CAOUTCHOUC—Exports to Foreign Countries—*continued.*

Years.	Arrobas.	Value in milreis.
1851–52	107,007	861,600
1852–53	109,619	1,407,800
1853–54	157,420	3,571,348
1854–55	195,285	2,830,545
1855–56	144,677	2,278,130
1856–57	111,908	1,596,219
1857–58	109,344	1,243,360
1858–59	116,355	1,844,522
1859–60	172,310	3,419,038
1860–61	167,021	2,910,531
1861–62	152,520	2,438,159
1862–63	208,513	3,275,913

CACÁO, OR COCOA.

This bean, from which chocolate is prepared, is the seed of an evergreen tree, growing about twelve to twenty feet high. The fruit resembles a short thick cucumber, and contains a number of the seeds enclosed in a pulp, somewhat like that of a water-melon, which is frequently used for food and sweetmeats. The tree is indigenous in Pará, being found in great abundance on the banks of the great rivers of that province, and from Pará come five-sixths of the exports from Brazil. It is, besides, grown to some extent in Bahia, and, in a trifling degree, in

Maranhão and in Rio de Janeiro, but, requiring little labour and capital, is well worthy of more attention.

The mode of forming a plantation is, after having cleared and burned off the suitable land near the bank of a river, small holes are made in the ground and a seed placed in each, and, in order to keep down weeds and to shelter the young plants from the sun and winds, banana trees are planted throughout the cocoa grounds.

At the end of three years the cocoa tree is well grown and productive of fruit. These are ripe about June and December, and are knocked off the trees with the aid of long forks. They are then piled in heaps on the ground, or under sheds, and are allowed to ferment for three or four days, after which they are cut open and the beans removed, which are spread on the ground, or on mats, to dry.

HERVA MATE.

CACÁO.—Exports to Foreign Countries.

Years.	Arrobas.	Value in milreis.
1840–41	139,249	385,000
1841–42	182,282	467,000
1842–43	151,526	370,000
1843–44	189,749	432,000
1844–45	132,755	351,000
1845–46	199,816	541,000
1846–47	205,749	541,000
1847–48	161,015	469,000
1848–49	251,682	577,000
1849–50	282,260	657,000
1850–51	262,670	581,000
1851–52	291,361	554,000
1852–53	229,986	492,000
1853–54	316,251	787,321
1854–55	147,901	418,659
1855–56	164,283	618,000
1856–57	240,448	1,476,000
1857–58	246,409	1,655,815
1858–59	276,938	1,320,119
1859–60	246,460	1,456,276
1860–61	270,974	1,681,079
1861–62	232,555	1,442,059
1862–63	313,152	1,578,937

HERVA MATÉ

(Yerba-Maté, Jesuits' or Paraguayan Tea).

The tree from which this tea, so much used by the inhabitants of the southern South American republics, is prepared, is a species of holly growing wild in the state of Paraguay and in the Brazilian provinces of Paraná and St. Pedro do Rio Grande. The natives of the countries where it is used ascribe to it many valuable medicinal qualities, and it certainly possesses, like opium, the double effect of soothing the nerves and stimulating the spirits.

At first Europeans do not like it, it having a herby and somewhat bitter taste, but among the inhabitants of the southern republics it is a much-prized article of luxury and necessity, and is the first thing offered by them to their visitors; indeed, their tables are rarely seen unoccupied by it, and the *gaucho* of the plains will travel on horseback for weeks, asking no better fare than dried beef washed down by copious draughts of maté. The demand being thus great and increasing, there is, unfortunately, continually going on a rapid destruction of the tree. The Jesuits foreseeing this started large plantations in Paraguay, and at their branch missions in the provinces of Paraná and St. Pedro do Rio Grande, some of which still exist, and furnish the best tea made; and of late years some of the land-owners, sensible

HERVA MATE.

of the short-sighted policy pursued, have established many plantations with the best results, as the quality of the tea improves with the cultivation of the tree.

The manufacture is very simple, and is thus conducted. At the proper season the leafy twigs are gathered and spread on scaffolds, under which slow fires are maintained until the twigs are sufficiently dry to be easily pulverised. After being pounded in rude wooden mortars the tea is forced into bags of raw hide, which are carefully sewn up; and contracting in drying still further compresses it into an almost solid mass.

This tea is mostly used without milk or sugar, and on account of its being in powder, the infusion is sucked up through a small tube having a strainer at the end; but in the province of Paraná another kind is manufactured from the leaves alone, and these being left unpulverised it is used in the same way as Chinese tea.

HERVA MATÉ.—Exports to Foreign Countries.

Years.	Arrobas.	Value in milreis.
1840–41	181,365	289,500
1841–42	161,475	272,700
1842–43	168,651	313,900
1843–44	161,404	317,600
1844–45	202,022	381,400
1845–46	173,853	362,300
1846–47	204,009	379,600
1847–48	311,238	590,200
1848–49	381,251	719,400
1849–50	380,808	651,100
1850–51	347,099	570,700
1851–52	497,929	890,900
1852–53	322,582	554,300
1853–54	472,683	851,292
1854–55	406,682	857,186
1855–56	465,421	1,785,500
1856–57	517,728	2,637,700
1857–58	404,271	2,304,066
1858–59	475,624	1,749,335
1859–60	579,293	2,115,043
1860–61	544,108	1,673,144
1861–62	467,704	1,404,376
1862–63	605,179	1,514,781

FARINHA DE MANDIOCA, OR CASSAVA, AND TAPIOCA.

These are prepared from the mandioca, which is the starchy root of a small shrub about six to eight feet high, largely cultivated for this purpose in Brazil. The root of the Brazilian species is sometimes 30 pounds in weight, and differs from the other known varieties by containing a very poisonous and acrid bitter juice. In preparing this root for food it is first well washed, and is then scraped or grated to a pulp, which is thoroughly pressed to remove the poisonous juice, and is afterwards dried. This is the farinha de mandioca, or cassava, a common food of the Brazilians. The pure and fine starch that settles from the expressed juice is well washed with cold water, and, when dried, forms the substance known as tapioca. Farinha de mandioca in its crude state is often seen on Brazilian tables, but is more frequently mixed with water and baked in thin cakes—in this state forming the ordinary bread of the poorer classes. It thus forms a nourishing and cheap food, and it is to be regretted that in Europe the vendors should palm off potato-starch, and other similar substances, for the more delicate and agreeable cassava and tapioca.

TABLE showing the Average Price, the Value, and the
Countries from the

Articles.	Years.	Average Price.	RIO DE Value.
Spirits	1858–59	448	200,008$590
	1859–60	429	145,111$771
	1860–61	633	64,931$880
	1861–62	367	170,845$660
	1862–63	302	242,209$960
Cotton	1858–59	...	...
	1859–60	...	...
	1860–61	...	...
	1861–62	...	...
	1862–63	9,712	58,351$920
Sugar (white)	1858–59	3,907	367,973$016
	1859–60	4,297	200,139$523
	1860–61	5,238	206,910$137
	1861–62	3,554	408,506$850
	1862–63	3,676	173,701$430
Sugar (brown)	1858–59	2,720	1,474,784$742
	1859–60	3,437	429,757$000
	1860–61	3,193	279,593$958
	1861–62	2,461	1,368,706$460
	1862–63	2,500	1,003,854$860
Coffee	1858–59	4,539	45,269,413$412
	1859–60	5,986	51,319,178$394
	1860–61	5,508	71,908,314$515
	1861–62	5,896	48,124,558$670
	1862–63	6,576	45,324,110$000
Hides (salt)	1858–59	5,864	201,284$000
	1859–50	7,478	370,122$400

Quantities of the Chief Articles Exported to Foreign Principal Ports.

JANEIRO.			BAHIA.	
Quantities.	Average Price.	Value.		Quantities.
can. 437,130	269	419,398$390	can.	1,555,059
,, 338,347	337	130,247$200	,,	385,675
,, 102,583	413	328,239$149	,,	793,636
,, 465,091	263	479,827$381	,,	1,826,259
,, 806,689	250	387,304$796	,,	1,511,871
...	7,915	67,356$324	arr.	9,361
...	7,588	70,137$171	,,	9,279
...	8,513	9,875$063	,,	1,160
...	9,678	178,981$940	,,	18,493
arr. 6,008	15,928	729,730$204	,,	45,814
,, 94,173	2,999	2,190,029$730	,,	730,012
,, 46,573	3,351	652,087$165	,,	194,562
,, 39,495	2,245	2,697,102$675	,,	1,201,363
,, 114,929	2,657	2,507,563$498	,,	943,722
,, 47,244	2,567	1,991,952$616	,,	775,971
,, 542,077	2,528	6,591,852$729	,,	2,607,006
,, 125,026	2,794	2,227,495$007	,,	797,044
,, 87,548	...	...		...
,, 556,167	1,951	5,197,127$916	,,	2,662,779
,, 401,541	1,647	4,942,407$509	,,	3,000,464
,, 9,972,347	3,989	933,168$794	,,	233,904
,, 8,573,063	5,121	1,001,812$292	,,	195,638
,, 13,054,061	5,099	1,011,074$414	,,	198,304
,, 8,162,195	5,678	1,126,125$526	,,	198,313
,, 6,891,872	6,160	1,762,940$318	,,	286,167
n°. 34,324	6,708	271,969$130	,,	40,541
,, 49,629	8,358	329,562$722	,,	39,428

Table showing the Average Price, the Value, and the Countries from the

Articles.	Years.	Average Price.	RIO DE Value.
Hides (salt)	1860-61	7,892	251,340$000
	1861-62	8,000	272,124$000
	1862-63	7,990	340,688$000
Hides (dry)	1858-59	11,841	382,820$300
	1859-60	11,649	123,986$380
	1860-61	10,803	192,123$760
	1861-62	10,338	266,898$700
	1862-63	8,351	112,317$450
Diamonds	1858-59	300,000	1,506,450$000
	1859-60	300,000	1,535,700$000
	1860-61	427,480	2,506,320$000
	1861-62	500,000	2,878,198$200
	1862-63	354,193	2,468,725$400
Tobacco (in leaf)	1858-59	...	...
	1859-60	...	...
	1860-61	...	...
	1861-62	...	...
	1862-63	...	...
Tobacco (in twist)	1858-59	9,576	581,051$149
	1859-60	10,108	667,761$559
	1860-61	12,969	837,449$127
	1861-62	8,248	473,507$000
	1862-63	7,542	688,706$709
Gold in dust and bar.	1858-59	3,617	797,251$210
	1859-60	3,640	1,364,463$046
	1860-61	3,645	1,628,992$970
	1861-62	3,595	2,121,349$300
	1862-63	3,869	766,177$300

Quantities, of the Chief Articles Exported to Foreign Principal Ports—*continued*.

JANEIRO.		Average Price.	Value.	BAHIA.	
Quantities.				Quantities.	
n°.	31,833	5,800	752,288$997	n°.	129,702
,,	34,013	6,695	235,098$040	,,	35,111
,,	42,636	4,636	224,065$700	,,	48,329
arr.	32,329	8,808	293,996$845	arr.	33.375
,,	10,643	9,980	397,649$184	,,	39,844
,,	17,784	...	...		...
,,	25,815	6,525	360,112$156	,,	55,182
,,	13,449	6,199	209,556$600	,,	33,806
oit.	5,021	300,000	1,536,600$000	oit.	5,122
,,	5,119	300,000	1,596,300$000	,,	5,321
,,	5,863	308,700	1,265,700$000	,,	4,100
,,	5.756	300,000	1,356,900$000	,,	4,523
,,	6,970	300,739	1,647,450$000	,,	5,478
	...	5,177	1,971,773$243	arr.	380,811
	...	5,419	2,768,975$251	,,	510,929
	...	6,176	1,538.986$612	,,	249,179
	...	6,487	3,933,279$978	,,	606,322
	...	5,183	5,372,666$099	,,	1,036,598
arr.	60,674	3,975	449,143$975	,,	112,980
,,	66,060	5,407	576,514$050	,,	106,625
,,	64,571	...	...		...
,,	57,408	4,512	465,615$190	,,	113,192
,,	91,314	...	...		...
oit.	220,362	3,600	43,213$150	oit.	12,003
,,	374,780	3,600	37,567$600	,,	10,435
,,	446,794	...	...		...
,,	590,070	...	...		...
,,	197,984	...	...		...

48

Table showing the Average Price, the Value, and the Countries from the

Articles.	Years.
Spirits...	1858–59 1859–60 1860–61 1861–62 1862–63
Cotton...	1858–59 1859–60 1860–61 1861–62 1862–63
Sugar (white)	1858–59 1859–60 1860–61 1861–62 1862–63
Sugar (brown)	1858–59 1859–60 1860–61 1861–62 1862–63
Coffee...	1858–59 1859–60 1860–61 1861–62 1862–63
Hides (salt)	1858–59 1859–60

Quantities of the Chief Articles Exported to Foreign Principal Ports—*continued.*

PERNAMBUCO.

Average Price.	Value.	Quantities.	
360	217,038$019	can.	602,682
394	281,635$640	,,	714,443
445	204,273$460	,,	458,476
351	172,318$120	,,	491,033
275	145,877$620	,,	529,222
8$037	670,762$230	arr.	83,457
8$247	1,078,492$360	,,	130,765
7$851	624,825$626	,,	79,586
10$348	1,207,864$057	,,	116,718
16$861	4,327,974$383	,,	256,649
3$489	4,502,777$048	,,	1,290,393
4$312	2,947,954$880	,,	683,636
3$656	2,133,400$096	,,	583,419
3$061	3,915,434$149	,,	1,279,056
2$967	2,955,089$230	,,	995,847
2$455	7,950,383$304	,,	3,238,323
2$669	5,705,509$800	,,	2,220,346
2$308	3,720,874$331	,,	1,611,715
2$040	6,331,186$261	,,	3,103,242
1$796	4,297,565$926	,,	2,391,858
5$334	1,867$144	,,	350
6$831	2,951$100	,,	432
7$298	1,043$647	,,	143
5$622	3,643$435	,,	648
7$864	1,698$702	,,	216
6$537	552,032$648	n°.	84,443
7$726	850,845$020	,,	110,118

E

50

Table showing the Average Price, the Value, and the Countries from the

Articles.	Years.
Hides (salt)	1860–61 1861–62 1862–63
Hides (dry)	1858–59 1859–60 1860–61 1861–62 1862–63
Diamonds	1858–59 1859–60 1860–61 1861–62 1862–63
Tobacco (in leaf)	1858–59 1859–60 1860–61 1861–62 1862–63
Tobacco (in twist)	1858–59 1859–60 1860–61 1861–62 1862–63
Gold in dust and bar	1858–59 1859–60 1860–61 1861–62 1862–63

Quantities of the Chief Articles Exported to Foreign Principal Ports—*continued*.

PERNAMBUCO.

Average Price.	Value.	Quantities.	
6$674	582,840$932	n°.	87,321
5$184	570,911$130	,,	110,122
4$577	471,114$899	,,	102,919
6$605	1,347$529	arr.	204
12$622	19,186$240	,,	1,520
9$688	32,213$540	,,	3,325
6$207	7,784$040	,,	1,254
4$525	29,437$150	,,	6,505
...	..	...	
...	..	...	
...	...	...	
...	...	...	
3$500	297$500	oit.	35
...	...	...	
3$603	1,447$200	,,	402

E 2

Table showing the Average Price, the Value, and the
Countries from the

Articles.	Years.	MARANHAO.	
		Average Price.	Value.
Cotton	1858–59	7$901	1,825,189$577
	1859–60	7$684	1,850,098$859
	1860–61	6$928	1,440,827$967
	1861–62	9$808	2,062,360$057
	1862–63	17$385	4,006,546$472
Hair	1858–59	...	...
	1859–60	...	...
	1860–61	...	...
	1861–62	...	...
	1862–63	...	...
Cocoa	1858–59	...	...
	1859–60	...	...
	1860–61	...	...
	1861–62	...	...
	1862–63	...	...
Hides (salt)	1858–59	7$208	310,563$460
	1859–60	8$566	372,648$110
	1860–61	7$294	341,219$316
	1861–62	5$561	235,934$800
	1862–63	5$672	288,160$730
Hides (dry)	1858–59	...	...
	1859–60	...	...
	1860–61	...	...
	1861–62	...	...
	1862–63	...	...

Quantities of the Chief Articles Exported to Foreign Principal Ports—*continued*.

MARANHAO.			PARA.	
Quantities.	Average Price.	Value.	Quantities.	
arr. 230,993	7$260	15,832$375	arr.	1,906
,, 240,777	8$762	15,466$494	,,	1,765
,, 207,954	6$823	14,622$375	,,	2,143
,, 210,259	8$445	29,549$625	,,	3,499
,, 230,451	16$237	79,333$937	,,	4,880
...	...	...	...	
...	...	...	...	
...	...	...	...	
...	...	...	...	
...	...	...	...	
...	4$801	1,180,954$038	,,	245,938
...	5$943	1,286,505$984	,,	216,460
...	6$233	1,475,799$029	,,	236,762
...	6$230	1,265,743$483	,,	203,155
...	5$495	1,369,531$273	,,	263,611
arr. 43,083	3$848	177,037$085	,,	46,000
,, 43,502	4$829	201,563$755	,,	41,753
,, 46,781	5$153	116,584$220	,,	22,622
,, 42,423	3$888	98,501$080	,,	25,333
,, 50,801	2$792	106,546$130	,,	38,151
...	3$515	164,391$750	n°.	46,761
...	2$552	367,232$408	,,	143,860
...	4$198	153,868$600	,,	36,645
...	3$666	290,626$520	,,	54,721
...	2$924	120,338$760	,,	41,141

Table showing the Average Price, the Value, and the Quantities of the Chief Articles Exported to Foreign Countries from the Principal Ports—*continued.*

Articles.	Years.	PARA.		
		Average Price.	Value.	Quantities.
Gum Elastic	1858–59	16$165	1,880,921$288	arr. 116,354
	1859–60	19$952	3,402,335$253	,, 170,522
	1860–61	17$432	2,863,946$576	,, 164,235
	1861–62	15$967	2,408,895$784	,, 150,865
	1862–63	15$846	3,233,386$738	,, 204,046
Sarsaparilla	1858–59	23$304	69,493$924	,, 2,982
	1859–60	23$423	74,063$559	,, 3,162
	1860–61	24$322	68,904$189	,, 2,833
	1861–62	21$737	35,322$249	,, 1,625
	1862–63	18$874	45,979$125	,, 2,436
		RIO GRANDE DO SUL.		
Hair	1858–59	7$797	207,463$978	arr. 26,604
	1859–60	8$959	261,387$359	,, 29,174
	1860–61	10$240	257,946$000	,, 25,188
	1861–62	9$369	258,739$017	,, 27,616
	1862–63	8$621	257,175$330	,, 29,830
Hides (salt)	1858–59	7$950	1,094,605$079	n°. 137,683
	1859–60	14$000	1,989,106$000	,, 142,079
	1860–61	5$376	2,135,576$850	arr. 397,184
	1861–62	4$592	1,753,303$600	,, 381,755
	1862–63	3$575	1,424,047$920	,, 398,283
Hides (dry)	1858–59	6$901	2,269,918$545	n°. 328,879
	1859–60	8$388	2,207,519$240	,, 263,162
	1860–61	11$131	2,084,514$371	arr. 187,271
	1861–62	8$213	1,798,156$250	,, 218,940
	1862–63	6$751	1,836,479$000	,, 271,991

Table showing the Average Price, the Value, and the Quantities of the Chief Articles Exported to Foreign Countries from the Principal Ports—*continued.*

Articles.	Years.	S. JOSE DO NORTE.		
		Average Price.	Value.	Quantities.
Hides (salt)	1858–59	8$327	1,046,399$208	nº. 125,649
	1859–60	11$603	2,282,407$098	,, 196,685
	1860–61	10$509	1,821,215$422	,, 173,289
	1861–62	8$546	2,063,396$971	,, 241,425
	1862–63	7$720	1,530,201$323	,, 200,799

SANTOS.

Coffee	1858–59	4$042	3,728,427$267	arr. 922,293
	1859–60	5$446	7,623,652$300	,, 1,481,730
	1860–61	5$030	6,481,855$679	,, 1,288,604
	1861–62	6$230	8,547,185$928	,, 1,371,729
	1862–63	6$047	8,410,981$025	,, 1,390,804

PARANAGUA.

Maté	1858–59	3$327	1,057,624$437	arr. 317,843
	1859–60	3$766	1,652,814$470	,, 438,865
	1860–61	2$946	1,072,005$514	,, 363,899
	1861–62	2$716	827,667$273	,, 305,340
	1862–63	2$548	1,031,589$362	,, 404,829

Table showing the Average Price, the Value, and the
Countries from the

Articles.	Years.	PARAHYBA.	
		Average Price.	Value.
Cotton	1858–59	7$642	1,193,443$736
	1859–60	7$466	1,654,107$000
	1860–61	7$142	1,273,233$152
	1861–62	9$740	1,791,313$503
	1862–63	14$963	3,021,124$036
Sugar (brown) ...	1858–59	2$038	1,630,820$000
	1859–60	1$965	1,639,336$658
	1860–61	1$822	738,658$800
	1861–62	1$513	1,123,703$000
	1862–63	1$323	821,120$250
Coffee	1858–59	...	...
	1859–60	...	...
	1860–61	...	...
	1861–62	...	...
	1862–63	...	...
Hides (salt) ...	1858–59	...	...
	1859–60	...	...
	1860–61	...	...
	1861–62	...	...
	1862–63	...	...

Quantities of the Chief Articles Exported to Foreign Principal Ports—*continued*.

PARAHYBA.			CERA.	
Quantities.	Average Price.	Value.	Quantities.	
arr. 156,151	7$080	526,206$715	arr.	74,324
,, 221,557	7$688	596,485$920	,,	77,581
,, 178,267	7$148	419,810$372	,,	58,728
,, 183,900	9$224	470,479$800	,,	50,785
,, 201,899	14$898	659,234$960	,,	44,250
,, 800,075	2$066	407,613$243	,,	197,258
,, 833,918	1$954	287,383$040	,,	147,083
,, 405,194	2$011	193,089$440	,,	95,972
,, 742,545	1$847	211,661$620	,,	114,595
,, 620,270	1$622	248,328$960	,,	153,085
...	5$107	200,287$515	,,	39,216
...	5$110	288,388$900	,,	56,430
...	5$837	257,693$680	,,	44,146
...	6$360	940,876$560	,,	147,939
...	6$976	1,031,005$140	,,	147,777
...	6$663	144,934$229	n°.	21,751
...	7$576	158,859$200	,,	20,970
...	6$944	327,659$540	,,	47,181
...	6$437	372,948$080	,,	57,937
...	5$492	292,898$100	,,	53,334

Table showing the Average Price, the Value, and the Quantities of the Chief Articles Exported to Foreign Countries from the Principal Ports—*continued*.

Articles.	Years.	ALAGOAS.		
		Average Price.	Value.	Quantities.
Cotton ...	1858–59	6$868	1,147,275$439	arr. 167,024
	1859–60	6$765	1,034,725$878	,, 152,951
	1860–61	6$311	823,251$281	,, 130,443
	1861–62	7$004	1,914,947$821	,, 273,396
	1862–63	13$198	3,737,808$389	,, 283,201
Sugar (brown)	1858–59	2$281	973,567$499	,, 426,818
	1859–60	2$147	521,303$627	,, 242,782
	1860–61	2$287	442,481$045	,, 193,467
	1861–62	1$817	1,035,676$110	,, 569,888
	1862–63	1$650	996,464$581	,, 603,608

		PORTO ALEGRE.		
Maté ...	1858–59	3$000	76,255$500	arr. 25,418
	1859–60	3$007	76,168$400	,, 25,323
	1860–61	2$853	153,518$695	,, 53,807
	1861–62	2$571	128,888$000	,, 50,115
	1862–63	2$075	173,931$450	,, 83,840

		URUGUAYANNA.		
Maté ...	1858–59	5$064	493,075$281	arr. 97,363
	1859–60	3$475	288,873$760	,, 83,105
	1860–61	4$498	204,229$233	,, 45,402
	1861–62	4$498	347,464$372	,, 77,249
	1862–63	3$236	88,832$100	,, 27,445

Table showing the Average Price, the Value, and the Quantities of the Chief Articles Exported to Foreign Countries from the Principal Ports—*continued*.

Articles.	Years.	SANTA CATHARINA.		
		Average Price.	Value.	Quantities.
Flour of Mandioca	1858–59	1$863	62,456$480	alq. 33,524
	1859–60	2$287	139,068$400	,, 60,790
	1860–61	1$143	102,833$760	,, 89,933
	1861–62	705	49,479$323	,, 70,124
	1862–63	799	49,128$980	,, 61,449

		SERGIPE.		
Sugar ...	1858–59	2$276	910,630$906	arr. 399,980
	1859–60	2$476	464,940$412	,, 187,712
	1860–61	2$469	212,669$380	,, 86,040
	1861–62	1$903	769,254$561	,, 404,092
	1862–63	1$699	1,073,539$524	,, 631,738

		RIO GRANDE DO NORTE.		
Cotton ...	1858–59	6$713	80,609$975	arr. 12,008
	1859–60	6$312	76,347$061	,, 12,094
	1860–61	6$179	9,665$461	,, 1,564
	1861–62	10$773	43,191$480	,, 4,018
	1862–63	19$168	105,694$520	,, 5,514
Sugar ...	1858–59	1$825	325,239$500	,, 178,130
	1859–60	1$883	482,805$070	,, 256,388
	1860–61	1$876	275,764$800	,, 146,975
	1861–62	1$542	124,832$000	,, 80,955
	1862–63	1$359	304,245$500	,, 223,745

Table showing the Average Price, the Value, and the Quantities of the Chief Articles Exported to Foreign Countries from the Principal Ports—*continued.*

Articles.	Years.	PIAUHY		
		Average Price.	Value.	Quantities.
Cotton ...	1858–59	6$166	99,420$360	arr. 16,123
	1859–60	7$220	56,711$500	,, 7,854
	1860–61	5$994	66,030$262	,, 11,015
	1861–62	7$762	86,455$887	,, 11,137
	1862–63	13$612	87,611$159	,, 6,436

Average Prices of the Chief Articles Exported:—

	Unit.	1858—59	1859—60	1860—61	1861—62	1862—63
Spirits	Canada...	335	387	447	299	273
Cotton	Arroba...	7$485	7$526	6$979	8$927	15$491
Sugar	,,	2$597	2$708	2$451	2$172	1$905
Hair	,,	8$224	9$263	10$237	9$103	8$489
Cocoa	,,	4$691	5$657	6$011	6$035	5$042
Coffee	,,	4$489	5$844	5$461	5$945	6$484
Hides {Salt	Um	8$024	11$221	9$263	8$352	7$145
{Dry	Arroba...	7$958	7$749	10$445	7$381	6$286
Diamonds	Oitava...	300$000	300$000	378$000	412$011	330$699
Tobacco ...	Arroba...	5$449	5$878	7$585	6$354	5$838
Gum Elastic	,,	16$090	19$836	17$239	15$717	15$710
Maté ...	,,	3$615	3$169	3$104	2$873	2$503

MANUFACTURES.

This branch of industry has been but slowly developing itself, notwithstanding the constant endeavours of the Government to foster and encourage all attempts at establishing manufactories. Whilst labour continues to be so much needed Brazil does not study her true interests in creating manufactures which can only be looked upon as exotics, to be supported by heavy tariffs and burdensome monopolies. Brazil is essentially an agricultural country, whose rich natural productions are eagerly sought for by other countries, which, possessing superabundance of labour, can furnish manufactures of every kind, only too glad to receive in exchange the overflowing abundance of Brazilian soils. To the products of his soil the Brazilian owes his present wealth, and to his soil he must, for many years to come, entrust the aggrandisement and development of his country.

In some of the minor manufactures the Brazilians show much taste and ingenuity, such as in their feather flowers, in which the varied hues of the real flowers are beautifully and exactly imitated with the feathers of the native birds ; and in their shell and fish-scale flowers, in which the petals are formed, in the one case of shells, and in the other with the scales of fishes. Cushion-lace is largely made in the northern provinces ; and also a peculiar kind of needlework called *crivé*, made on fine linen, threads of which are drawn out so as to leave a multitude of square holes, which are afterwards filled up with elaborate and elegant needlework.

MONETARY.

In September, 1864, there occurred in Rio de Janeiro perhaps the most extraordinary monetary crisis which has occurred since the days of Law and the South Sea scheme. On the 10th of that month there took place the failure of a very important private banking establishment, that of Souta & Co., who carried on not only a considerable business with the mercantile and monied community of Rio, but were also the bankers of a large number of tradesmen and mechanics, whose earnings were deposited in the hands of this well-known and trusted firm. On the failure becoming known, an indescribable panic took place. The streets were crowded by persons hurrying to withdraw their money from the hands of the private bankers with whom it was deposited, and speedily became blocked up in the neighbourhood of these establishments by a dense crowd, some denouncing in unmeasured terms the rascality of all bankers, some weeping and lamenting, while others, who were fortunate enough to obtain their money, throwing themselves on their knees, held it up to heaven within their clasped hands, and, abandoning themselves to the extravagance of their unlooked-for happiness, pressed it rapturously to their lips, time after time, before they could induce themselves to withdraw their treasure from their gaze.

At length, so great became the confusion that the police were ordered out to patrol and guard the streets, to quell any anticipated disturbance of the public peace; which delicate undertaking they performed by riding furiously up and down the narrow and crowded streets, cutting and slashing indiscriminately at every one in their way who was not agile enough to find a shelter in some adjoining house, and severely injuring many of the unfortunates, who, whatever their extravagance of gesture and manner, had acted with a forbearance which would probably find no parallel in any other country under similarly trying circumstances.

The two following days similar scenes took place; the depositors, reinforced and increased by those from the surrounding country, bore steadily and persistently on the private banks,

F

and in despite of all the efforts of individuals, of the aid rendered quickly and generously by their friends, and of that given by the English banks, which, with a view to restore confidence, themselves paid the deposit receipts of Gomes and Sons, several of these bankers finally succumbed in a conflict which no providence could have foreseen, and no experience have enabled them to withstand.

While these events were going on, the Government, in order to meet, in some measure, the emergenc which was pressing not only on the private bankers, but was also beginning to be felt by other banks, and by the Bank of Brazil itself, using their constitutional power under the Bank Act, authorised this bank to issue notes to the value of three times its disposable capital, and finally, the whole commerce and credit of the city being paralysed, and the panic taking the form of a rapid withdrawal of the bullion of the banks, issued, on the petition of most of the bankers and chief merchants of the place, an order, not only suspending specie payments, but even going to the extraordinary length of decreeing a suspension of payment of all debts for a period of sixty days, during which time no one could be made a bankrupt, the courts being all forbidden to receive any petitions for declaration of bankruptcy, and also decreeing that the broken banks should be wound up by commissions, and not by the ordinary officers of the law.

These measures, unusual, and in some degree unconstitutional, are not to be judged of by European standards, for in South America there are no kindred great national banking establishments interested in the maintenance of public credit, which, in case of emergency, aid each other to withstand the drain upon their coffers, nor are there the rich Exchanges wherein sales can be made, or large loans effected, on the evidences of credit possessed by banks and individuals, so that in case of such a panic as occurred here, the Brazilian banks have to depend on their own slender resources, for at least two months, until recourse can be had to Europe for the assistance of a loan, or for the bullion requisite to meet the unforeseen demand upon the specie in their treasuries.

BANKS OF

Name.	Place of Business.	Capital. Authorised. Milreis.
Banco do Brazil...	Rio de Janeiro ...	33,000,000
,, branch at ...	Bahia ...	...
,, ,, ...	Pernambuco ...	...
,, ,, ...	Maranhão ...	...
,, ,, ...	Pará ...	...
,, ,, ...	Ouro Preto ...	...
,, ,, ...	Rio Grande do Sul	...
,, ,, ...	St. Paulo...	...
Banco da Bahia...	Bahia ...	8,000,000
Novo Banco de Pernambuco ...	Pernambuco ...	2,000,000
Banco do Maranhão ...	Maranhão ...	1,000,000
Banco Rural e Hypothecario ...	Rio de Janeiro ...	16,000,000
London and Brazilian Bank ...	Ditto ...	13,333,333
,, branch at ...	Bahia ...	...
,, ,, ...	Pernambuco ...	...
,, ,, ...	Rio Grande do Sul	...
Brazilian and Portuguese Bank ...	Rio de Janeiro ...	8,888,888
Banco Mauà (M'Gregor and Co.) ...	Ditto ...	6,000,000
Sociedade Commercial ...	Bahia ...	...
Companhia Commercial...	Ditto ...	...
,, Reserva Mercantil	Ditto ...	...
,, Hypothecaria ...	Ditto ...	...
,, Econonmica ...	Ditto ...	...
,, de Economias ...	Ditto ...	...
Caifa Commercial das Alagôas ...	Alagôas ...	...
Banco do Rio Grande do Sul ...	Rio Grande do Sul	1,000,000

BRAZIL.

Capital.	Reserve Fund.	Issue.		Guarantee Fund.
Paid up. Milreis.	Milreis.	Actual. Milreis.	Authorised. Milreis.	Milreis.
33,000,000	1,552,092	25,416,940	41,131,155	15,565,577
...	...	...	...	...
...	...	...	...	...
...	...	...	...	...
...	...	...	...	...
...	...	...	...	...
...	...	...	...	...
...	...	...	...	...
4,000,000	48,080	3,113,200	2,582,911	2,586,660
2,000,000	108,280	950,000	...	1,486,000
750,000	58,701	376,000	468,027	376,000
8,000,000	1,000,000	...	...	...
4,622,200	...	...	...	...
444,444	...	...	...	...
888,880	...	...	...	...
444,444	...	...	...	...
4,444,444	...	...	...	...
6,000,000	304,288	...	...	...
5,547,900	32,346	...	...	...
2,480,000	55,468	...	...	...
2,209,600	88,190	...	...	...
875,300	14,322	...	...	...
2,683,503	187,287	...	...	...
829,955	418	...	...	...
243,000	12,160	...	...	...
600,000	17,462	...	...	...

COMMERCE.

THE commerce of Brazil is yearly developing itself in proportion to the increase in her agricultural wealth, and such is the desire of other countries to obtain her products, that the demand seems limited only by the production. The chief articles which she exports are cotton, coffee, sugar, tobacco, cacao, gum-elastic, hides, rum, furniture and dye-woods, hair, nuts, gums, resins, balsams, diamonds, gold, &c., &c.

The principal imports are flour, wine, cotton, woollen and silk goods, linens, fancy goods, machinery, iron, coals, &c., &c.

The countries which have the largest trade with Brazil are England, United States, France, and Portugal.

IMPERIAL EXPORTS for 1862-63 compared with 1853-54,

Destination.	Total. 1853-54.	Total. 1862-63.
British Possessions..	24,903,429	46,247,527$695
English Channel ...	...	15,985,724$229
French Possessions..	6,110,146	15,446,522$175
Portuguese Possessions	3,342,086	7,702,825$626
United States ...	21,785,501	15,258,117$682
River Plate ...	3,265,875	5,152,288$687
Chile	786,920	961,051$432
Denmark	2,025,202	1,026,378$753
Belgium	1,367,938	1,043,753$017
Hanse Towns ...	6,356,926	5,050,770$518
Spain	646,079	2,364,147$160
Sweden	1,681,673	2,347,471$910
Russia	113,093	591,557$070
Sardinia	679,856	571,219$256
Austria	2,710,087	374,395$650
Turkey	116,242	366,668$000
Mediterranean ...	...	701,738$000
Mexico	...	135,800$000
For consumption ...	...	69,930$505
Holland	102,950	117,851$081
Africa	...	441,863$168
Ports not specified...	848,490	522,395$990
Total ...	76,842,493	122,479,997$604

and showing the Imports at each Port in 1862–63.

Rio de Janeiro.	Bahia.	Pernambuco.
9,194,203$688	10,147,887$789	4,013,987$626
12,181,822$912	...	1,254,652$677
10,333,520$652	974,822$946	986,614$765
1,734,966$743	1,464,871$946	1,863,745$866
9,696,039$860	471,358$375	1,277,399$591
1,611,929$642	483,697$315	1,509,072$231
85,180$100	...	451,067$000
912,734$400	...	...
945,497$950	...	...
1,408,765$970	3,184,271$697	...
220,453$700	183,710$004	1,037,118$172
1,913,512$400	361,730$942	72,228$568
591,557$070	...	...
339,256$430	198,307$826	...
374,395$650	...	...
366,668$000	...	...
701,738$000	...	...
135,800$000	...	...
62,663$047	...	5,691$270
...	116,845$081	207$000
...	441,863$168	...
...	...	...
52,810,706$214	18,029,367$089	12,471,784$766

Imperial Exports for 1862-63 compared with 1853-54,

Destination.	Maranhao.	Pará.
British Possessions..	3,126,255$179	1,929,715$488
English Channel ...	...	...
French Possessions..	206,634$810	1,325,649$738
Portuguese Possessions	1,131,850$965	576,631$038
United States ...	209,430$960	1,633,177$847
River Plate ...	...	...
Chile	...	...
Denmark	...	...
Belgium	...	...
Hanse Towns ...	...	74,140$860
Spain	47,829$650	...
Sweden	...	...
Russia	...	...
Sardinia ...	...	33,655$000
Austria	...	...
Turkey	...	...
Mediterranean ...	...	...
Mexico	...	...
For consumption ...	...	...
Holland	...	799$000
Africa	...	...
Ports not specified...	...	...
Total ...	4,722,001$564	5,573,768$971

and showing the Imports at each Port in 1862-63—*cont.*

Rio Grande do Sul.	S. José do Norte.	Porto Alegre.	Uruguayana.
1,381,893$816	1,720,966$150	1,740$104	...
...	...	...	...
433,949$015	79,884$310	...	...
450,258$660	20,057$760	...	...
1,166,287$190	3,879$960	...	...
195,189$910	9,610$400	203,496$700	168,795$916
...	...	...	...
...	...	...	...
95,146$387	...	...	...
667$790	...	...	...
309,797$100	...	...	...
...	...	...	...
...	...	...	...
...	...	...	...
...	...	...	...
...	...	...	...
...	...	...	...
...	...	...	...
...	...	...	...
...	...	...	...
...	...	...	...
4,033,189$868	1,834,398$580	205,236$804	168,795$916

Imperial Exports for 1862–63 compared with 1853–54,

Destination.	Santos.	Paranaguá.
British Possessions	6,478,686$235	...
English Channel	...	...
French Possessions	363,853$458	...
Portuguese Possessions	306,695$000	...
United States	624,552$400	...
River Plate	...	677,022$310
Chile	...	396,864$861
Denmark	...	...
Belgium	...	...
Hanse Towns	380,664$701	...
Spain	256,943$643	...
For consumption	1,576$188	...
Ports not specified	...	...
Total	8,412,971$625	1,073,887$171

Destination.	Alagoas.	Sergipe.
British Possessions	4,158,720$566	...
English Channel	475,433$839	867,887$921
French Possessions	...	...
Portuguese Possessions	35,408$428	118,339$220
River Plate	39,515$572	6,508$800
Denmark	...	113,644$353
Spain	56,381$942	...
Ports not specified	...	...
Total	4,765,460$347	1,106,380$294

and showing the Imports at each Port in 1862-63—*cont*.

Antonina.	Parahiba.	Ceará.	Santa Catharina.
...	2,648,890$201	1,244,380$720	2,807$202
...	514,630$000	691,296$880	...
...	317,357$092	345,998$620	...
...	...	...	...
...	165,144$519	...	10,846$980
156,844$292	...	...	90,605$599
27,939$471	...	...	...
...	...	...	...
...	...	...	3,108$680
...	...	2,259$500	...
...	251,912$949	...	...
...	...	...	...
...	...	...	...
184,783$763	3,897,934$761	2,283,935$720	107,368$461

Espirito Santo.	Rio Grande do Norte.	Piauhy.	Mato Grosso.
*52,528$440	...	144,864$491	...
...	...	...	...
...	...	78,236$744	...
...	...	...	...
...	...	...	...
...	...	...	...
...	...	...	...
...	472,608$910	...	49,787$080
52,528,$440	472,608$910	223,101$235	49,787$080

IMPERIAL EXPORTS to

Whence Exported.	1857-58.	1858-59.
Rio de Janeiro	44,421,609$	51,974,658$
Bahia	13,419,612$	15,465,597$
Pernambuco	14,259,269$	14,005,585$
Maranhão	2,770,627$	2,454,967$
Pará	3,549,631$	3,917,104$
Rio Grande do Sul	3,294,691$	4,154,379$
S. José do Norte	1,169,023$	1,235,800$
Porto Alegre	57,665$	87,200$
Uruguayana	295,046$	614,731$
Santos	3,278,767$	3,733,158$
Paranaguá	1,898,019$	1,074,163$
Antonina	92,962$	61,618$
Parahyba	3,139,734$	2,897,876$
Ceará	1,141,087$	1,291,953$
Santa Catharina	127,672$	120,341$
Alagoas	2,121,204$	2,248,789$
Sergipe	715,163$	929,177$
Espirito Santo	...	...
Rio Grande do Norte	374,903$	422,107$
Piauhy	73,051$	130,227$
Mato Grosso	47,728$	23,750$
Total	96,247,463$	106,843,180$

Foreign Countries.

1859-60.	1860-61.	1861-62.	1862-63.
57,592,639$	79,083,786$	57,845,011$	52,810,706$
10,822,944$	8,422,986$	16,791,101$	18,029,367$
11,105,818$	7,444,534$	12,339,859$	12,471,785$
2,511,211$	2,049,484$	2,757,912$	4,722,001$
5,912,860$	5,341,304$	4,604,137$	5,573,769$
4,880,873$	4,894,490$	4,342,677$	4,033,190$
2,410,067$	2,195,210$	2,471,997$	1,834,398$
94,524$	210,206$	291,775$	205,237$
415,498$	282,977$	417,252$	168,796$
7,633,610$	6,486,027$	8,549,369$	8,412,972$
1,666,381$	1,124,034$	856,686$	1,073,887$
63,806$	78,949$	118,452$	184,784$
3,355,301$	2,030,760$	2,969,741$	3,897,935$
1,356,572$	1,254,984$	2,032,124$	2,283,936$
202,414$	142,374$	83,038$	107,368$
1,606,064$	1,317,969$	3,011,454$	4,765,460$
479,497$	222,007$	788,688$	1,106,380$
...	...	...	52,528$
678,111$	328,074$	195,208$	472,609$
133,438$	198,895$	201,839$	223,101$
36,344$	62,113$	51,622$	49,787$
112,957,972$	123,171,163$	120,719,942$	122,479,996$

Imperial Exports to

Articles Exported.	1857-58.	1858-59.
Spirits	1,318,363$	921,442$
Cotton	6,655,321$	5,624,097$
Sugar (white)	8,393,960$	7,905,083$
Sugar (brown)	14,311,851$	19,761,780$
Hair	341,127$	413,911$
Cocoa	1,655,815$	1,320,119$
Coffee	43,502,851$	50,138,253$
Hides (salt)	4,185,589$	3,957,434$
Hides (dry)	2,925,374$	3,244,041$
Diamonds	2,308,500$	3,049,965$
Tobacco	2,374,307$	3,046,636$
Gum Elastic	1,243,360$	1,884,522$
Rose Wood	527,048$	614,995$
Slate	2,304,066$	1,749,335$
Gold (in dust and bar)	703,583$	840,464$
Other articles	3,496,348$	2,371,103$
Total	96,247,463$	106,843,180$

Foreign Countries—*continued.*

1859-60.	1860-61.	1861-62.	1862-63.
570,486$	660,544$	858,371$	819,231$
6,432,572$	4,682,141$	7,786,151$	16,817,808$
4,049,008$	11,055,679$	7,399,630$	7,006,400$
11,672,251$		15,936,169$	12,274,627$
364,596$	376,296$	345,013$	318,932$
1,456,276$	1,681,079$	1,442,059$	1,578,937$
60,238,437$	79,663,552$	58,746,993$	56,574,935$
6,653,871$	9,090,335$	5,852,751$	4,834,589$
3,342,131$		2,833,770$	2,415,845$
3,132,000$	3,772,300$	4,241,248$	4,116,175$
4,022,455$	2,382,567$	4,878,619$	6,202,010$
3,419,038$	2,910,531$	2,438,159$	3,275,913$
964,433$	653,690$	927,837$	782,057$
2,115,043$	1,673,144$	1,404,376$	1,514,781$
1,402,031$	1,629,290$	2,121,399$	777,625$
3,123,344$	2,940,015$	3,507,397$	3,170,131
112,957,972$	123,171,163$	120,719,942$	122,479,996$

TABLE of Chief Articles of Importation.

Articles.	1st Period. 1852-53 and 1856-57. Average Value.	2nd Period. 1857-58 and 1861-62. Average Value.	1862-63.
Oils	615,623$	1,005,152$	926,733$
Fish	2,339,815$	3,324,448$	1,489,532$
Spirits	729,136$	1,620,437$	1,457,471$
Shoes and boots	778,916$	1,507,270$	1,235,116$
Meat	1,580,044$	4,829,370$	5,497,468$
Coal	1,357,860$	2,440,482$	2,076,342$
Leather	882,650$	861,703$	975,066$
Drugs	1,003,238$	1,522,409$	999,610$
Wheat flour	4,608,141$	8,509,636$	4,922,627$
Iron goods	3,972,655$	6,188,012$	5,207,886$
Iron	629,002$	1,303,689$	1,450,728$
Earthenware and glass	1,757,352$	1,818,360$	1,841,750$
Machinery	226,190$	721,912$	850,927$
Butter	1,501,954$	2,087,177$	2,206,326$
Manufactures—			
Cotton	29,186,376$	32,832,171$	23,827,407$
Wool	5,440,707$	5,828,278$	3,967,059$
Linen	2,578,665$	2,776,280$	2,170,397$
Silk	2,436,480$	3,175,648$	2,187,718$
Mixed	4,022,984$	2,813,371$	2,486,071$
Gold and silver money	7,380,085$	4,780,404$	4,388,887$
Gold and silver work	2,310,049$	4,011,489$	2,298,741$
Powder	433,830$	544,434$	601,595$
Salt	775,156$	1,026,108$	1,168,076$
Wines	3,304,859$	4,283,939$	4,708,738$

TABLE of Chief Articles of Exportation.

Articles.	1st Period. 1852-53 and 1856-57. Average Value.	2nd Period. 1857-58 and 1861-62. Average Value.	1862-63.
Spirits	943,887$	865,841$	819,231$
Cotton	5,461,672$	6,236,056$	16,817,808$
Sugar	19,204,537$	20,097,082$	19,281,027$
Hair	415,646$	368,189$	318,932$
Cocoa	758,472$	1,511,070$	1,578,937$
Coffee	43,990,621$	58,458,017$	56,574,935$
Hides (salt)	3,192,505$	8,417,059$	4,834,589$
Hides (dry)	3,264,186$		2,415,845$
Diamonds	3,650,907$	3,300,802$	4,116,175$
Tobacco	2,162,353$	3,340,917$	6,202,010$
Gum Elastic	2,336,995$	2,379,122$	3,275,913$
Maté	1,336,207$	1,849,193$	1,514,781$
Gold in dust or bar	181,867$	1,339,353$	777,624$

Quantities of Articles Exported.

Spirits	can. 2,875,340	2,189,807	2,995,186
Cotton	arr. 976,037	831,997	1,085,628
Sugar	,, 8,450,374	8,143,355	10,121,719
Hair	,, 47,690	40,614	37,567
Cocoa	,, 219,773	260,398	313,152
Coffee	,, 11,265,529	11,132,679	8,724,142
Hides (salt)	lib. 502,796	594,152	676,562
Hides (dry)	arr. 444,860	355,603	384,208
Diamonds	oit. 12,181	9,707	12,448
Tobacco	arr. 570,568	525,534	1,140,467
Gum Elastic	,, 143,065	144,546	208,513
Maté	,, 436,946	519,193	605,179
Gold in dust or bar	oit. 50,390	369,876	198,386

IMPERIAL IMPORTS from Foreign Countries,

From	Total. 1853-54.	Total. 1862-63.
British Possessions..	46,499,478$168	50,765,699$972
Hanse Towns ...	5,192,313$690	5,379,327$668
Belgium	1,785,857$032	1,008,111$262
Portuguese Possessions	5,792,749$250	5,966,136$876
Sardinian States ...	657,125$395	587,571$050
River Plate ...	4,474,046$135	6,550,567$568
Imperial Ports. ...	688,217$763	907,402$646
Spain	686,513$770	1,854,551$364
Denmark	262,133$841	68,111$384
Sweden	245,099$906	116,675$734
French Possessions .	9,955,097$132	18,382,574$545
Austria	674,791$164	791,929$002
United States ...	8,053,483$733	6,044,133$780
Holland	60,081$187	131,201$125
Fishery	...	2,156$417
African Ports not specified ...	811,765$154	292,366$944
Other Ports not specified ...		224,195$506
Total ...	85,838,753$320	99,072,712$843

showing the Import at each Port in 1862-63.

Rio de Janeiro.	Bahia.	Pernambuco.
25,670,172$415	8,614,433$074	8,310,377$321
1,654,771$643	1,165,096$518	586,362$710
472,367$420	117,010$000	105,254$350
2,195,162$195	1,230,959$742	876,005$931
368,575$703	127,965$354	37,315$084
3,974,152$238	1,291,915$300	608,678$516
72,980$863	536,913$179	99,277$580
751,638$773	288,446$230	229,743$278
24,784$083	4,635$900	...
96,386$173	13,550$450	...
10,771,787$290	2,896,384$416	2,888,777,567
390,713$126	190,719$750	152,657$066
3,178,112$461	275,977$744	1,134,595$018
...	91,167$141	40,033$984
...	...	...
...	292,366$944	...
...	...	...
49,621,604$383	17,137,541$742	15,069,078$405

Imperial Imports from Foreign Countries, showing

From	Maranhao.	Para.
British Possessions..	2,106,647$445	2,151,588$875
Hanse Towns ...	29,803$480	148,186$653
Belgium	30,773$754	49,622$206
Portuguese Possessions	358,139$761	734,957$197
Sardinian States ...	...	...
River Plate ...	...	...
Imperial Ports ...	8,358$290	5,115$312
Spain	53,883$276	45,755$963
Denmark	...	9,748$021
Sweden	...	...
French Possessions..	722,559$747	451,122$017
Austria	17,184$560	11,034$750
United States ...	277,051$615	863,182$659
Holland	...	...
Fishery	...	...
African Ports not specified	...	...
Other Ports not specified	...	...
Total ...	3,604,401$928	4,470,313$653

the Import at each Port in 1862-63—*continued*.

Rio Grande do Sul.	Porto Alegre.	Uruguayana.	Santos.
1,014,602$127	40,985$212	...	1,463,092$392
738,926$400	587,286$372	...	240,025$039
194,755$703	25,846$925	...	6,132$296
383,449$357	26,798$265	...	151,495$940
23,883$290	18,788$519	...	11,043$100
101,286$886	13,295$491	135,109$739	1,124$667
30,603$120	10,833$399	...	56,113$337
444,562$650	...	...	28,609$600
...	...	...	...
...	...	...	...
467,030$350	...	...	48,099$401
24,276$000	...	...	...
302,146$213	...	...	13,068$070
...	...	...	...
...	...	...	...
...	...	...	...
...	...	...	...
3,725,522$096	723,834$183	135,109$739	2,018,803$842

Imperial Imports from Foreign Countries, showing

From	PARANAGUA.	ANTONINA.
British Possessions ...	...	...
Hanse Towns	...	...
Belgium	...	...
River Plate	271,603$673	1,008$000
Imperial Ports... ...	31,677$252	...
Spain	...	...
Denmark	...	...
French Possessions ...	...	...
Austria...	...	...
Fishery...	...	...
Other Ports not specified	40$083	...
Total	303.321$008	1,008$000

From	ALAGOAS.	SERGIPE.
British Possessions ...	88,334$857	24,418$712
Portuguese Possessions .	529$000	8,197$488
Imperial Ports... ...	14,484$141	8,751$020
Spain	...	430$800
Denmark	...	11,243$535
Sweden	...	6,739$111
French Possessions ...	405$000	...
Other Ports not specified	...	...
Total	103,752$998	59,780$666

the Import at each Port in 1862-63—*continued.*

Parahiba.	Ceara.	Santa Catharina.
49,153$370	1,004,484$873	14,155$000
...	121,912$159	106,956$694
...	...	6,348$608
...	...	152,393$058
1,674$794	13,715$644	9,638$135
11,480$794	...	...
...	17,699$845	...
...	134,972$671	...
...	5,343$750	...
...	...	2,156$417
...	...	...
62,308$958	1,298,128$942	291,647$912

Espirito Santo.	Rio Grande do Norte.	Piauhy.	Mato Grosso.
...	...	213,254$299	...
...	442$000	...	...
3,952$680	3,283$900	30$000	...
...	...	...	...
...	...	...	...
...	...	...	...
...	...	436$086	...
...	...	...	223,792$423
3,952$680	3,725$900	213,720$385	223,792$423

IMPORTS FROM

	1857-58.	1858-59.	1859-60.
Rio de Janeiro	69,539,746$	68,540,352$	60,229,412$
Bahia ...	19,679,531$	19,464,440$	16,205,951$
Pernambuco...	24,784,040$	23,286,579$	19,492,110$
Maranhão ...	3,631,000$	3,949,012$	3,141,352$
Pará	3,688,601$	3,946,364$	4,709,896$
Rio Grande do Sul ...	4,210,030$	4,530,887$	5,206,198$
Porto Alegre	721,602$	562,465$	687,961$
*Uruguayana...	849,102$	361,855$	460,722$
Santos ...	408,593$	374,162$	567,532$
Paranaguá ...	150,182$	221,332$	54,943$
Antonina ...	5,652$	5,131$	1,121$
Parahyba ...	290,381$	247,311$	140,249$
Ceará ...	1,103,015$	917,987$	906,061$
Santa Catharina	109,031$	163,668$	175,962$
Alagôas ...	376,922$	494,027$	158,491$
Sergipe ...	80,907$	55,362$	27,178$
Espirito Santo	1,061$	992$	469$
Rio Grande do Norte ...	596,117$	321,825$	511,699$
Piauhy ...	139,060$	170,497$	182,938$
Mato Grosso...	75,600$	108,371$	167,750$
Total ...	130,440,173$	127,722,619$	113,027,995$

FOREIGN COUNTRIES.

1860-61.	1861-62.	Average.	1862-63.
72,979,831$	58,222,834$	65,902,435$	49,621,604$
14,107,549$	17,385,000$	17,368,494$	17,137,542$
17,426,058$	17,838,320$	20,565,421$	15,069,078$
2,891,801$	3,263,470$	3,375,327$	3,604,402$
5,704,745$	3,619,393$	4,333,800$	4,471,314$
5,668,634$	5,140,064$	4,951,162$	3,725,522$
940,381$	1,100,642$	802,610$	723,834$
397,847$	207,619$	455,429$	135,110$
1,374,931$	1,777,204$	900,484$	2,018,804$
57,583$	79,484$	112,705$	303,684$
...	4,537$	3,288$	1,008$
226,978$	37,006$	188,385$	62,309$
889,364$	1,016,674$	966,620$	1,298,129$
291,886$	213,241$	190,757$	291,648$
77,099$	77,301$	236,768$	103,753$
15,608$	47,612$	45,333$	59,781$
470$	1,989$	996$	3,953$
209,888$	28,373$	333,580$	3,726$
254,136$	257,025$	200,731$	213,720$
205,556$	213,401$	154,135$	223,792$
123,720,345$	110,531,189$	121,088,460$	99,072,713$

Imports from

	1857-58.	1858-59.	1859-60.
Oils	932,987$	1,087,749$	1,045,924$
Fish	4,242,183$	4,530,545$	3,609,020$
Spirits	1,251,797$	1,301,016$	1,190,600$
Boots & shoes	1,574,464$	1,585,872$	1,576,463$
Meat	3,134,666$	4,013,338$	3,419,283$
Coal	1,574,411$	2,107,447$	2,120,706$
Hats	2,000,259$	1,706,015$	1,766,875$
Leather	993,640$	876,173$	902,835$
Drugs	1,329,603$	1,443,143$	2,109,580$
Wheat flour	9,071,278$	9,705,634$	10,685,862$
Iron goods	5,307,965$	6,655,831$	5,654,007$
Iron	1,505,367$	1,482,428$	1,141,724$
Earthenware and glass	2,368,980$	1,892,451$	1,585,948$
Machinery	480,365$	733,459$	938,687$
Butter	1,892,893$	2,323,851$	2,359,987$
Manufactures:			
Cotton	35,479,684$	31,791,897$	27,514,978$
Wool	8,264,235$	6,059,915$	5,783,570$
Linen	2,968,130$	2,861,796$	2,986,218$
Silk	3,738,568$	3,606,554$	3,405,531$
Mixed	3,199,148$	3,324,678$	2,531,633$
Coin	6,680,512$	5,849,252$	4,045,184$
Gold & silver work	4,917,820$	5,995,251$	4,123,334$
Paper	1,151,700$	881,551$	1,029,059$
Powder	543,477$	506,254$	560,141$
Clothing	1,457,094$	1,449,544$	1,635,318$
Salt	1,166,501$	893,301$	1,128,794$
Wines	3,094,806$	3,891,288$	4,710,361$
Other articles	20,117,640$	19,166,386$	13,466,373$
Total	130,440,173$	127,722,619$	113,027,995$

Foreign Countries—*continued*.

1860-61.	1861-62.	Average.	1862-63.
993,216$	965,887$	1,005,152$	929,733$
2,725,635$	1,514,857$	3,324,418$	1,489,532$
1,408,432$	2,950,344$	1,620,437$	1,457,471$
1,479,236$	1,320,319$	1,507,270$	1,235,116$
5,568,618$	8,010,944$	4,829,370$	5,497,468$
3,594,381$	2,805,465$	2,440,182$	2,076,342$
1.437,780$	1,373,091$	1,656,804$	1,393,021$
766,853$	769,014$	861,703$	975,066$
1,490,426$	1,239.205$	1,522,408$	999,610$
7,285,613$	5,799,797$	8,509,636$	4,922,627$
7,123,886$	6,198,371$	6,188,012$	5,207,886$
1,356,913$	1,032,012$	1,303,680$	1,450,728$
1,619,446$	1,624,975$	1,818,300$	1,841,740$
692,841$	764,209$	721,912$	850,927$
2,007,996$	1,851,159$	2,087,177$	2,206,326$
34,435,526$	34,938,768$	32,832,171$	23,827,407$
5,116,674$	3,916,984$	5,828,278$	3,967,059$
2,699,187$	2,366 073$	2,776,280$	2,170,397$
2,988,048$	2,139,542$	3,175,648$	2,187,718$
2,213,819$	2,797,581$	2,813,371$	2,486,071$
5,322,068$	2,005,006$	4,780,404$	4,388,887$
3,215,737$	1,805,302$	4,011,189$	2,298,741$
1,206,273$	1,089,158$	1,071,548$	993,495$
543,338$	568,061$	544,134$	601,595$
1,609,389$	1,265,926$	1,483,454$	1,730,897$
812,671$	1,129,272$	1,026.108$	1,168,076$
5,557,514$	4,165,730$	4,283,939$	4,708,738$
18,448,829$	14,123,147$	17,064,475$	16,010,039$
123,720,345$	110,530,189$	121,088,460$	99,072,713$

FOREIGN TRADE OF THE EMPIRE.—

Ports.		1857-1858.	
		Entered.	Sailed.
Rio de Janeiro	Ships	1,121	1,095
	Tons	513,103	508,598
	Crew	14,524	14,034
Bahia	Ships	319	326
	Tons	103,248	106,052
	Crew	3,831	3,851
Pernambuco	Ships	453	450
	Tons	105,111	146,848
	Crew	5,235	5,313
Maranhão	Ships	83	78
	Tons	21,105	24,520
	Crew	1,039	836
Pará	Ships	102	104
	Tons	28,760	30,394
	Crew	1,090	1,206
Rio Grande do Sul	Ships	111	87
	Tons	10,423	18,559
	Crew	930	796
S. José do Norte	Ships	79	78
	Tons	13,210	18,109
	Crew	729	526
Porto Alegre	Ships	12	9
	Tons	1,806	1,240
	Crew	79	67

Entries of Vessels Inwards and Outwards.

	1858-1859.		1859-1860.	
	Entered.	Sailed.	Entered.	Sailed.
	1,157	1,089	1,153	1,212
	507,030	466,421	505,834	522,361
	13,655	12,305	14,217	14,452
	416	393	311	355
	146,129	140,316	105,221	122,553
	4,809	4,758	3,647	4,160
	475	462	438	461
	108,888	144,955	101,164	147,380
	5,333	5,254	4,823	5,254
	79	81	76	74
	22,421	28,262	20,515	26,625
	1,044	885	959	804
	104	104	109	119
	28,411	29,376	31,300	32,047
	1,160	1,172	1,279	1,290
	206	105	133	68
	34,180	20,878	27,164	13,065
	1,641	700	1,253	510
	...	88	...	76
	...	19,199	...	16,165
	...	569	...	473
	14	6	17	8
	2,070	907	2,418	1,407
	97	50	93	47

Foreign Trade of the Empire.—Entries

Ports.		1857-1858.	
		Entered.	Sailed.
Uruguayana	Ships	284	177
	Tons	1,402	1,413
	Crew	448	312
Santos	Ships	58	65
	Tons	18,469	20,648
	Crew	499	593
Paranaguá	Ships	45	48
	Tons	15,697	15,340
	Crew	473	497
Antonina	Ships	2	4
	Tons	473	557
	Crew	21	39
Parahyba	Ships	71	70
	Tons	24,423	24,268
	Crew	849	839
Ceará	Ships	23	19
	Tons	7,966	6,859
	Crew	283	238
Santa Catharina	Ships	39	36
	Tons	8,297	7,416
	Crew	490	425
Alagôas	Ships	45	48
	Tons	18,207	19,608
	Crew	596	629

of Vessels Inwards and Outwards—*continued.*

| 1858-1859. || 1859-1860. ||
Entered.	Sailed.	Entered.	Sailed.
353	128	249	51
1,127	474	1,607	381
370	177	432	104
66	63	105	110
20,156	20,293	36,465	39,029
565	588	1,008	1,123
31	44	44	48
8,281	12,049	13,421	13,778
314	456	419	456
3	3	1	4
597	497	126	683
30	31	10	37
72	70	77	75
22,073	20,953	26,252	25,111
816	787	860	819
26	28	25	25
8,571	9,865	8,930	8,946
321	351	311	315
52	50	45	44
15,531	14,997	11,518	10,762
781*	693	737	694
51	41	33	38
19,007	15,285	13,232	17,154
640	501	423	506

H

Foreign Trade of the Empire.—Entries

Ports.			1857-1858.	
			Entered.	Sailed.
Sergipe	{	Ships	21	20
		Tons	4,650	4,392
		Crew	195	185
Rio Grande do Norte	{	Ships	15	12
		Tons	5,373	4,682
		Crew	185	154
Piauhy	{	Ships	3	3
		Tons	896	896
		Crew	34	34
Total	{	Ships	2,886	2,729
		Tons	911,619	960,399
		Crew	31,580	30,574
National	{	Ships	374	270
		Tons	28,447	27,272
		Crew	1,556	1,426
Foreign	{	Ships	2,512	2,459
		Tons	883,172	933,127
		Crew	30,024	29,148

of Vessels Inwards and Outwards—*continued*.

1858-1859.		1859-1860.	
Entered.	Sailed.	Entered.	Sailed.
34	35	16	18
6,819	7,006	3,216	3,714
197	208	99	114
13	14	25	27
3,755	4,133	7,961	8,376
135	147	309	326
3	3	4	4
971	971	1,238	1,238
34	34	47	47
3,155	2,807	2,861	2,817
956,017	956,837	917,582	1,010,775
31,942	29,666	30,931	31,564
449	248	325	143
27,510	32,693	28,610	25,469
1,740	1,635	1,638	1,257
2,706	2,559	2,536	2,674
928,507	924,144	888,972	985,306
30,202	28,031	29,293	30,307

Foreign Trade of the Empire.—Entries

Ports.		1860—61.	
		Entered.	Sailed.
Rio de Janeiro	Ships	1,204	1,190
	Tons	527,353	554,662
	Crew	15,651	15,507
Bahia	Ships	259	292
	Tons	125,845	134,827
	Crew	5,170	5,122
Pernambuco	Ships	381	384
	Tons	154,420	185,106
	Crew	9,499	9,503
Maranhão	Ships	73	72
	Tons	19,924	25,961
	Crew	916	803
Pará	Ships	131	128
	Tons	36,302	37,835
	Crew	1,580	1,323
Rio Grande do Sul	Ships	153	76
	Tons	25,154	15,134
	Crew	1,337	652
S. José do Norte	Ships	...	61
	Tons	...	13,487
	Crew	...	385
Porto Alegre	Ships	24	18
	Tons	3,488	3,332
	Crew	157	144

of Vessels Inwards and Outwards—*continued*.

	1861-62.		1862-63.	
	Entered.	Sailed.	Entered.	Sailed.
	1,130	1,011	1,040	846
	407,601	498,302	369,323	441,167
	18,512	18,145	18,744	15,202
	356	375	433	492
	166,566	173,843	182,135	208,747
	6,951	7,166	7,472	8,496
	413	409	402	406
	151,463	183,465	147,220	179,121
	9,172	9,129	9,763	9,652
	67	62	85	87
	20,645	23,828	24,793	33,067
	870	776	1,053	1,044
	85	84	130	126
	25,452	24,292	36,366	36,008
	1,000	927	1,384	1,351
	207	82	232	76
	35,640	17,245	36,504	14,548
	1,758	677	1,952	661
	...	114	...	129
	...	25,834	...	26,952
	...	710	...	747
	23	21	28	32
	3,373	3,406	4,963	5,566
	141	140	199	211

Foreign Trade of the Empire.—Entries

Ports.			1860-61.	
			Entered.	Sailed.
Uruguayana	{	Ships	500	234
		Tons	4,183	2,573
		Crew	1,193	590
Santos	{	Ships	93	92
		Tons	32,364	31,780
		Crew	846	842
Paranaguá	{	Ships	31	41
		Tons	9,986	12,445
		Crew	349	409
Antonina	{	Ships	2	3
		Tons	431	683
		Crew	21	35
Parahyba	{	Ships	45	40
		Tons	15,832	14,497
		Crew	551	503
Ceará	{	Ships	21	20
		Tons	6,295	6,332
		Crew	233	233
Santa Catharina	{	Ships	43	43
		Tons	10,580	11,750
		Crew	589	558
Alagôas	{	Ships	25	25
		Tons	9,974	10,266
		Crew	315	315

of Vessels Inwards and Outwards—*continued.*

1861-62.		1862-63.	
Entered.	Sailed.	Entered.	Sailed.
116	24	223	25
689	211	1,277	187
384	78	408	60
113	113	108	109
40,726	41,221	35,414	36,852
1,012	1,041	847	930
30	50	53	59
9,155	14,277	15,455	17,485
279	505	496	569
3	8	2	10
680	1,935	357	2,754
22	48	17	99
61	62	59	59
21,495	22,125	21,345	21,302
716	733	666	668
30	30	32	30
8,050	7,989	8,832	8,109
343	336	309	336
46	44	55	58
10,661	10,995	14,818	15,191
716	718	949	949
40	35	50	52
20,477	17,597	23,098	25,415
531	454	710	768

Foreign Trade of the Empire.—Entries

Ports.		1860-61.	
		Entered.	Sailed.
Sergipe	Ships	8	7
	Tons	1,480	1,252
	Crew	65	54
Rio Grande do Norte	Ships	17	16
	Tons	5,204	5,032
	Crew	193	148
Piauhy	Ships	23	23
	Tons	3,667	3,667
	Crew	261	261
Total	Ships	3,033	2,765
	Tons	992,482	1,070,801
	Crew	38,926	37,387
National	Ships	513	305
	Tons	25,279	31,710
	Crew	1,935	1,768
Foreign	Ships	2,520	2,460
	Tons	967,203	1,039,091
	Crew	36,991	35,619

of Vessels Inwards and Outwards—*continued.*

	1861-62.		1862-63.	
	Entered.	Sailed.	Entered.	Sailed.
	31	32	51	49
	7,039	7,368	10,860	10,751
	183	197	298	346
	14	14	16	16
	4,862	4,862	5,346	5,346
	163	163	180	180
	28	28	34	36
	4,333	4,333	5,542	5,924
	283	283	355	375
	2,793	2,598	3,033	2,697
	938,907	1,083,128	943,649	1,094,492
	43,036	42,226	45,852	42,747
	214	128	386	167
	30,215	27,934	41,064	39,682
	1,721	1,319	2,389	1,883
	2,579	2,470	2,647	2,530
	908,692	1,055,194	902,585	1,054,810
	41,315	40,907	43,463	40,864

COASTING TRADE OF THE EMPIRE.—

Ports.		1857-58.	
		Entered.	Sailed.
Rio de Janeiro	Ships	1,059	1,096
	Tons	143,621	154,033
	Crew	11,036	11,528
Bahia	Ships	352	352
	Tons	47,673	49,145
	Crew	3,331	3,496
Pernambuco	Ships	106	320
	Tons	20,952	39,292
	Crew	1,151	2,890
Maranhão	Ships	59	64
	Tons	8,480	8,992
	Crew	587	626
Pará	Ships	57	57
	Tons	21,135	22,285
	Crew	1,562	1,578
Rio Grande do Sul	Ships	154	175
	Tons	28,637	34,786
	Crew	1,916	2,269
S. José do Norte	Ships	19	12
	Tons	5,505	2,903
	Crew	333	134
Porto Alegre	Ships	70	67
	Tons	11,234	11,086
	Crew	734	681

of Vessels Inwards and Outwards—*continued.*

	1858-1859.		1859-1860.	
	Entered.	Sailed.	Entered.	Sailed.
	958	996	1,016	1,045
	130,584	141,550	141,470	147,291
	9,489	10,077	9,722	10,053
	403	374	362	335
	53,458	50,680	46,180	48,882
	3,798	3,530	3,301	3,183
	106	288	354	357
	17,672	34,197	123,465	121,704
	1,043	2,495	6,009	6,107
	68	65	73	68
	9,347	9,148	10,178	9,529
	777	729	1,092	958
	50	52	67	64
	22,463	22,597	27,592	27,125
	1,116	1,114	955	923
	140	163	189	172
	27,020	30,262	41,875	33,871
	1,571	1,578	2,302	1,631
	19	14	25	28
	4,862	3,162	8,498	5,681
	312	143	391	263
	67	59	92	107
	11,028	9,446	9,162	18,057
	694	634	622	1,076

Coasting Trade of the Empire.—Entries

Ports.			1857-58.	
			Entered.	Sailed.
Santos		Ships	286	221
		Tons	40,503	28,284
		Crew	4,654	3,135
Paranaguá		Ships	143	133
		Tons	23,468	24,041
		Crew	1,555	1,455
Antonina		Ships	85	65
		Tons	18,633	15,855
		Crew	1,372	1,194
Parahyba		Ships	240	220
		Tons	5,899	5,687
		Crew	832	734
Ceará		Ships	90	65
		Tons	46,076	36,974
		Crew	2,891	2,260
Santa Catharina		Ships	121	105
		Tons	14,446	13,122
		Crew	957	795
Alagôas		Ships	206	92
		Tons	28,046	25,510
		Crew	2,259	1,831
Sergipe		Ships	136	107
		Tons	19,708	14,427
		Crew	1,483	985

of Vessels Inwards and Outwards—*continued*.

1858-59.		1859-60.	
Entered.	Sailed.	Entered.	Sailed.
254	211	223	172
36,841	28,469	38,895	23,902
4,237	2,943	3,571	2,328
145	83	92	89
22,532	5,337	9,162	8,275
1,530	454	622	573
75	79	81	94
15,011	14,410	18,557	19,240
1,339	1,296	1,359	1,405
166	167	150	130
4,782	5,048	5,897	5,311
658	668	661	574
95	93	95	86
54,987	55,227	56,641	55,788
3,411	3,412	3,530	3,580
128	115	112	102
14,886	14,066	13,722	13,227
1,001	847	941	853
152	68	143	97
24,817	20,896	24,950	24,087
1,637	1,224	1,718	1,553
162	113	156	113
27,314	15,769	26,522	13,565
1,833	1,107	1,828	922

Coasting Trade of the Empire.—Entries

Ports.		1857-58.	
		Entered.	Sailed.
Espirito Santo	Ships	51	45
	Tons	4,287	3,739
	Crew	423	358
Rio Grande do Norte	Ships	51	41
	Tons	10,203	9,937
	Crew	990	946
Piauhy	Ships	24	24
	Tons	1,469	1,437
	Crew	160	161
Total	Ships	3,309	3,261
	Tons	499,975	501,535
	Crew	38,226	37,056

of Vessels Inwards and Outwards—*continued.*

1858-59.		1859-60.	
Entered.	Sailed.	Entered.	Sailed.
45	44	36	34
3,894	4,143	3,971	3,869
390	357	320	321
47	39	55	53
9,836	9,639	15,486	15,386
814	784	1,124	1,120
36	36	37	37
3,322	3,322	2,989	2,989
452	452	825	825
3,116	3,059	3,358	3,183
494,656	477,368	631,295	597,779
36,102	33,864	41,192	38,248

Coasting Trade of the Empire.—Entries

Ports.		1860-61.	
		Entered.	Sailed.
Rio de Janeiro	Ships	894	921
	Tons	126,849	127,892
	Crew	9,512	10,016
Bahia	Ships	356	300
	Tons	85,750	42,907
	Crew	4,654	2,979
Pernambuco	Ships	313	303
	Tons	95,927	93,443
	Crew	5,858	5,278
Maranhão	Ships	70	65
	Tons	9,409	9,226
	Crew	1,008	939
Pará	Ships	64	64
	Tons	23,639	23,556
	Crew	1,389	1,792
Rio Grande do Sul	Ships	223	218
	Tons	59,094	58,822
	Crew	3,358	3,075
S. José do Norte	Ships	18	14
	Tons	4,383	4,134
	Crew	202	174
Porto Alegre	Ships	81	81
	Tons	14,077	14,423
	Crew	852	787

of Vessels Inwards and Outwards—*continued*.

1861-62.		1852-63.	
Entered.	Sailed.	Entered.	Sailed.
706	834	1,071	1,280
101,146	117,081	188,384	270,079
7,513	9,467	14,473	17,145
437	388	445	379
99,968	63,211	100,266	59,915
5,928	4,195	6,141	4,133
304	276	288	269
92,510	85,327	92,418	84,811
5,437	5,074	5,409	4,957
69	60	64	64
14,111	12,294	9,757	10,125
1,208	1,091	970	1,010
67	66	65	64
23,015	22,926	26,030	25,583
1,995	1,987	1,939	1,915
182	196	212	208
34,399	36,993	41,387	41,044
2,175	1,918	2,555	2,107
17	21	18	18
4,183	4,907	4,422	4,364
206	152	247	187
72	72	62	58
13,162	11,787	10,549	9,948
817	767	658	508

Coasting Trade of the Empire—Entries

Ports.		1857-58.	
		Entered.	Sailed.
Santos	Ships	213	158
	Tons	39,078	22,866
	Crew	3,705	2,427
Paranagua	Ships	120	85
	Tons	19,710	10,131
	Crew	1,209	676
Antonina	Ships	27	30
	Tons	2,905	2,267
	Crew	199	185
Parahyba	Ships	97	82
	Tons	4,796	3,626
	Crew	432	357
Ceará	Ships	97	72
	Tons	56,625	37,472
	Crew	3,614	2,123
Santa Catharina	Ships	86	81
	Tons	8,288	8,348
	Crew	714	655
Alagôas	Ships	178	99
	Tons	39,607	27,230
	Crew	777	1,718
Sergipe	Ships	145	145
	Tons	25,612	26,189
	Crew	1,952	1,936

of Vessels Inwards and Outwards—*continued*.

	1858-59.		1859-60.	
	Entered.	Sailed.	Entered.	Sailed.
	242	234	225	168
	41,664	40,579	45,874	26,223
	4,232	4,064	4,190	2,606
	94	73	104	91
	10,054	5,398	10,619	7,603
	615	426	719	600
	62	67	27	37
	20,016	19,737	5,467	5,562
	1,407	1,459	428	467
	110	100	107	88
	4,955	4,572	4,740	3,934
	514	476	519	423
	81	74	102	92
	51,909	49,729	56,893	56,360
	3,463	3,311	3,713	3,668
	99	83	104	73
	9,764	8,009	11,354	8,136
	832	667	873	624
	169	85	189	137
	35,588	25,459	31,684	25,635
	2,292	1,515	2,246	1,811
	230	221	192	199
	38,122	37,940	34,638	32,207
	2,915	2,688	2,609	2,402

Coasting Trade of the Empire.—Entries

Ports.		1857-58.	
		Entered.	Sailed.
Espirito Santo	Ships	38	40
	Tons	3,651	3,879
	Crew	336	314
Rio Grande do Norte	Ships	66	58
	Tons	34,253	35,397
	Crew	2,215	2,426
Piauhy	Ships	33	33
	Tons	4,075	4,075
	Crew	784	784
Total	Ships	3,119	2,849
	Tons	657,728	555,873
	Crew	42,770	38,641

of Vessels Inwards and Outwards—*continued.*

	1858-59.		1859-60.	
	Entered.	Sailed.	Entered.	Sailed.
	43	40	50	47
	4,374	4,050	5,883	5,615
	390	454	524	488
	96	93	83	76
	56,100	56,105	39,643	39,117
	3,763	3,758	2,456	2,421
	36	36	39	36
	4,600	4,600	5,172	4,676
	914	914	935	905
	3,116	3,019	3,447	3,384
	659,643	610,704	725,180	720,937
	46,616	44,383	51,705	48,377

GOVERNMENT.

BRAZIL is a hereditary constitutional monarchy. The constitution was granted by Pedro I., on the 25th of March, 1824, who then took the title of Constitutional Emperor and Defender of Brazil. It provides for an Emperor, an Imperial Parliament or General Assembly, and the right of trial by jury.

The monarch is hereditary, the succession is in the heirs of Dom Pedro I., and these failing, a new dynasty is to be chosen by the General Assembly during the lifetime of the last of the race. The new dynasty is to be a native one. The Emperor (or Empress, as females are not excluded) is the representative and executive of the nation. He appoints the officers of the army and navy, the archbishops and bishops, the judges, the presidents of the provinces, and all the other officials of the government. He appoints seven ministers who are responsible for their acts—namely, of the Empire, of Justice, of Foreign Affairs, of Marine, of War, of Finance, and of Agriculture and Commerce. These ministers carry on the administrations of the empire, through the officials appointed by them, subject to the approval of the Emperor. The Emperor has also the right to pardon criminals, and all acts of provincial presidents must receive his approval. The General Assembly consists of two Chambers, that of the Senate, which comprise 57 members who are elected for life, and approved of by the Emperor, and that of the Deputies, 118 members, who are elected for four years. Both houses are chosen by electors, who represent every fifteen families, and are themselves chosen by other electors, who must possess an income of 200$000 per annum. The senators receive an annuity of 3600$0 and deputies 2,400$000.

The General Assembly makes the laws, votes the sums for the necessary expenses of the Empire, and chooses a new dynasty if necessary, but all bills must receive the consent of the majority in each Chamber, and of the Emperor, before becoming law.

The judges are appointed for life, and are removable only by impeachment. The constitution recognises only two kinds, the first and second, namely, *juizes de direito* (judges of rights), and *juizes de relacões* (judges of appeal). But, besides these, there are the municipal judges, who take cognizance of civil causes, and originate all criminal processes, and the Supreme Tribunal, which guards the uniformity and justice of procedure in the lower courts, and has also jurisdiction over offences committed by its own members, those of the *relacões*, *diplomats*, bishops, and presidents of provinces. The Supreme Court and those of *relacões* are presided over by the perpetual judges, called *desembargadores*.

There are also other exceptional judges for particular purposes, namely—*juizes des feitos*, *juizes do commercio*, and *Tribunals do Commercio* in Rio, Bahia, and Pernambuco, and the two last also in Maranhão. Auditors of war and marine, a Supreme Military Tribunal, and ecclesiastic judges and *relacão* for clerical causes.

The population is not exactly known for want of accurate enrolment, but, according to the best authorities, it is estimated at 9,083,725, including about 1,357,416 slaves, and excluding about 200,000 Indians, which last are chiefly in the provinces of Amazonas, Pará, Piauhy, Goyaz, and Mato Grosso, a part of them being domesticated, while others, especially in Amazonas and Goyaz, are yet uninfluenced by civilisation, and remain almost unknown.

The population of Brazil consists of three essentially distinct races, the European, the Indian, and the Negro ; a proportion of which remain pure, but the majority is composed of an intermingling of these races in every conceivable degree. No prejudice as regards colour exists in Brazil, and both political and social distinction is open alike to white, black, and red, many of the chief families priding themselves on their descent from celebrated Indian notabilities.

The religion of the people and of the State is Roman Catholic, but all others are tolerated. The Empire is divided into two archiepiscopal sees, those of Rio de Janeiro and Bahia, and into eleven bishoprics, which contain 1,124 parishes. The patronage of the Church is in the gift of the Minister of the Empire.

TITLES AND ORDERS OF MERIT.

The Emperor can create barons, viscounts, and marquises. There are, besides, four orders of merit, the orders of the Cruzeiro do Sul, of the Rosa, of Aviz, and of Christo.

EDUCATION.

Public instruction is liberally provided for by law, and a free school must be maintained in every parish. There exist two colleges for lawyers, one in S. Paulo, and one in Pernambuco; two for medical students, one in Rio and one in Bahia; engineering, and military and naval colleges; 21 lyceums in the provinces, and about 2,000 primary schools.

Few of the free population cannot read and write.

There are also many literary and scientific associations and libraries, and in Rio de Janeiro is a school of the fine arts.

The *army* consists of about 22,000 men, distributed throughout the Empire, and of about 560,000 men of the National Guard, liable to be called on to serve in case of necessity. There are, besides, about 4,000 police.

The *navy* consists of 42 vessels of all kinds, manned by 3,617 men. Of these vessels, 29 are steamers, with an aggregate of 4,944 horse-power.

MILITARY AND NAVAL ESTABLISHMENTS.

There are a powder manufactory near Rio Janeiro, a foundry at Ipauéma, and arsenals of war at Maranhão, Rio Janeiro, and Porto Alegre. Arsenals of marine exist at Pará, Pernambuco, Bahia, and Rio Janeiro.

LIGHTHOUSES.

On the coast of Brazil are 16 lighthouses.

Colonies existing in 1862.

Provinces.	Colonies.	To whom belonging.	Population.
Santa Catharina	Blumenau	Government	2,058
,,	Itajahy	,,	833
,,	Theresopolis	,,	1,282
,,	Santa Isabel and Vargem Grande	,,	1,016
,,	Donna Francisca	Aided undertaking	3,676
,,	Angelina	Provincial Government	207
,,	Flor da Silva	Private	212
Paraná	Assunguy	Government	85
,,	Theresa	,,	289
S. Paulo	Cananéa	,,	67
Minas Geraes	Mucury	,,	487
,,	Pedro II.	Aided undertaking	1,219
Espirito Santo	Santa Isabel	Government	801
,,	Santa Leopoldina	,,	1,130
,,	Rio Novo	,,	433
,,	Guandú	,,	...
S. Pedro	Santa Cruz	Provincial Government	3,767
,,	Santo Angelo	,,	508
,,	Nova Petropolis	,,	612
,,	Santa Maria da Soledade.	Aided undertaking	1,403
,,	S. Lourenço	,,	213
,,	Conventos	Private	332
,,	Estrella	,,	294
Maranhão	Petropolis	,,	60
,,	Santa Isabel	,,	97

RAILROADS.

Railroads in Brazil have hitherto been very unprofitable speculations, both for the companies which have made them and for the Government which guarantees their dividends. For this there are several causes, one of which lies in the nature of the country itself. Along the ocean the eastern seacoast is in general fringed with a narrow belt of comparatively low level land, from twenty to one hundred miles wide, which offers few obstacles to the construction of roads and railways, but, this passed, the mountains that gird the elevated plateau of the interior, raise themselves almost abruptly from the plains below, and give rise to engineering difficulties of the highest order. Add to this, that, supported by English capitalists, planned by extravagant engineers, and superintended by extravagant *employés* at extravagant salaries, they have been constructed with costly stations, and with grades, tunnels, curves, and ways suited, no doubt, to the great speed and traffic of an English railway, but utterly incommensurate with the circumstances of a new and undeveloped country; so it is not to be wondered at that these enterprises have disappointed and disheartened, not only the companies themselves, but also the Government and people of Brazil, among whom they have unfortunately created a fear and horror of the English system of construction.

Another great drawback to the prosperity of these lines, and, indeed, of Brazil in general, is that entailed on the country from former years, when large grants of land were made by the kings of Portugal for services rendered to the State, and thus the at present most valuable and accessible parts of the country are in the hands of a few large landowners, who (with some exceptions) are unwilling either to colonise or sell any portion of their large domains.

Aware of this, the companies egregiously erred in not stipulating with the Government for a law of disappropriation to oblige the landed proprietors to sell or surrender to them all the land within a certain distance along the road, thus to open it to the immigration and the enterprise which would gladly take advantage of the facilities of railroad communication to settle and cultivate the land along the lines, furnishing, by their labour and consumption, the traffic necessary to give a fitting return for the funds invested, and to relieve the Government from the incubus of the payment of the guarantee of dividend.

In this little difficulty was to be apprehended. The Government and statesmen of Brazil are too enlightened not to have long been fully alive to the evils resulting from the ancient grants, and, while rightly unwilling to take away the vested rights of the *donatorios*, would gladly have availed themselves of any project by which, while giving to the latter just compensation for their loss, large tracts of land in most favourable situations would be afforded for the encouragement of the emigration of the working and farming classes of Europe.

FINANCES.

The Imperial revenue is derived from import and export duties, stamp and other excise taxes, house and other taxes in the municipality of Rio de Janeiro, produce of the Government gold and diamond mines, and other minor sources. The collections are made through the various custom-houses of the provinces, and by officers in each province appointed by the general Government. The receipts and collections made are paid into the Imperial treasury of each province, and are subject to the orders of the Minister of Finance.

The Government owned (December, 1863) 1,481 slaves, and 28 large estates, together with about 50,000 cattle, horses, mules, &c. From want of proper management these estates yield but little revenue. In July, 1864, 840 of the Government slaves were set free by order of the Minister of Justice.

IMPERIAL REVENUE AND EXPENDITURE.

IMPERIAL REVENUE from all sources, including Deposits.

Derived from	1848-49.	1849-50.	1850-51.	1851-52.
Importation Duties	15,455,014$299	17,429,436$256	20,506,637$454	24,840,292$032
Coasting Export Duties	573,974$916	557,035$400	523,479$567	558,576$541
Exportation Duties	3,834,369$966	3,815,941$825	4,718,941$123	4,538,306$709
Excise and Interior	4,297,393$768	3,884,420$510	4,462,830$552	4,466,726$331
Taxes in the Municipality	878,321$651	1,009,603$914	995,013$949	984,898$789
Extraordinary	165,204$712	281,398$525	325,862$048	398,021$451
Deposits	958,749$129	1,222,313$146	1,164,137$290	1,925,776$067
Total	26,163,028$441	28,200,149$576	32,696,901$983	37,712,597$920

Imperial Revenue from all sources, including Deposits—*continued*.

Derived from	1852-53.	1853-54.	1854-55.	1855-56.
Importation Duties...	24,758,150$637	23,527,067$603	23,687,616$134	25,485,031$773
Coasting Export Duties	199,156$984	199,559$275	239,510$644	249,081$598
Exportation Duties...	4,982,343$356	3,833,442$512	4,476,455$104	4,662,445$594
Excise and Interior...	4,702,748$096	5,045,894$837	5,906,719$033	6,229,737$446
Taxes in the Municipality	1,163,807$113	1,191,722$614	1,305,260$187	1,426,058$498
Extraordinary ...	584,825$822	718,768$817	370,037$380	582,001$203
Deposits	1,711,770$834	2,531,761$184	2,590,565$317	3,307,869$319
Total	38,102,802$842	37,048,216$842	38,576,163$799	41,942,225$424

Imperial Revenue from all sources, including Deposits—*continued.*

Derived from	1856-57.	1857-58.	1858-59.	1859-60.
Importation Duties...	32,856,263$294	32,213,399$156	29,021,792$408	27,247,145$562
Coasting Export Duties ...	249,445$573	264,477$199	280,057$130	282,102$648
Exportation Duties...	6,910,998$779	6,661,891$249	7,380,069$913	5,569,626$548
Excise and Interior...	7,065,737$685	7,945,088$851	7,921,970$360	8,329,532$121
Taxes in the Municipality ...	1,531,753$718	1,742,638$764	1,571,917$549	1,759,827$276
Extraordinary ...	542,215$675	919,511$968	744,188$115	619,112$295
Deposits ...	3,599,694$512	3,664,159$326	3,455,727$863	3,503,608$776
Total .	52,756,109$236	53,411,166$713	50,375,723$338	47,310,955$226

Imperial Revenue from all sources, including Deposits—*continued.*

Derived from	1860-61.	1861-62.	1862-63.	Estimate for 1865-66.
Importation Duties...	30,022,732$152	31,365,424$056	27,011,114$150	29,822,331$000
Coasting Export Duties	265,127$843	281,496$076	248,342$548	264,221$000
Exportation Duties...	7,266,288$809	8,226,809$805	8,166,795$706	8,636$000
Excise and Interior...	9,140,939$290	9,413,979$726	9,021,114$585	10,306,303$000
Taxes in the Municipality	2,508,265$619	2,079,496$851	2,119,405$190	2,203,404$000
Extraordinary ...	852,619$923	1,104,693$680	983,887$774	767,634$000
Deposits	3,525,425$670	3,381,917$934	3,173,374$960	2,856,949$000
Total	53,581,399$306	55,853,818$128	50,724,034$913	54,856,949$000

IMPERIAL REVENUE

Custom-houses.	1858-59.	1859-60.
Rio de Janeiro	18,293,733$919	17,407,651$207
Bahia	5,319,860$497	4,067,919$317
Pernambuco	6,825,217$847	5,368,094$370
Pará	1,285,995$450	1,490,163$402
Maranhão	1,274,795$669	990,388$422
Rio Grande do Sul	1,446,492$258	1,585,778$558
Santos	473,930$313	625,734$188
Porto Alegre	360,797$907	340,627$529
Ceará	375,217$887	346,648$258
Alagôas	217,615$586	115,619$183
Parahiba	275,666$596	225,851$056
Paranaguá	112,762$370	123,456$414
Uruguayana	173,120$233	147,436$372
Albuquerque	41,521$557	54,053$626
Aracajú	121,135$168	63,290$424
Santa Catharina	69,093$860	83,552$016
Parnahiba	67,645$217	71,739$108
Rio Grande do Norte	134,989$575	211,941$602
Espirito Santo	21,085$467	23,150$449
	36,890,637$376	33,349,095$495

DERIVED FROM COMMERCE.

1860-61.	1861-62.	1862-63.	1st half of 1863-64.
22,171,321$483	20,179,730$519	17,219,751$950	9,290,148$526
3,622,465$813	5,755,675$997	5,967,210$002	2,166,475$249
4,403,796$091	6,217,718$703	5,267,205$020	2,516,306$665
1,921,235$817	1,488,695$365	1,358,993$480	974,909$149
977,480$693	1,222,251$554	1,441,995$995	1,054,607$982
2,058,997$475	1,949,234$518	1,485,255$363	746,444$764
703,872$522	982,406$111	1,035,017$376	413,882$587
429,572$711	637,557$082	370,460$807	110,564$011
375,936$330	512,434$417	633,688$040	434,407$391
121,570$706	248,957$228	387,158$027	139,524$940
209,786$203	260,081$228	328,626$756	135,052$605
134,731$018	113,947$215	129,170$073	76,759$774
153,986$140	108,816$182	90,876$963	55,091$247
71,551$034	106,698$076	84,698$823	28,997$775
49,449$567	99,064$063	126,106$393	50,656$871
97,048$843	93,241$733	110,464$257	71,355$372
98,342$130	109,575$443	97,075$110	38,468$138
99,929$776	44,431$932	53,945$768	89,515$566
27,269$996	34,281$438	35,361$444	13,477$284
37,728,344$348	40,164,798$864	36,223,061$647	18,406,645$896

IMPERIAL EXPENDITURE,

Year.	Empire.	Justice.
1844–45	2,934,492$795	1,338,261$425
1845–46	3,197,141$243	1,426,009$181
1846–47	3,461,095$630	1,567,182$909
1847–48	3,493,818$059	1,575,832$745
1848–49	3,617,373$283	1,720,082$313
1849–50	4,427,124$837	1,833,777$634
1850–51	4,077,067$918	2,012,168$463
1851–52	3,377,472$774	1,916,368$558
1852–53	4,400,084$498	2,190,527$299
1853–54	4,781,379$085	2,478,187$914
1854–55	6,000,712$854	2,862,494$629
1855–56	7,992,885$206	2,873,960$704
1856–57	6,656,227$301	3,309,732$618
1857–58	8,342,889$954	3,730,665$458
1858–59	10,304,411$041	4,371,775$828
1859–60	10,029,718$926	4,713,184$553
1860–61	8,046,406$912	4,017,174$719
1861–62	4,361,711$868	2,857,745$270
1862–63	3,850,047$485	2,881,067$024

SHOWING THAT OF EACH DEPARTMENT.

Foreign.	Marine.	War.
579,178$237	3,357,427$673	7,414,189$720
466,532$456	3,421,481$963	6,464,733$622
447,253$427	3,969,450$502	6,120,440$080
450,245$036	3,793,997$134	6,019,239$185
513,585$165	3,909,508$381	7,852,024$677
387,910$462	4,239,191$070	7,317,879$547
1,060,045$720	5,165,676$734	9,096,592$143
3,039,846$323	4,764,741$715	15,679,741$137
816,730$301	4,473,296$466	8,190,301$670
1,389,551$440	5,299,643$194	9,142,063$818
1,108,403$516	6,066,008$190	10,637,965$905
640,462$375	5,201,161$924	11,013,196$528
639,374$130	5,510,457$578	106,417,68$406
1,598,670$157	10,496,297$671	14,207,026$416
892,178$371	9,561,468$595	12,539,546$280
860,586$413	9,306,836$687	12,925,385$852
858,884$096	7,905,253$790	11,505,722$527
787,471$248	7,502,891$163	11,365,441$369
1,610,574$615	7,821,027$955	11,112,648$780

Imperial Expenditure, showing that of each Department—*continued.*

Year.	Finance.	Agriculture, Commerce, and Public Works.	Total.
1844–45	9,834,980$484	...	25,458,530$334
1845–46	9,269,615$067	...	24,245,513$532
1846–47	9,403,645$167	...	24,969,067$715
1847–48	9,649,809$297	...	24,982,941$456
1848–49	10,270,998$648	...	27,883,572$467
1849–50	10,356,970$595	...	28,562,854$145
1850–51	11,244,250$175	...	32,655,801$153
1851–52	13,462,850$840	...	42,241,021$347
1852–53	10,858,392$060	...	30,929,332$294
1853–54	13,143,663$604	...	36,234,489$055
1854–55	12,064,734$694	...	38,740,319$788
1855–56	12,520,981$970	...	40,242,648$707
1856–57	13,616,403$403	...	40,373,963$436
1857–58	13,380,107$250	...	51,755,656$906
1858–59	15,049,200$553	...	52,718,580$668
1859–60	14,770,439$338	...	52,606,151$769
1860–61	16,153,431$629	3,871,543$615	52,358,417$288
1861–62	18,828,325$453	7,594,842$704	53,298,429$075
1862–63	20,630,491$465	7,181,999$886	55,087,857$210

The Department of Agriculture, Commerce, and Public Works was created in 1860, previous to which time it was included in that of the Empire.

FUNDED IMPERIAL DEBT, COINAGE, &c.

FUNDED IMPERIAL DEBT.

Loans.	Original Capital.	
	Real.	Nominal.
	£	£
Of 1824 due 1864	2,999,940	3,686,200
,, 1839 ,, 1869	312,512	411,200
,, 1843 ,, 1864	622,702	732,600
,, 1852 ,, 1882	954,250	1,040,600
,, 1859 ,, 1879	508,000	508,000
,, 1863 ,, 1893	3,300,000	3,855,300
	8,697,404	10,233,900
For the Railroad Pedro II., contracted May 19th, 1858, due 1888	1,425,000	1,526,500
Contracted March 16th, 1860, due 1890, for the Co. União e Industria	675,000	765,930
For the Railroad of Pernambuco	400,000	453,884
For the Co. do Mucury	135,000	153,186
Total	11,332,404	13,133,400

State on 6th of April, 1864.

Extinguished.				Nominal Circulation.
Real.			Nominal.	
£	s.	d.	£	£
2,999,940	0	0	3,686,200	...
85,138	5	0	86,000	325,200
622,704	0	0	732,600	...
139,950	5	0	150,600	890,000
80,707	10	0	80,800	427,200
...			...	3,855,300
3,929,440	0	0	4,736,200	5,497,700
185,200	0	0	203,200	1,323,800
47,679	2	6	52,661	713,269
28,254	6	0	31,207	422,677
9,535	16	6	10,532	142,654
4,200,109	5	0	5,033,800	8,099,600

FUNDED INTERNAL DEBT.—State on 31st March, 1864.

	Issued.	Extinguished.	Total Circulation.
Bonds at 6 per cent., Rio de Janeiro	78,492,000$000	3,672,000$000	74,820,000$000
,, 5 ,, Ditto	1,333,800$000	161,200$000	1,172,600$000
,, 5 ,, Bahia	290,200$000	...	290,200$000
,, 5 ,, Pernambuco...	63,400$000	...	63,400$000
,, 5 ,, Maranhão ...	36,400$000	...	36,400$000
,, 5 ,, S. Pedro ...	77,800$000	...	77,800$000
,, 5 ,, Goyaz	41,000$000	...	41,000$000
,, 5 ,, Mato Grosso...	156,400$000	...	156,400$000
,, 4 ,, Rio de Janeiro	119,600$000	...	119,600$000
Total	80,610,600$000	3,833,200$000	76,777,400$000

Their Circulation is thus Distributed:—

	Bonds.			Total Circulation.
	6 Per Cent.	5 Per Cent.	4 Per Cent.	
Amongst Nationals	45,897,600$000	657,800$000	3,800$000	46,559,200$000
,, British	7,029,400$000	23,400$000	...	7,052,800$000
,, Other Countries	1,178,700$000	117,400$000	...	1,296,000$000
,, Banks of Rio...	20,714,400$000	374,000$000	115,800$000	21,204,200$000
,, Provinces	...	665,200$000	...	665,200$000
Total	74,820,000$000	1,837,800$000	119,600$000	76,777,400$000

COINAGE.—Mint Returns of the New Coinage.

	Gold Coins.			Total.
	20$000	10$000	5$000	
From 1849 to 1862	31,410,660$000	6,590,460$000	504,390$000	38,505,510$000
In 1863	163,040$000	18,000$000	$	181,040$000
	31,573,700$000	6,608,460$000	504,390$000	38,686,550$000

	Silver Coins.			Total.
	2$000	1$000	500	200	
From 1849 to 1862	2,921,808$000	6,126,220$000	2,591,148$000	307,271$000	11,946,447$000
In 1863	46,746$000	488,798$000	232,287$000	28,000$000	795,831$000
	2,968,554$000	6,615,018$000	2,823,435$000	335,271$000	12,742,278$000

| Total value of Gold and Silver Coins | | | 51,428,828$000 |

From what Coined.

	Gold.			
	Foreign Coins.	Old National Coins.	Dust and Ingots.	Total.
From 1849 to 1862	21,422,754$000	134,970$000	16,947,786$000	38,505,510$000
In 1863	...	...	181,040$000	181,040$000
	21,422,754$000	134,970$000	17,128,826$000	38,686,550$000

	Silver.		
	Foreign Coins and Ingots.	Old National Coins.	Total.
From 1849 to 1862	10,052,715$950	1,893,731$050	11,946,447$000
In 1863	779,599$034	16,231$966	795,831$000
	10,832,314$984	1,909,963$016	12,742,278$000

The EMPIRE is divided into Twenty

Names.	Area.
Municipality of Rio de Janeiro	60
Province of Amazonas	64,000
,, Parú	39,000
,, Maranhão	12,500
,, Piauhy	11,000
,, Ceará	4,500
,, Rio Grande do Norte	1,500
,, Parahyba	1,500
,, Pernambuco	6,000
,, Alagôas	1,200
,, Sergipe	1,200
,, Bahia	14,000
,, Espirito Santo	1,400
,, Rio de Janeiro	2,400
,, São Paulo	11,000
,, Paraná	6,000
,, Santa Catharina	2,200
,, São Pedro do Sul	9,000
,, Minas Geraes	20,000
,, Goyaz	21,000
,, Mato Grosso	51,000
Total	280,460

Provinces and One Municipality.

Total Population.	Slaves.	Capitals.
400,000	50,000	Rio de Janeiro
70,000	5,000	Manáos
250,000	15,000	Belém
400,000	70,000	S. Luiz
175,000	10,000	Teresina
486,000	30,000	Fortaleza
210,000	20,000	Natal
260,000	5,000	Parahyba
1,180,000	250,000	Recife
250,000	45,000	Macció
250,000	50,000	Aracajú
1,200,000	250,000	Bahia
55,000	10,000	Victoria
850,000	200,000	Nitherohy
800,000	60,000	São Paulo
105,000	20,000	Coritiba
120,000	15,000	Desterro
392,725	77,416	Porto Alegre
1,350,000	150,000	Ouro Preto
200,000	15,000	Goyaz
80,000	10,000	Cuiabá
9,083,725	1,357,416	...

The RAILROADS already Constructed or yet Constructing are—

	Length.	How much Completed.
	Miles.	
The Pedro II., from Rio de Janeiro.	...	...
,, Bahia, from Bahia to Alagoinhas.	77	all.
,, Pernambuco, from Recife to the Una.	77	all.
,, São Paulo, from Santos to Jundiahy.	...	all.
,, Mauá, from Mauá to Fragoza.	...	all.
,, Porto das Caixas, from Porto das Caixas to Cantagallo.	...	all.
,, Tejuca, from Rio de Janeiro to Andarahy.	4	all.

Of these the Pedro II., the Bahia, the Pernambuco, and the São Paulo were built by English companies with English capital.

PROVINCES OF BRAZIL.

THE provincial Government consists of the President of the province, appointed by the Emperor and a Provincial Assembly chosen by the people. All laws relating to the internal management are passed by the Assembly and agreed to by the President, who has a veto, but whose acts are subject to the approval of the Emperor. Besides the Provincial Assembly each city has its Municipal Council, the members of which are elected, and who look to the economy of their city; each parish also possesses its Elective Government.

The municipality of Rio de Janeiro, like the district of Columbia in the United States of North America, is cared for by the Imperial Government. It also possesses a Municipal Council for strictly local matters.

RIO DE JANEIRO.

The municipality of Rio de Janeiro consists of the city of Rio de Janeiro (once called St. Sebastião), and a small extent of territory around it, the whole being about sixty square leagues. This is the *corte* of the empire, and, like the district of Columbia in the United States, is under the direct administration of the Government and General Assembly. It is the capital of the empire, and in it reside the Emperor, the Ministers of State, and the other high functionaries. Here, also, the Imperial Chambers hold their sessions for four months every year, opening on May 3, and closing on September 3.

The *city of Rio de Janeiro* is the most important and most populous town in Brazil, being at once the capital of the empire and the foreign shipping port for the province of Rio de Janeiro. The town cannot be less than six miles long from Botafogo to the Gamboa, and lies along the west side of the beautiful bay of Rio de Janeiro. It is situated in 22° 54' 7" south latitude, and 43° 9' west longitude of Greenwich, and has a population of about 400,000. A military force of about 9,000 is kept here, and about 1,000 police, who wear a similar uniform to that of the soldiers, but are distinguished by wearing a sword. Judging from the extent of ground it covers Rio might be supposed to have a much larger population than it really possesses, but a large part of the space is taken up in the suburbs by the beautiful gardens attached to many of the houses. Rio, at one time, was proverbial for its filthiness, but, of late years, much has been done to facilitate the traffic and improve the sanitary condition of the city. The streets have been carefully paved with squared stones, the roads in the suburbs well macadamised, and a magnificent system of sewerage has been inaugurated, and in part completed, under the practical skill of Mr. Gotto, the engineer of the Company; but there is still needed the great desideratum—a large supply of water to make the working perfect, which, however, will no doubt be obtained, as the

Government is doing all in its power to improve the sanitary state of the city.

The modern houses in Rio are in general well constructed, but the old ones afford miserable accommodation, more especially as the sleeping closets, called *alcovas*, are all without windows, the Brazilians usually devoting their best rooms to ostentation, and sacrificing the useful to the ornamental. Each floor is generally laid out for the use of a family.

The only private buildings worthy of particular notice as specimens of architectural beauty are the Bank of Brazil, and the *palacete* of the Baron of Novo Friburgo, a handsome building, but with the great disadvantage of being located immediately on a thoroughfare.

Of the public buildings of the city one of great importance is the Hospital da Misericordia, which is not far from the Gardens of the Passeio Publico. This hospital is an establishment conducted on a magnificent scale, under the direction of a committee of gentlemen, and zealously ministered to by the sisters of charity, whose Christian care of the inmates sees no distinction of sect or creed. It is daily attended by clergymen to administer spiritual aid to the sick, and connected with it is a school of medicine and surgery. Close by it are the military arsenal and the barracks, neither of which has anything to recommend it. Advancing along Rua da Misericordia you enter Rua Direita, passing the Chamber of Deputies and the city palace of the Emperor, in contiguity with the Imperial Chapel. This edifice may be taken as a fair sample of the style of building which prevails in all the churches of Brazil. Passing along the Rua Direita you come to the Exchange, which structure contains offices of different brokers and a commodious reading-room. Close on the right is the Post-Office, a building affording little of the accommodation required by such an important department.

The Custom House is near the Rua Direita. Its external and internal arrangements, as also its administration, are continually undergoing changes, but without the end of facilitating the despatch of commercial business, unnecessary impediments and delays being caused by the needless multiplicity of forms. The Marine Arsenal, which is at the end of the street, is perhaps not surpassed by any other edifice in Rio, and the buildings enclose a square planted with trees, and surrounded by seats for the use of idlers. Opposite, in the Ilha das Cobras, is a splendid graving dock for the repairs of vessels, and capable of accommodating the largest vessel in the British navy. This great work, after 13 years of fruitless labour, was finally undertaken by Mr. Henry Law, who successfully completed it. It is entirely cut out of the solid rock, and is a beautiful and imperishable monument of the ingenuity and skill of its constructor, who has also contracted for another close by it, to cost 855,000 milreis.

Rua do Ouvidor, being the Regent Street of Rio, is sure to be visited by all strangers. The shops in this street are very neatly kept, and, though small, are furnished with every European article of luxury and utility. Many of the shops of this, and, still more, of the adjoining street, Rua dos Ourives (Goldsmiths' Street), are devoted to valuable jewellery, a partiality for which is a weakness of the Brazilian ladies, and unfortunately leads to great extravagance among many who can ill afford it. From this charge we must, however, except the Empress, who sets her subjects a good example by never appearing in public or private decorated with this expensive manufacture of France and Germany.

Leaving Rua do Ouvidor you come to the Largo do St. Francisco do Paula, one side of which is occupied by a church of the same name, and another by the military college. From this you pass to the Largo do Rocio. Here is the theatre of St. Pedro d'Alcantará. This square is laid out as a promenade, and in its centre is a fine equestrian statue of the Emperor Dom Pedro I., the founder of the empire and the father of the present Emperor. This statue, considered to be one of the finest bronze statues in the world, is by the French sculptor Louis Rochet, a pupil of David d'Angers, and who is well known by his celebrated group of "Count Ugolin and his Children," and by other remarkable works. Executed in the sculptor's best style, it represents the Emperor on the plain of Ypiranga, near S. Paulo, with outstretched arm, declaring to the surrounding people the independence of Brazil, in the words—"Independence or Death"—words which lost to Portugal the finest jewel in her crown, and will render September 7, 1822, a day memorable in the annals of the Brazilian empire. On each side of the square pedestal, which rests on a large mass of granite, are colossal Indian figures, emblematic of the great rivers of the country.

From this you pass to the Campo de Santa Anna, one of the largest squares in Rio, but devoid of embellishment, if we except that of some hundreds of black laundresses washing at the fountains, whose primitive mode of beating the linen on a stone until clean is somewhat novel to English eyes. Notwithstanding its devotion to these black nymphs of cleanliness, this square has on one side the Senate, on another the offices of the Minister of War and the military barracks, on another those of the Minister of Commerce, and on a fourth side is located the provisional Italian Opera House and the Museum. This last cannot boast of very rare specimens, but a visit to the mineralogical department will be repaid, and there is a rich collection of all the woods of the country in a polished state. The interior of the senate affords little accommodation. The senators harangue from their places, and find it necessary to pitch their voices high to ensure their being heard. It contains a gallery for the convenience of their private friends, of the diplomatic corps, and a separate one for strangers.

The new quays and docks now constructing under the superintendence of Mr. Neat, an experienced engineer, are yet far from completion, and, owing to many difficulties during their construction, have already cost the Government 3,500,000$. Besides these undertakings the new mint is worthy of mention. This work, on which already 1,000,000$ has been expended, is in charge of a native, and deserves a recognition of its merit—a merit which Brazilians do not appreciate, as they repose in general more confidence in the abilities of strangers, thus neglecting native talent, a result perhaps arising from the engineering education of the academies, though administered by gentlemen of undoubted powers, being too strictly confined to the theoretic.

There are several public institutions in Rio, of which the Historical, the Geographical, the Fine Arts, and the Agricultural Societies, and the Academy of Medicine are frequently attended by the Emperor.

Education in Rio is given in 46 primary schools for both sexes, a commercial school, a marine academy, a military college, and a first-class college, that of Pedro II., all of which are supported by the Government. In addition to these there are about 20 private schools and colleges, the most important of which is conducted by an English gentleman named Hitchings, who has made it the first in Brazil, and one which would compare favourably with any in Europe.

MASONIC LODGES.

The Grand Orient of Brazil hold their meetings at the Masonic Temple, in Rua dos Benedictinos, the most zealous members of the society having separated from the old edifice in Rua do Lavradio, and having formed about 30 subordinate lodges, which acknowledge only the new organisation, and hold their meetings in the large and spacious rooms of the Temple in Rua dos Benedictinos.

There are three different rites admitted, which are subordinate to their respective High Consistories, every one, however, being subject to the legislative power of the Grand Orient of Brazil, presided over by the Grand Master of the Order, his Excellency Joaquim Saldanho Maranho.

The high orders are:—A Supreme Consistory of the General Inspectors, 33; a Grand Lodge of the Princes Kadosk, 30, for the Red or Scotch rite; a Chapter of the Princes Rose Croix for the Blue or Modern rite; and a Council of the Prussian Knights for the Adonhiramit rite.

STEAM COMMUNICATION.

Fine steamers carrying the mails leave on the 7th and 23rd of each month for the northern ports of Bahia, Maceio, Pernambuco, Parahyba, Rio Grande do Norte, Ceará, Maranhão, and Pará; and on the 6th of each month for the southern ports of Desterro, Rio Grande, Porto Alegre, and Monté Video. Other small steamers carry on a lively intercourse with the other ports north and south of Rio.

The foreign steamers leaving this port are:—

On the 8th of each month, the English mail steamers for Southampton; calling at Bahia, Pernambuco, S. Vincente, and Lisbon.

On the 24th of each month, the French mail steamers for Bordeaux; calling at Bahia, Pernambuco, S. Vincente, and Lisbon 48 hours after their arrival. The English and French mail steamers for Monté Video and Buenos Ayres; these connect with the respective European lines, and carry the mails and passengers to and from Monté Video and Buenos Ayres.

The foreign steamers arriving are:—

Due on the 3rd of each month, the English mail steamers from Southampton; calling at the ports above mentioned.

Due on the 18th of each month, the French mail steamers from Bordeaux; calling at the ports above mentioned.

About the 5th and 18th of each month, the English and French steamers from Buenos Ayres.

Besides these there are two lines of screw-steamers between Liverpool and Buenos Ayres, which touch at the Brazilian ports of Bahia and Rio de Janeiro.

BANKS.

There are five banking establishments in Rio—

Banks.	Capital.	Paid-Up.
The Banco do Brazil...	33,000,000$	33,000,000$
,, Banco Rural e Hypothecario ...	8,000,000$	8,000,000$
,, London and Brazilian Bank, Limited ...	13,333,333$	4,622,200$
,, Brazilian and Portuguese Bank, Limited ...	8,888,888$	4,444,444$
,, Banco, Mariú McGregor and Co., Commandita...	6,000,000$	6,000,000$

and in addition to these there are many discount houses. The Bank of Brazil is the national bank of the empire, and is the only bank of issue in Rio, it being allowed to circulate notes to double the amount of its metallic deposit. It thus enjoys an important and lucrative privilege; but, unfortunately, the directors are not always judiciously chosen, and the great evil exists of too much of the red-tape system. As it justly deserves, the Brazilian and Portuguese Bank enjoys the highest credit, from the ability with which it is managed by Mr. Hobkirk and two excellent directors, chosen from the first mercantile houses in Rio. The London and Brazilian Bank affords great commercial facilities, issues circular letters of credit payable throughout Europe and South America, and has branches at Bahia, Pernambuco, and Rio Grande do Sul.

COMMERCE AND MANUFACTURES.

The *industry*, *commerce*, and *manufactures* of Rio are greatly progressing. There are about fifty cotton, paper, hat, soap, glass, carriage, and other manufactories. Telegraph wires run through the city to Petropolis, and also along the first section of the Railway Pedro II., and to and between the different police stations of Rio.

The commerce of Rio is yearly augmenting, as may be seen by the statistics. It was formerly almost entirely in the hands of foreigners, but the natives, who are many of them men of great natural talent, and possessed of great zeal and integrity, are eagerly entering into all kinds of enterprises.

The foreign commerce of Rio has considerably increased since the cessation of the slave-trade, in 1850. The great decrease, since 1860-61, was owing to failure in the coffee crops.

FOREIGN TRADE of Rio de Janeiro.—Value of Exports and Imports.

Years.	1849-50.	1853-54.	1854-55.
Exports	Milreis. 26,343,000	Milreis. 37,711,431	Milreis. 51,171,340
Imports	...	47,034,190	47,431,056
Total	26,343,000	84,745,621	98,602,396

Years.	1857-58.	1858-59.	1859-60.
Exports	Milreis. 44,421,609	Milreis. 51,974,658	Milreis. 57,592,639
Imports	69,539,746	68,540,352	60,229,412
Total	113,961,355	120,515,010	117,822,051

Years.	1860-61.	1861-62.	1862-63.
Exports	Milreis. 79,083,786	Milreis. 57,845,011	Milreis. 52,810,706
Imports	72,979,831	58,222,834	49,621,604
Total	152,063,617	116,067,845	102,432,310

FOREIGN TRADE of Rio de Janeiro.—Value of Exports and Imports.

1862-63.	British Possessions.	English Channel, to Order.	French Possessions.
	Milreis.	Milreis.	Milreis.
Exports to ...	9,194,203	12,181,822	10,333,520
Imports from ...	25,670,172	...	10,771,787
Total	34,864,375	12,181,822	21,105,307

1862-63.	United States.	Portuguese Possessions.	La Plata.
	Milreis.	Milreis.	Milreis.
Exports to ...	9,696,040	1,734,966	1,611,930
Imports from ...	3,178,112	2,195,162	3,974,152
Total	12,874,152	3,930,128	5,586,082

1862-63.	Hanse Towns.	Other Countries.	GRAND TOTAL.
	Milreis.	Milreis.	Milreis.
Exports to ...	1,408,766	6,649,459	52,810,706
Imports from ...	1,654,771	2,177,448	49,621,604
Total	3,063,537	8,826,907	102,432,310

The Exports to the English Channel to order were mostly for Great Britain.

This great commerce makes Rio de Janeiro the emporium of South America, and yields to the general Government a revenue of from 17,000,000$ to 22,000,000$, annually; being one half of the Imperial revenue derived from commerce.

The commerce of Rio is very great, and employs a large number of vessels. The coasting trade is almost entirely confined to national vessels, and furnishes employment to a yearly increasing number.

COASTING TRADE of Rio de Janeiro.—Number and Tonnage of Vessels which entered and sailed during Seven Years from 1857-8 to 1863-64.

	1857-58.		1858-59.	
	Entered.	Sailed.	Entered.	Sailed.
Ships	1,059	1,096	958	996
Tonnage	143,621	154,033	130,584	141,550

Coasting Trade of Rio de Janeiro.—Number and Tonnage of the Vessels which Entered and Sailed during Seven Years, from 1857-58 to 1863-64—*continued.*

	1859-60.		1860-61.	
	Entered.	Sailed.	Entered.	Sailed.
Ships	1,016	1,045	894	921
Tonnage	141,470	147,291	126,849	127,892

	1861-62.		1862-63.	
	Entered.	Sailed.	Entered.	Sailed.
Ships	706	834	1,071	1,280
Tonnage	101,140	117,081	188,384	270,079

	1863-64.	
	Entered.	Sailed.
Ships	2,054	2,280
Tonnage	282,688	343,206

Foreign vessels are allowed to carry coastwise certain articles of food, and also soap. It is believed that the Assembly will abolish the **navigation laws**, and open the coasting trade to foreign vessels.

Coasting Trade of Rio.—Entries and Departures for the Year 1863-64.

Foreign Vessels Entered ...	63	Measuring 16,539 tons	Sailed ...	195	Measuring 73,927 tons.
National Vessels Entered ...	1,595	Sailing Vessels ...	,, ...	1,690	Sailing Vessels.
Ditto	396	Steamers ...	,, ...	395	Steamers.
	2,054	Vessels	,, ...	2,280	Vessels.

City and Province of Rio de Janeiro, January 1st, 1864, owned—

...	74	Sailing Vessels...	...	913 men	in Foreign Trade.
28 steamers ...	205	Ditto ...	...	8,397 ,,	in Coast Trade.
27 ,, ...	1,499	Ditto ...	...	3,590 ,,	in Ports and Rivers.
...	...	...	1,238	Barges, Boats, &c. 1,852 ,,	Fishing.
55 steamers ...	1,778	Sailing Vessels...	1,238	Barges, Boats, &c. 14,752 men	

The foreign trade of Rio is mostly carried on in foreign vessels. There has been a considerable falling off since 1860, caused by a partial failure in the coffee crop, coffee being the greatest article of export.

FOREIGN TRADE of Rio de Janeiro.—Number and Tonnage of the Vessels which entered and sailed during Seven Years from 1857-58 to 1863-64.

	1857-58.		1858-59.	
	Entered.	Sailed.	Entered.	Sailed.
Ships	1,121	1,095	1,157	1,089
Tons	513,103	508,598	507,030	466,421

	1859-60.		1860-61.	
	Entered.	Sailed.	Entered.	Sailed.
Ships	1,153	1,212	1,204	1,190
Tons	505,834	522,361	527,353	554,662

RIO DE JANEIRO. 169

Foreign Trade of Rio de Janeiro.—Number and Tonnage of the Vessels which entered and sailed during Seven Years from 1857–58 to 1863–64—*continued.*

	1861-62.		1862-63.	
	Entered.	Sailed.	Entered.	Sailed.
Ships	1,130	1,011	1,040	846
Tons	407,601	498,302	369,323	441,167

	1863-64.	
	Entered.	Sailed.
Ships	1,021	808
Tons	373,117	398,545

In 1863-64, Fifty-eight Steamers entered and Fifty-four sailed.

BRAZIL.

FOREIGN TRADE of Rio de Janeiro.—Nationality of the Vessels which entered and sailed 1863–4.

1863-4.	English.	Portuguese.	French.	Danish.	United States.	Swedish.	Spanish.	Hamburg.
Entered ...	207	105	96	86	84	62	45	43
Sailed ...	177	75	86	76	83	57	29	31

1863-4.	Norwegian.	Dutch.	Bremen.	Argentine.	Italian.	Hanoverian.	Austrian.	Russian.
Entered ...	36	26	24	22	21	16	11	9
Sailed ...	24	17	14	23	12	18	5	8

1863-4.	Prussian.	Uruguayan.	Oldenburg.	Belgian.	Lubeck.	Mecklenburg.	Chilean.	Total.
Entered ...	8	8	8	5	4	3	1	930
Sailed ...	7	9	...	3	1	6	...	761

SCENERY.

Sailing to Rio de Janeiro from the north, the first place of note which is seen is Cape Frio, a rugged and remarkable headland, situated about twenty leagues from the entrance of the harbour of Rio, from which it lies due east.

The land from this to the bay of Rio is low and sandy near the beach, but at a short distance inland is more elevated and irregular; and the varying contour of the mountains is interesting and picturesque.

Cape Negro, twelve leagues west of Cape Frio, is the first notable prominence in this direction. This cape is formed by a small hill at the extremity of a range of mountains, and is covered with blackish verdure, whence its name. Within three miles of it vessels may approach the shore in safety, as there is 18 to 26 fathoms water, with a soft oozy bottom.

From Cape Frio to Rio de Janeiro strangers can view a fair specimen of Brazilian scenery, and, as all vessels keep within a short distance of the land, an opportunity is afforded of seeing every inlet along the coast, some of which, enclosed by lofty masses of granite, are very beautiful.

Straight before you, when near the harbour, are the Pão de Assucar (sugar-loaf), the Corcovado (hunchback), the Gavéa (top-sail), and the Dois Irmãos (two brothers), besides other mountains of singular form and great height. During foggy mornings many of these raise their heads high above the mists, and serve as guides to the port. The Gavéa is the most westerly, and is remarkable for its perpendicular sides and flat table-like top. The Corcovado is more to the east, and its high point seems to pierce the heavens.

Close to this is the Pão de Assucar, a conical mountain, with its steepest side to the west, and which forms one side of the entrance to the harbour. When near to this the gorge opens, and through it is seen the calm expanse of what is generally deemed the finest harbour in the world. The entrance is here about one mile wide, and guarded on both sides by solid masses of granite, and the strong fortification of Santa Cruz is placed on its right side. The Ilha de Rasa, near the mouth of the harbour, appears from the east like a slipper with the sloping side northward, and on it is a lighthouse whose light may be seen ten leagues off, and which revolves every ten seconds, presenting, alternately, white and red lights.

The first appearance of the Bay of Rio de Janeiro to a stranger is certainly the most picturesque in the world, with its surrounding verdure-adorned mountains, and their easy slopes covered with the richest green. Plantations of all kinds, handsome country seats, and well-cultivated islands ornament and diversify the surface of this little inland sea of 105 miles circumference; and, taken in all, there is not perhaps a sight elsewhere more imposing and agreeable. To the north you see, at a distance of 40 miles, the Organ mountains reaching along the horizon; to the left, the Corcovado extends its peak over the Sugar-loaf; hill after hill meets the eye, until the city, expanding to the view, spreads, like ancient Rome, over the amphitheatre of its seven hills and intervening valleys.

Every traveller on coming to a city for the first time should see it from an eminence, and Rio has numerous ones from which to acquire an acquaintance with the relative bearings of the buildings and the scenery. The best point for this purpose is the Castle-hill ; but if you enjoy a really magnificent prospect, if your soul hangs with delight on a rich and diversified grandeur of hill and vale, of city and country, of land and water, of fertile gardens and uncultivated woodlands, go to the height terminating the hill of Santa Thereza, and ascend to the top of the Corcovado, an elevation of 2,600 feet above the sea, where the surrounding beauty is chiefly derived from the impressive variety of forms assumed by the different ranges of mountains, whose relative distances are marked by the position of the clouds resting on their summits.

To diversify this view it should be revisited before sunrise on some foggy morning, when the scene becomes indescribably sublime and beautiful. The mountains that before had formed a continuous amphitheatre, now in the low fog seem like islands and separate headlands, and, when the fog vanishes in the morning glow, the eye can wander in rapturous observation over an endless variety of picturesque and glorious combination ; a scene of wondrous beauty, whose general effect must defy alike verbal and pictorial descriptions.

This place can be ascended with facility by going along the hill of Santa Thereza, and, if ladies are among the excursionists, the same route should be taken to return, as to descend by Larangeiras is somewhat difficult; still this beautiful valley is well worth the exertion, and if you wish to luxuriate in " Adam's ale " of the purest quality, you will find at the base of the hill the famed fountain, Bica da Rainha, opposite the *palacete* of Commendador José de Carvalho Pinto, who, like all his countrymen, proverbial for their courtesy, will not refuse you a cup wherewith to drink.

This water is deliciously cool, and quite a contrast with the tepid beverage which you have to drink elsewhere, and it is strange so copious and unfailing a supply should be found so near the top of a hill. A large deposit must indeed exist to supply the many fountains of the city which are fed by the springs of the Corcovado, as they are never known to fail even in the dryest seasons.

The environs of Rio are occupied by some beautiful houses, and with extensive gardens that furnish the town with abundance of vegetables. The most rocky and uncultivated places produce spontaneously delicate plants and flowers, which it would be very difficult to rear in Europe ; and the trees, of which there are great numbers, have a varied richness of leaf, form, and colour. Of these the mangas are the most common, and there is not perhaps a more delightful feast for the eye than an avenue of these trees, some years laden with their much-prized fruit, and at all times clothed in a beautiful verdure that perfumes the air for many a yard around.

An evening will be agreeably spent in an equestrian excursion to the Cova d' Onça (den of the ounce), to which you ascend the hill of Santa Thereza. When you reach this elevated point the magnificent sight in front and rear will be enjoyed with undiminished delight, in the unbounded view of mountain and valley and harbour intermingled in one wide expanse of beauty and grandeur. To the south-east the horizon is bounded by the peaks of the Corcovado, to the north lie the beautiful bay and all the rich alternation of precipice and valley, and form together a panorama of the most diversified and impressive character. In truth, whatever point the traveller may ascend in the suburbs of the town, his eye rests only on a scene of beauty needing no aid from the art or enterprise of man.

The lovely locality of Botafogo, situated about three miles from the city southward, is one of the many pretty inlets surrounding the bay of Rio de Janeiro.

It is a place of easy access, steamboats going to it morning and evening, and omnibuses every half-hour. Taking the steamer and returning by the omnibus, you can obtain an idea of Brazilian rural architecture, as the road is lined with beautiful *palacetes*, and while at Botafogo the splendid view of the entrance to the Botanic Gardens should not be missed, as the avenue of magnificent palm-trees is unsurpassable in the world. This, however, is the only attraction of the gardens, excepting some plants and trees interesting to botanists. On returning from Botafogo you have another view of the cliff of the Corcovado uprearing its enormous mass to the skies.

The neighbourhoods of Botafogo and of the Glória are in general chosen by English people for their residences, and may be looked upon as the west-end of Rio.

The scenery is fine, and many of the houses command a view of the mouth of the harbour, and of all the vessels entering and leaving it. The Glória has been much improved of late years by the enterprise and talent of the late Dr. Cajueiros.

Returning to the city you come to the Passeio Publico, or Public Walks, which is close to the town, and open to every one. It forms an agreeable promenade, and is much frequented by the citizens during the summer months. The entrance is unpretentious, but there are a serpentine canal and some small *jets d'eau*, and from the terrace, which is neatly constructed and has at each end an octagonal house, there is a fine view of the forts, and of the man-of-war anchorage.

The traveller should take the earliest opportunity of paying a visit to Tijuca, which he can reach in two hours by taking the tramway to Andarahy, and thence riding on horseback to the beautiful valley, which forms a pleasant and convenient place of residence, and where the mansions of Dr. Cochrane and Mr. Ginty seem almost more appropriate for dreaming poets than for such energetic and business-like individuals. The views descried from the mountains here are lovely beyond description, in the undulation of the forest-covered hills; and a few days spent in seeing the Cascades will be well repaid. Here, in the midst of the fairy-scene, the traveller can avail himself of the well-known courtesy and hospitality of Mr. Bennett, whose hotel, perhaps the best in Brazil, is located in this beautiful region.

From the hills of Tijuca you can see the deep blue South Atlantic, and when commencing the descent on your return to the city, there will open before you an extensive view of cultivated lands interspersed with *chacaras* (country seats).

At St. Christovão is the palace of the Emperor, which is about three miles from the city, and is the Emperor's residence. Until lately it was not an edifice deserving the name of palace, but at present, with additions and repairs, affords more or less suitable reception-rooms and accommodation for the Imperial household.

On the 10th of October, 1864, Rio was visited by a storm such as had never before been experienced in that city. The fierce wind was accompanied by heavy showers of rain, and by hailstones as large as pigeons' eggs, which demolished fully one-half of the windows and skylights of the city, the suburbs, and the Emperor's palace at S. Christovão—plate-glass panes being pierced with holes as if by pistol bullets. Branches of trees were broken and twisted off, and the leaves riddled and destroyed by the hail, which poured down in such quantities that piles remained at the corners of the streets until the afternoon of the following day. The lightning was vivid, and such was the amount of electricity present that an iron railing at Andarahy, struck by a thunderbolt, was destroyed and melted into a shapeless mass. In the harbour the effects were still more distressing. The English admiral, Admiral Elliott, and his wife, attempting to get on board his flag-ship, the "Bombay," were swamped in their boat, and were saved only by the courageous gallantry of the captain of a French merchant-ship, who succeeded in rescuing them and in taking them on board.

Three English officers belonging to the supply-ship, "Egmont," while trying to reach their own ship in a shore-boat, were capsized, and they and the boat's crew drowned. The

English merchant vessel, "Leighton," was also blown over, and the captain lost his son, his wife escaping, but with a broken arm. Numerous other disasters took place among the coasting vessels and the small craft of the harbour, and the shores of the sea and bay were strewn with wrecks.

PROVINCE OF MATO GROSSO.

HISTORY.

The first knowledge of this district was acquired about 1550, and for three quarters of a century it was exposed to the incursions of the Paulists and others, who carried off great numbers of Indians, without making any settlement on its territory. In 1719, however, Pascoal Moreira Cabral notified the governor of São Paulo of his discovery of gold in the river Cuxipó, and the country was soon overrun by adventurers in search of mines and washings of gold, many of whom died of want and fatigue, or were cut off by the Indians. Others, however, founded several small towns, and, in 1724, the governor of São Paulo visited his new district and raised the town of Cueabá to the rank of a city. In 1730, the first gold escort, with 2,000 pounds of gold, destined for the treasury of São Paulo, was cut off in the marshes of Fecho dos Morros, on the Paraguay, only seventeen escaping. And though avenged in the following year by a boat expedition of 600 men and two cannons, which destroyed an Indian armada at the mouth of the Imbotetiú, the Indians continued for many years to attack both the escorts and the settlements. Notwithstanding, the colonisation of the country and the search for gold continued to progress until the three years' drought, which, following the great earthquake of 1746, that destroyed Lima and was felt in Mato Grosso, caused great want and disease among the settlers. In 1748, it was disannexed from São Paulo, and made a captaincy, and, in 1751, the first governor arrived and fixed his residence at the city of Villa Bella, now Mato Grosso. For many years the Spaniards sought to acquire districts of this province, and, in 1801, they assaulted Nova Coimbra, but were received so warmly that they abandoned their invasion and returned to Paraguay. In 1824 the present form of government was established in the province.

GEOGRAPHY.

This province lies between 7° and 24° south latitude, and 50° 4' and 65° 29' west longitude from Greenwich. It is bounded on the north by Pará and Amazonas, the separating rivers being Vertentes, Fresco, Aboary, Tres Barras, Tapajos, Oreguatus, Machado, and Madeira: on the west by Bolivia, the Madeira, Paragaú, Serra de Albuquerque, and Paraguay forming the principal bounding lines; on the south by Paraguay, the Appa, and the Serra do Maracujù being the frontier; and on the east by Paraná and Goyaz, the Paraná, Pardo, Pitombas, and Araguaya dividing the provinces. It has a length of 340 leagues, a breadth of 300 leagues, and a superficies of 51,000 square leagues.

The capital is the city of Cuiabá.

The *climate*, owing to the elevation of the surface, is in general moderate and healthy, except where there are swamps and lands subject to overflow, as at Mato Grosso and along the course of the Paraguay.

The *surface* is mostly elevated, and the mountains which traverse it are, in general, but table lands of no great altitude. The most important is the range which stretches from west of the Madeira, in a south-easterly direction, over the province, and forms a part of the great Brazilian system of mountains and elevated *plateaux*, having the same general course, and dividing the rivers of the north from those of the south. The chief mountains are the Cordilheras, Geral and do Norte, the Serras dos Paracys, Tapirapuan, Diamantina, Arapus, and Vertentes, mostly vast table lands, yet the most elevated ground of Brazil, and the Serra de Sta. Barbara, and others, lying between the Paraguay and the Paraná, among which are the best cultivated lands of the province. Between these serras the land sweeps from one table-land to another, rising here and there into the minor elevations which vary the general features of the plains.

All the rivers which drain this immense province flow into either the basin of the Amazonas or that of the Paraguay and Paraná. The largest belonging to the northern system, are the Araguaya and its chief affluent the Das Mortes, the Xingú and its streams, the Tapajos and its great tributary the Arinos, and the Madeira, into which flows the fine river

Guaporé. Those of the southern, are the Paraguay with its important affluents the Jaurú, Lourenço (into which empties the Cuíabá), Taquary, Mondego and Appa, and the Paraná, into which flow the useful Pardo and Ivinheima (the latter swelled by the Brillante), and the Igatiny.

The lakes of this province are numerous, but they are mostly formed by the expansion of the rivers, or by their overflow during the season of high waters, such as that of Xaraes, formed by inundations of the upper Paraguay and some of its affluents, which extends 80 leagues in length by 40 in breadth.

The mineral wealth of this province was at one time very productive in gold, copper, and diamonds, the last of which, though small, being of the purest water; but the great abundance of early days is no longer obtained. Besides these are iron, found in all directions, granite, limestone, salt, especially near the Jaurú, saltpetre, clays, crystal, and precious stones.

The soil is in general very fertile, except on the sandy dividing ridge already mentioned, which only grows a low grass. Like Goyaz, a large proportion of the plains is covered with brush, but there are many immense forests of excellent timber.

The native animals are abundant, such as the ounce and its kin, the deer or mountain goat, wolves, tapirs, &c. There are also rare and beautiful birds both aquatic and terrestrial, together with bees, &c. Large herds of cattle and horses are reared, and form the chief dependence of the inhabitants. The rich soil produces spontaneously rice, maté, cacáo, vanilla, jalap, indigo, dragon's blood, gum-elastic, and balsams; and cochineal is easily procurable. The chief articles of cultivation are sugar-cane, maize, wheat, legumes, &c., and those of export gold, diamonds, drugs, and a large number of hides and cattle.

MEANS OF COMMUNICATION.

The chief roads are those connecting the cities of Mato Grosso, Diamantina, and Cuiabá, with Goyaz, Minas Geraes, and S. Paulo.

The Araguaya, the Arinos and Tapajos, and the Guaporé and Madeira, furnish a somewhat interrupted communication with the Amazonas, while the upper tributaries of the Paraguay and Paraná, give outlet to the south.

In former times, before the free navigation of these last was conceded, advantage was taken of the fact that the head waters of many of the tributaries of the chief rivers of the province almost meet, to keep up a difficult and toilsome boat intercourse with S. Paulo, by means of these rivers and numerous portages. That from the cities of Mato Grosso and Cuiabá followed, from the first up the Guaporé, reaching by a portage of $3\frac{1}{2}$ miles the Aguapahy, down which and the Jaurú it went to the Paraguay, and by this last to the mouth of the S. Lourenço, where it met that from Cuiabá, which came down the Cuiabá and S. Louranço to the Paraguay. Further down, the communication with the Paraná took two courses, the one up the Taquary, arrived by a portage of 10 miles to the Pardo, an affluent of the Paraná, while the other, following up the Mondego, reached, by a portage of 12 miles, the Brillante, and descended that river and the Ivanheima to the Paraná. Both courses then proceeded up the Paraná to the Tiete, which allowed approach by water to within 50 miles of the city of S. Paulo.

By these tedious ways, embarrassed by rapids and endangered by the savages who infested the rivers, all the trade with the south-east was for a long time carried on. But of late the commerce takes its natural course to the river Plate, and is rapidly developing.

The *population* is about 80,000, including the settled Indians and 10,000 slaves, and excluding the savage tribes, some of whom are troublesome.

The *representation* is one senator and two deputies to the Imperial Assembly, and twenty-two deputies to the Provincial Chamber.

The *military force* consists of about 5,000 national guards. Garrisons are maintained on the frontier, and a steam squadron on the rivers.

Public instruction is provided for by an episcopal seminary, three advanced schools, and sixteen primary schools.

The *provincial revenue* is about 50,000$, and the *imperial revenue* 140,000$.

Steam navigation exists between the city of Cuiabá and Montevideo, by the rivers Cuiabá, S. Lourenço, Paraguay, Paraná and La Plata. At Montevideo, Brazilian and other steamers sail to Rio de Janeiro.

TOPOGRAPHY.

The chief places are the cities of Cuiabá, the capital, and Mato Grosso, the towns of Diamantina, Maria, Miranda, Corumbá, and Coimbra.

Cuiabá is the capital, and the residence of the bishop of Cuiabá. It is situated in south latitude 15° 28' and 55° 45' west longitude from Greenwich, and is about a mile from the river Cuiabá. Its population is about 16 to 18,000. It has an arsenal of war and one of marine, a lazar hospital, another hospital, and seven churches.

Mato Grosso, on the Guaporé, south latitude 10° 2' and west longitude 60° 12', at one time called Villa Bella, and which was once the capital, is a small unhealthy town, owing to its liability to overflow by the Guaporé. It is well laid out, but is falling to decay, as is likewise *Diamantina*, north-west of Cuiabá.

Maria, on the upper Paraguay, and *Miranda* on the Mondega, are improving towns. At *Albuquerque* on the Paraguay, south latitude 14° 28', is the custom-house of the province; 40 miles below is *Coimbra*, where is a fort. In the hill on which it is built is an immense cavern, with several large rooms and large quantities of stalactites.

PROVINCE OF PERNAMBUCO.

HISTORY.

This province was founded by Duarte Coelho Pereira in 1530, who established himself at Iguarassú, and afterwards a colony at Olinda. The territory of the province was conferred on him by royal charter, March 10, 1534, and it was governed by him and his descendants until the invasion and capture of Olinda in 1630 by the Dutch, who, in 1635, obtained possession of the whole province. On their expulsion Dom João IV., King of Portugal, made it a captain-generalship, with dominion over the adjacent provinces of Alagôas, Rio Grande, Parahyba and Ceará, whose captains were subordinated to the captain-general of Pernambuco, the same laws, both civil and ecclesiastic, ruling throughout these provinces. In 1716 the ownership of the land was taken from the descendants of Senr. Pereira, who were, however, indemnified for its loss.

In 1676, Pernambuco was raised to a bishopric, and February 6, 1821, a superior tribunal was created by charter.

If Pernambuco is not the first province it can scarcely be styled the second of the empire; and had it not been injured by continual wars it would be now the richest in Brazil. But from 1630 to 1654 it had to contend against the invasion of the Dutch; in the beginning of this century, against the civil war with the Mascatos; from 1817 to 1824 against the revolts of the revolutionary democrats; and again at intervals from 1831 to 1848 against a continuance of those sanguinary outbreaks which have acquired for the Pernambucans some notoriety in the history of Brazil.

GEOGRAPHY.

This province is situated between the 6° 57' and 11° 3' south latitude, 34° 32' and 41° 48' west longitude.

It is bounded on the north by Parahyba and Ceará, from which it is separated by the rivers Abiahy and Popoco, and by the Serra das Imburanas; on the north-west by Piauhy, the

Serra da Borborema being the boundary; on the south by Bahia and Alagôas, from which it is divided by the rivers S. Francisco, Casanova, and Persinunga; and on the east by the Atlantic. Its extension along its coast is 44 leagues; westward from Cape Agostinho to the Serra do Araripe 147 leagues, and its area about 6,000 square leagues.

The *climate* of Pernambuco, situated as it is within ten degrees of the equator, is of a high temperature, but this heat is so much modified by proximity to the sea or rivers, by the elevation of the land in the interior, and by the large and shady forests of the country, that it is in a great part of the province even genial, and, with some few exceptions, healthy for Europeans. In the stripe of low land of from 40 to 60 miles wide which borders the coast, the climate is humid and warm, and, during the wet season, lassitude and weakness prevail, predisposing to disease. This season, lasting from March to July, is therefore more unhealthy than the dry one, which, though warmer, is more healthy, with the exception of those places where, from November to March, the yellow fever has become epidemic. In the interior, where the

o

ground is high and in part mountainous, the elevation of the land has its due effect, and the climate becomes dry and healthy, with the exception of some cases of intermittent fever.

The surface of the country along the seacoast is generally flat and sandy for 10 to 15 miles, but beyond that the ground becomes hilly and broken, and rises gradually—still preserving a comparatively low altitude—until, at a distance of from 40 to 60 miles from the sea, it elevates into extensive table-lands and mountains. A good deal of the mountainous regions and of the southern part of the province is covered with dense forests, which produce the páo de Brazil, and other valuable articles, but other districts are well suited to the extensive rearing of cattle. Few ferocious beasts are found here, or indeed in any part of Brazil, but poisonous reptiles are common. Here, also, is abundance of parrots, and of the little monkey called the marmozet, whose body is only four or five inches long. This animal is a favoured pet of the Brazilian ladies.

Little has been done in the exploration of the mineral resources of this province, but it is said that many districts abound with the precious metals, that marble is found in abundance, and that coal has been discovered near the city of Recife.

There are on the coast many islands, the largest of them being the island of Fernando de Noronha, which is the Van Dieman's Land of Brazil, though a dependency of this province. The others are the island of Itamaracá, where are raised the best mangas of Pernambuco, that of Nogueira, Santo Aleixo, and a group of little isles on the bar of S. Francisco.

The reef, which seems placed like a breakwater at a short distance from the coast of a large extent of Brazil, has numerous openings along this province, giving access to several small ports, which, however, are used only for the coasting trade, Pernambuco being the only port open to the foreign trade.

This province cannot boast of first-class rivers, except the S. Francisco, which in part separates it from Bahia and Alagôas. The chief are the Formoso, the Beberibe, the Capiberibe, the Serinhaem, and some others of less importance.

The land throughout this province is very extile, and produces all tropical plants, and

o 2

most table vegetables. It also yields abundance of fruit, among which the pine-apple is perhaps the finest in the world. It also furnishes Brazil and other dyewoods, gums, balsams, and medicinal roots, but it is to its great crops of sugar and cotton that it owes its largest commerce, these two articles forming eleven-twelfths of its export.

Of these *sugar* takes the first place. In 1711 there were only 246 sugar-houses, which annually exported to Lisbon 12,300 boxes of sugar, weighing 430,500 arrobas, worth 834,140$; in 1840, 512 large sugar-houses, and about 200 smaller ones, making *rapadura* (a kind of cake sugar); in 1844, 712 ; and in 1859, 1,272 sugar-houses of both kinds.

PERNAMBUCO.

Foreign Export of Sugar from the Province of Pernambuco.

		Arrobas.		
In	1711	430,500	1$940	834,140$
Average of 10 yrs. ending	1810	520,972	...	...
,, ,, ,,	1820	510,196	...	...
,, ,, ,,	1830	958,548	...	...
,, ,, ,,	1850	2,665,009	1$976	5,139,955$
In	1853	3,688,264	2$141	7,879,000$
,,	1854	4,001,523	2$201	8,834,000$
,,	1855	4,181,198	2$699	11,284,000$
,,	1858	4,528,716	...	12,453,160$
,,	1860	2,195,134	...	5,854,274$
,,	1862	3,387,705	...	7,252,654$
Besides Sugar, Spirits were exported in	1862	Canadas. 529,222	$275	145,877$

Cotton.—Until 1778 this province exported no cotton, but since then it has gradually grown up to be one of the great articles of export. Previous to the year 1800 the cotton of the province was the most esteemed in the English market, but this repute was lost chiefly through the carelessness and fraud of the producers and exporters. Since the outbreak of the war in the United States the growth of cotton has taken rapid strides, and the planters have awakened to the necessity of improving the quality of the fibre, and of facilitating its separation from the seed.

EXPORT OF COTTON from Pernambuco to Foreign Countries.

		Arrobas.
Average of Ten Years ending ...	1810	216,573
,, ,, ,, ...	1820	230,425
,, ,, ,, ...	1830	190,786
,, ,, ,, ...	1850	162,728
,, Four ,, ...	1855	146,503
For the Year ending ...	1858	83,457
,, ,, ...	1859	130,765
,, ,, ...	1860	79,586
,, ,, ...	1861	116,718
,, ,, ...	1862	256,619

These statistics would seem to show a decrease from 1802 to 1861, for unhappily no data exist to show the proportion belonging to the provinces of Alagôas and Parahyba, which at one time shipped almost all their cotton through Pernambuco, but of late years ship mostly through their own ports.

The *population* is about 1,180,000, of whom 250,000 are slaves.

The *representation* is 6 senators and 13 deputies to the Imperial Assembly; and 39 deputies to the Provincial Chamber.

The *military force* consists of about 1,600 soldiers and police, and about 42,000 national guards.

Public education is provided in 1 college of arts, 1 seminary, 1 gymnasium, and 108 primary schools. There are, besides, the Faculdade Juridica, the Ecclesiastic Seminary, the Orphan College, and the School of the Arsenal.

The provisional *revenue* is about 1,160,000$, and the Imperial, 6,500,000$.

Steam navigation.—By the steamers of the Campanhia Brazileira de Paquetes, Recife is placed in bi-monthly communication with the chief ports to the north and south; and by the English and French mail steamers, with Maceio, Bahia, and Rio de Janeiro. Other steamers also trade twice a month to Aracajú and Fortaleza, and intervening ports, and make a trip, each two months, to Fernando de Noronha.

Of the *railroad* designed to connect the Recife with the river S. Francisco, 77 miles have been finished as far as the river Una.

TOPOGRAPHY.

Pernambuco, as it is commonly called, consists of three towns adjoining one another—

Recife, Boavista, and St. Antonio, and of the town of Olinda, three miles distant.

Pernambuco is the third city in importance in the empire, the united population of the four towns being about 80,000. Of these Recife, or the reef, is the most important, it being the capital of the province, and also the port through which all its foreign commerce must be carried on. It is situated in 8° 3' 42" south latitude, and 34° 51' 42" west longitude from Greenwich. It takes its name from the curious reef already referred to as enclosing a considerable part of the coast of Brazil with a natural breakwater. Here, for five miles, it runs almost parallel to the shore, at a distance of 400 yards, and being only 30 to 50 feet wide, and flat on the top, with almost perpendicular sides, it has all the appearance of an artificial wall. This is the only defence of the port from the long swell of the Atlantic, which, checked by the shoals outside, expends its force against the reef, and rarely, even in stormy weather, affects the smooth water within, in which vessels lie safe at anchor, or moored to the reef, while discharging or receiving cargo.

The entrance to the port is formed by a sudden breaking away of the reef, leaving an open space free from rocks, but which is injured by a bar of sand washed there, having but 14 feet of depth at low water. Vessels drawing more than about 15 feet have to anchor in the exposed roadstead outside the reef, but this the Brazilians hope to remedy, and large sums have already been expended in deepening the port and bar. On the north end of the reef is the lighthouse, and close to it is the small ancient tower, Picão, on which are mounted eight guns. On the other side of the entrance is Fort Bruno. The Observatorio, called the "Tower of Malakoff," is a striking sight when entering the port, but the first view of Recife from the sea is not favourable, as, from the dampness and warmth of the climate, and the perishability of the materials used in the construction, the town looks old, mouldy, and decaying. Recife is built on the low sandy peninsular that faces the reef. Its streets are narrow, filthy, and disagreeable, and, with the exception of the Naval Arsenal, a new building with all the modern improvements, has no constructions of note. This district is devoted to the commerce of the place, and in it are the custom-house and the offices of the merchants.

Santo Antonio lies between Recife and Boavista, on the sandy island formed by the Capibaribe and Beberibe, and is connected with them by bridges, one of which is an elegant structure.

In this district are many fine buildings, including the Government Palace, the Theatre, the House of Correction, and some churches. It contains about 3,500 houses, is much better laid out than Recife, and is the shopkeepers' district. On the mainland is Boavista, built like the other two districts on low sandy soil. This is the newest district, and the streets are wider, and the houses more elegant and better planned than in the others.

Olinda is built on the high ground which shelters the port to the north, and along the winding river Beberibe. With its pretty cottages interspersed among mango and cocoa groves and fruitful vineyards, it presents a very pleasing effect. This was the first town built in Pernambuco, being commenced by Duarte Coelho Pereira. It suffered much from the wars with the Dutch, and also from the buccaneers.

Pernambuco has been much improved of late. All the streets have been well paved, and a system of sewerage has been inaugurated, which, when completed, will be of great benefit to the health and cleanliness of the place. Hotels have also been introduced—a great accommodation to the stranger, who in former times was altogether dependent on the hospitality of the citizens, a hospitality, however, always eagerly tendered, and which has caused many a pleasant reminiscence of Pernambuco and the Pernambucans to linger in the memory of the traveller.

Visitors should take a drive to Cashingar and Monteiro, which will be well repaid by the views of the country and of the pretty residences and gardens of the notables of the town. At both places are hotels, perhaps the best in the province.

The most attractive, because the most changeful, to a stranger is, perhaps, the seaward view from Recife. The green Atlantic, relieved here and there with ships—some at anchor, more with swelling sails—bound east and west, north and south; the restless swell beating against the reef—now dashing up into one long wall of spray—now pouring like a cataract over the top—contrasting well in its ceaseless activity with the calm river-like basin a few feet within; the groves of masts; the gaudy boats shooting around; the frail rafts of the fishermen; the people on the quay of every shade of white, yellow, and black, but, whether working or lounging, all with their characteristic look of *laissez-faire*—all form a most fitting introduction to Brazil, that real *terra incognita* of the European.

As a port Pernambuco is, from its situation, one of the most important in Brazil, it being in the centre of the coasting trade of the empire, and, as the most easterly part of the country, the point of departure of all the ships bound to Europe and North America. Besides these advantages, it possesses a foreign commerce, inferior only to that of Rio and Bahia, serving as a port, not only for the productions of the province, but also of a large proportion of those of the neighbouring provinces of Alagôas and Parahyba.

FOREIGN EXPORTATION

Articles.		1857—58.	
		Quantity.	Average Price.
Spirits	Canadas	1,588,859	$637
Cotton	Arrobas	130,344	8$173
White Sugar	,,	2,023,156	3$910
Mascava Sugar	,,	2,460,760	2$747
Salt Hides	Pounds	3,147,419	$266
Dry Hides	,,	5,870	$241
Honey	Canadas	739,579	$258
Leather	Sides	64,353	4$490

Articles.		1860-61.	
		Quantity.	Average Price.
Spirits	Canadas	772,867	$446
Cotton	Arrobas	91,731	7$933
White Sugar	,,	1,353,055	3$703
Mascava Sugar	,,	1,908,384	2$730
Salt Hides	Pounds	2,795,487	$216
Dry Hides	,,	108,870	$331
Honey	Canadas	182,958	$251
Leather	Sides	50,168	2$748

The Foreign Exportation for ,, ,, Importation for

OF RECIFE.

1858-59.		1859-60.	
Quantity.	Average Price.	Quantity.	Average Price.
1,116,140	$411	1,051,806	$409
92,543	8$027	144,823	8$321
1,938,161	3$472	1,430,153	4$365
3,297,694	2$476	2,437,768	2$605
2,621,245	$210	3,508,255	$242
6,516	$206	48,645	$394
129,495	$237	277,539	$252
50,717	3$987	71,933	3$482

1861—62.		1862-63.	
Quantity.	Average Price.	Quantity.	Average Price.
842,240	$372	639,791	$308
128,810	10$563	257,147	18$930
1,828,347	3$089	1,382,910	2$967
3,126,666	2$042	2,413,805	1$770
3,531,159	$179	3,293,416	$143
44,107	$206	208,209	$189
154,088	$203	158,597	$199
53,902	2$549	31,880	2$866

1862-3, amounted to ... 12,471,785$
1862-3,   ,,   ... 15,069,078$

27,540,863$

Goianna is 15 leagues from Recife. Its population has increased very much of late years, and it sends to the capital large quantities of sugar raised on the rich plain surrounding it, between the rivers Tracunhaem and Capiberibe.

Rio Formoso, situated on the coast near the river Formoso, is located in a fine sugar-growing district, and has a good port for the small vessels which convey the produce to Recife.

There are also many small towns and villages, one of which, Ponta de Pedra, is situated between the mouths of the Iguarassú and the Goianna, and is the most eastern point in South America.

The group of islands called *Fernando de Noronha*, which are sometimes visited by ships in distress, are, though upwards of 260 miles distant, a dependency of this province. The chief island gives its name to the group, and is used by the Imperial Government as a place of punishment for criminals. It is about 20 miles in circumference, and on it is a conical mountain about 1,000 feet high, which at the top is very steep, and at one side overhanging.

The island is covered with wood, and various articles are raised, but often suffer from the aridity of the climate. Fish abound in the sea around. In August, 1864, the inhabitants consisted of 305 military prisoners, 776 male judicial prisoners, and 20 female judicial prisoners, 85 wives and 257 children of prisoners, 206 soldiers and officers; and of other persons, 33 men, 103 women, and 50 children, making in all 1,835 persons.

PROVINCE OF GOYAZ.

HISTORY.

The first travellers who passed through this region were the Paulist Manoel Correa and his companions, who traversed it from Guaporé, in 1647, and brought to São Paulo some gold and a large number of Indians. In 1682, the adventurous Bartholemeo Bueno da Silva started from the city of S. Paulo, with his son, twelve years old, and a numerous company; and, following the traces of Manoel Correa, entered Goyaz as far as the Rio Vermelho, where he found gold in the possession of the Indians. Having terrified these by burning some spirits on a plate and threatening so to treat their lakes and rivers, he induced them to discover to him whence they procured the gold, and to aid him in its collection. He thus obtained a considerable amount; and, possessing himself, at the last moment, of the persons of a great many of his labourers, returned in

GOYAZ.

triumph to São Paulo. In 1722, his son was charged by the governor of São Paulo with an expedition intended to revisit these mines, and to procure gold and emeralds; but, failing in his search, he returned home disheartened at this result of three years' travel. The same governor, however, encouraged him to a new attempt, and, in 1725, after several months' march, he was recognised by two Indians of great age, and conducted to the lost mines, where he collected a very large quantity of gold, and, after establishing several small towns, returned to São Paulo with 8,000 *oitaves* of gold, upon which he received the appointment of *capitão mor* of the district. In 1746, Goyaz was made a captaincy, with Boavista as capital; and, in 1749, the first diamonds were found at the rivers Claro and Pilões. In 1773, the Tocantins was navigated to Pará; and in 1824, Caetano Lopez da Gama was appointed the first president.

GEOGRAPHY.

This province lies between 6° and 21° 40' south latitude, and 44° 39' and 53° 29' west longitude from Greenwich. It is bounded on the north by Maranhão and Pará, the Manoel Alves Grande, the Tocantins, and the Araguaya separating them; on the west by Mato Grosso, the Araguaya and the Pardo being the dividing rivers; on the south by São Paulo and Minas Geraes, the Paraná and Parnahiba parting them: and on the east by Minas Geraes, Bahia and Piauhy, the line of division running along the Cordilhera, which has the various names along its range of Serra dos Crystaes, Chapada da St^a. Maria, Serra da Tabatinga, and Serra das Coroadas.

It has a length of 300 leagues from the confluence of the Tocantins and Araguaya, to that of the Pardo and Paraná; an extreme breadth of 120 leagues, and a superficies of about 21,000 square leagues. Its capital is the city of Goyaz.

The *climate* is dry and moderate. The thunder-storms of the hot and wet season begin in October and end, usually, in April. It is in general healthy, except near stagnant ponds, in the dry season.

The *surface* of the country is diversified. Besides the range of mountains which bounds it on the east, it is traversed through nearly its whole length by the Cordilhera Grande, which separates the courses of the Tocantins and Araguaya, and whose elevation culminates, south-east and south-west of the city of Goyaz, into the dividing ridge of the two great basins of the province, where it sends out a number of spurs in several directions. Between these spurs and the various ranges, and along the courses of the rivers, lie valleys and large plains, mostly covered with brush.

The two great watersheds of the province are, that of the rivers flowing into the Amazonas, and that of those emptying into the Paraná. The former is subdivided into the basins of the Araguaya, and of the Tocantins, with its chief tributaries the Almas, Manoel Alves Pequeno, Sono, and the Manoel Alves Grande, which divides Goyaz from Maranhão. Of the rivers flowing into the Paraná, the largest are the Parnahiba, with its affluent, the Corumbá, and the Pardo.

The chief lakes are the Lagôa Grande, 25 leagues; and the Formosa, four leagues long, at the head of the Almas. The mineral productions are abundant and valuable, chiefly consisting of gold, iron, diamonds, and crystal; but the gold mines, which up to the beginning of this century had yielded nearly 150 tons of gold, seem almost exhausted.

The province possesses but few forests, and timber is not abundant, except in some localities, such as the banks of the Corumba, and where the great virgin forest of Mato Grosso lies between Meia Ponte and the city of Goyaz; the rest of the surface being covered, in a great measure, with brush, which, with the forests, give shelter to deer, boars, ounces, and other animals of the chase, and to many curious beasts and birds.

Where timber covers the ground the soil is excessively rich; but, in general, the province is most suited to the rearing of cattle, owing to its dryness and comparative isolation. It produces spontaneously, among other things, Brazil and Campechy wood, and many medicinal plants.

The chief products of cultivation are sugar, spirits, tobacco, lentils, &c., but owing to the cost of carriage its exports are mainly cattle, hides, gold, and a little tobacco.

Its commerce is carried on principally with

Pará and Rio Janeiro. That, with the former, by way of the rivers Araguaya and Tocantins, amounted during the year 1863, to upwards of 200,000$, carried on in *dugouts*, which brought down more than 40,000 hides, and returned laden with iron and other heavy goods, salt, &c.

The *population* is supposed to be about 200,000, of whom 15,000 are slaves, including about 25,000 Indians, some of whom are very fierce, while others are settled and apply themselves to agriculture and grazing.

The *representation* is one senator and two deputies to the Imperial Assembly; and 22 deputies to the Provincial Chamber.

The *military force* consists of about 300 soldiers in garrisons, and 13,000 national guards.

Public instruction is supplied in one lyceum, six advanced schools, and 33 primary schools.

The Imperial *revenue* is about 20,000$; the provincial about 75,000$.

MEANS OF COMMUNICATION.

The city of Goyaz is connected by roads with the chief rivers and towns, and with Cuiabá in

Mato Grosso, Minas Geraes, Maranhão, and Belem in Pará. Boats on the Araguaya and Tocantins serve to carry on a trade with the Amazonas, and others, on the Parnahiba, Pardo, and Paraná, with the south.

TOPOGRAPHY.

The city of *Goyaz*, once Villa Boa, situated, in 16° 24' south latitude, and 49° 4' west longitude, on the river Vermelho which divides it, has two bridges, a cathedral, five chapels, and among the most notable buildings, the Government Palace, the Hall of the Chamber, and the Treasury.

The city of *Meia Ponte*, situated in 16° 5' south latitude, and 47° 37' west longitude, near the head waters of the das Almas, has a church and four chapels. A road from Goyaz to Minas Geraes passes through it, and it is in the centre of a most agricultural and industrious district, where, also, are manufactured cotton and woollen cloth.

Pedro Affonso, a little town about 200 leagues north of Goyaz, where are several settlements of Indians. One of the tribes, the Guayajaras, lately immigrated from Maranhão, having, despite the remonstrances of the missionary, made continuous depredations on the property of the neighbouring tribe of the Chavantes, who apply themselves to agriculture and cattle-rearing; these, taking advantage of the absence of the missionary, armed themselves, and utterly exterminated the Guayajaras on the 13th of July, 1864, destroying even the women and their infants.

THE ARAGUAYA AND ITS NAVIGATION.

The population of the margins of the Araguaya have an animated aspect; their skin is smooth, fine, and shining; the muscles design themselves, vigorous in pleasing curves, in the robust bodies of the men; the appetite, stimulated by that pure air of plains of hundreds of leagues in width, where its circulation is uninterrupted by a single obstacle, requires an abundant nutrition that carries every day its tribute to the blood, that repairs the powers, and increases life.

As a commercial centre, we do not possess in the province, I might even say, in the empire, another more considerable.

To Pará navigation extends itself for nearly 1,600 miles; towards the south it can go, even now, to Rio Grande, and, in a not very remote future, may be established to the Taquary (130 miles by land), and from the Taquary, where a created navigation already exists, to the ocean.

The Araguaya being an affluent of the Tocantins, all that northern part of the province which lies to the rise of the Cordilheira remains, through the medium of the latter river, in communication.

Finally, when the region there will cease to be a wilderness, the river das Mortes (dos Araés) will furnish a majestic navigation.

If the price of transport be reduced, by way of the Araguaya, our production must augment, and exportation must be created, a thing which either does not exist, or is on so small a scale that it is not worth mention.

The reader will see further on that, after the regular establishment of navigation, the carriage of an *arroba* could not cost more than 2$ the *arroba*; therefore, coffee, cotton, sugar, rum, tobacco, dried beef, hides, leather, wheat, will be commodities that will abound on the

Araguaya, but which, so far, are produced in the province almost exclusively for its consumption.

From this will follow, therefore, the richness of the province, and the perfecting of our agricultural industry through division of labour.

At present we have no *fazendeiros* with a determined industry; each cultivator is an encyclopedian; he plants maize, beans, rice; rears cattle; manufactures rum; plants coffee, &c., &c.

And why is this? Because, if the planter devoted himself, in the present circumstances, to the growth of any one article, he could not find a purchaser for it, and would lose the greater part. If, however, the Araguaya were utilised he would find a sufficient market for all.

A common argument against navigation by the Araguaya is, the falls upon the Tocantins, and the unsettled extent upon the banks of the Araguaya; but, with all the difficulties in the way, once that navigation is established, the goods will come more cheaply by that river than by the roads from Rio de Janeiro.

By the last examinations made in this province and Mato Grosso, we find that the Araguaya is navigable to the port of Rio Grande; that thence to the Taquary, where the Coxim enters it, is merely 150 miles; that the Taquary is navigable from that place downwards to the Paraguay; so we have the mouth of the Amazonas bound to the River Plate by a fluvial navigation, interrupted by 150 miles; or perhaps less, as the Araguaya at Rio Grande is 650 yards wide, and no examination has been made above that point, so it is probable that it may yield navigation many leagues above.

What the productions are of the part of Goyaz adjacent to the Araguaya, and of the part of Mato Grosso in the valleys of the Taquary and Paraguay, it is easy to imagine, when we consider that the first of these rivers offers the most varied and rich products of Pará, without the excessive heat and the diseases of that province. The fertility of Mato Grosso is known to all. Consider then, reader, the immense impulse that our industry will have from the moment that the smoke of the steamer undulates through the blue sky of these new Indias!

On the banks of the Araguaya the cotton-plant grows in a form unknown to the persons who travel there; the reproduction of cattle is annual, and they are always fat; for at the time of overflows the pastures of the hills and high grounds are green, and in the dry season they have the borders of the rivers from which, as the waters withdraw, they can browse on pastures of a grass peculiar to those grounds, whose stalk is almost the size of cane, and which, yielding seeds like rice, gives a food that is highly prized by every kind of ruminant.

There can be nothing more picturesque than the view of the margins of the lakes formed by the river. Let the reader imagine those immense plains of hundreds of miles, uninterrupted by a single mountain, or even by the smallest hill; figure a calm basin of water of 15 or 20 miles in diameter, blue and deep, and reflecting in itself a sky in which a cloud rarely appears; figure this circle fringed with high reeds and grass; imagine, around, the herds of cattle confounded at times with others of deer, stags, antelopes, hogs, capivaras, covered with flocks of jabúrus, ducks of many kinds, colheireiros with rose-coloured plumage, divers and all kinds of aquatic fowls, and he will have a notion of the fertility of those lands.

The navigation of the Araguaya is more easy than that of the Paraguay; yet what a difference in the result! The latter serves Mato Grosso—or, to speak rightly, Villa Maria and Cuyabá; the former would open to industry the provinces of Pará, Maranhão, Goyaz, and Mato Grosso, that is, it would give to Brazil a second coast as considerable and vast as that offered by the Atlantic Ocean.

PROVINCE OF MARANHAO.

HISTORY.

The whole territory of this province was bestowed on the great Portuguese historian and statesman, Joãs de Barros, and two of his sons made two attempts to colonise it, but, both expeditions being disastrously shipwrecked on the coast, no further efforts were made until 1612, when French colonists were established, under the direction of La Ravardière, upon the Island of S. Luiz, where is now the capital, but they were expelled in 1615 by Jeronymo d'Albuquerque, and their place occupied by the Portuguese.

In 1641, however, the Dutch possessed themselves of the island, and of the coast of the province, but becoming wearied of the continual conflicts with the troops of Captain Antonio Terxeira, they abandoned their occupation in 1653.

In 1752 Piauhy was entirely separated from Maranhão, of which it had, until then, formed a dependency.

GEOGRAPHY.

It is bounded on the north by the Atlantic, on the west by Pará, from which it is divided by the river Gurupy; on the south-west by Goyaz, the Tocantins and Manoel Alves Grande separating them; and on the south and east by Piauhy, the river Parnahiba being their boundary. Its length from north to south is 195 leagues, from east to west, 163 leagues; its seacoast, 130 leagues, and its area about 12,500 square leagues. It lies between 1° and 10° 45′ south latitude, and 40° 54′ and 49° 16′ west longitude.

Its climate is very warm and humid, and during the months of November and December there fall heavy rains, accompanied by thunder and lightning.

The temperature is somewhat modified by the vapours which rise from the rivers and dense woods, and by the frequent rains, but varies little throughout the year. The province is in general healthy, except in the neighbourhood of the Parnahiba, where intermittent fevers prevail.

The surface of the northern half of the province is in general without mountains. Towards the coast it is low and flat, but in the south becomes elevated, and in parts hilly, and a large proportion of it is covered with dense forests, particularly along the valleys of the rivers.

There are eighteen rivers in the province, many of them navigable for long distances. The most important are the Parnahiba on the boundary line with Piauhy, which is navigable, with some obstructions, nearly 250 leagues, the Itapicurú, 150 leagues long, the Mearim, 130 leagues long, the Pindaré, 80 leagues long, the Turiassú, and the Gurupy.

There are also many deep lakes which afford facilities for transport, and at the mouths of the rivers are excellent ports, two of the best of which are the bays of S. Marcos and S. José. The chief island is S. Luiz, on which is the capital of the province; there are also other smaller ones, on one of which is placed the lighthouse of Santa Anna.

There are various mines of gold, silver, and

bismuth, some of which have been explored by a company and found to be very rich. This province produces cotton, rice, sugar, tapioca, maize, oil of cupaiva, nuts, cocoa, coffee, vanilla, castanha nuts, tobacco, arrowroot, gum elastic, castor oil beans, pepper, sarsaparilla, uruçu, carnaúba, tallow, and fibre, and all kinds of tropical plants. A valuable silkworm is also found here that feeds on orange and pine-trees.

The woods are full of birds and game, the rivers and lakes of fish, and from the sea, besides fish, are collected large quantities of shrimps, which, when dried, form an important article of consumption and export.

The chief exports are cotton, tapioca, rum of superior quality, maize, oil of cupaiva, gum-elastic, hides, and dried fish and shrimps.

Of these cotton is the most important export to foreign countries. The quality of Maranhão cotton is good, and that grown in the vicinity of Alcantará is considered to rank next to Sea-island. During the ten years ending 1862 the export of cotton remained between 200,000 to 300,000 *arrobas*, but since that year efforts have been made to increase the production, and with some result in spite of the scarcity of labour. In 1862 there were exported 230,451 *arrobas*. The total exports of all kinds were, in 1861-62,—

Coastwise 296,092$

Foreign 2,757,912$
_____
3,054,004$

but in 1862-63 the foreign exports alone amounted to 4,722,000$, this great increase being caused by the advance in the value of the chief article of export, cotton.

The *population* of the province is about 400,000, including 50,000 slaves.

The *representation* is—six deputies and three senators to the Imperial Assembly, and 30 deputies to the Provincial Chamber.

The *military force* is about 1,000 soldiers and policemen, and 28,000 national guards.

Public education is provided in one seminary for theology, one normal school, 14 grammar, and 78 primary schools.

The provincial *revenue* is about 500,000$, and the Imperial about 1,500,000$.

STEAM NAVIGATION.

S. Luiz do Maranhão is connected with the chief ports of the empire by the steamers of the Companhia Brazileira de Paquetes, which call from the north and south twice a month; and with Fortaleza and Belém, and the intervening ports, by a line of steamers for that purpose. Small steamers also ply on the Itapicurú to Caxias, and on the Parnahiba and some other rivers. The inhabitants of the province deserve great praise for their spirited endeavours to develope the steam trade.

TOPOGRAPHY.

S. Luiz do Maranhão, often called Maranhão, the capital, and foreign port of the province, is situated in 2° 30' south latitude, and 44° 17' west longitude, on the island of the same name, which is about 20 miles long and 15 broad. This town contains about 30,000 inhabitants, and about 3,000 houses, of which 700 are two stories and upwards, and many of them fine buildings. The palace of the government and the cathedral are worthy of a visit, though the exterior of the latter is coarse and devoid of architectural beauty. It, however, possesses some good paintings. The arsenal of marine is prettily situated and well defended, and there are a museum, a theatre, two hospitals, a relacão, or high court of appeal, and a tribunal of commerce. Six papers are published in the city, two of which are dailies.

The port of S. Luiz is excellent, commodious, and well sheltered, and is frequented by many vessels in need of repairs. The entrance is somewhat difficult to sailing vessels of large size, but, in general, vessels not drawing more than 20 feet of water can enter at all seasons.

S. Luiz carries on a foreign and coasting trade of importance. The foreign exports of 1862-3 amounted to . . . . . 4,722,001$
The direct foreign imports to . . 3,604,401

Total   8,326,402$

Alcantará is situated about five leagues from S. Luiz, and is a nice town with many handsome buildings. Its trade is not increasing like that of the village of S. Bento, which is nearer the interior, and is situated in a district where cotton of a superior quality is largely grown.

Vianna is an interior town, which is fast becoming important through its agricultural and commercial industry.

Caxias, a town on the bank of the river Itapicurú, distant about 120 leagues from the capital, is the second city in the province, and has a considerable trade with the surrounding country and Piauhy. A small steamer keeps up communication with S. Luiz, and is of great benefit to the agriculture of this part of the province.

PROVINCE OF PARANÁ.

HISTORY.

THIS province belonged, with São Paulo, Minas Geraes, and others, to the captaincy of S. Vincente, the grant made to Martim Affonso da Sousa.

It remained a part of São Paulo until 1853, when, at the petition of its inhabitants, it was made a province, with the city of Curitiba as its capital. The first president was Zacharias de Goes e Vasconcellas.

GEOGRAPHY.

It lies between 22° 18' and 27° 33' south latitude, and 47° 46' and 54° 35' west longitude. It is bounded on the north-east and north by São Paulo, the Itaréré, and Paraná Panema separating them in great part; on the west by Mato Grosso, Paraguay and the Argentine Confederation, the Paraná Iguassú, S. Antonio, and Pipiryguassú dividing them; on the south-east by Sta. Catharina, the Timbo, Serra do Mar, and Sahy, being the chief boundaries; and on the east by the ocean. It is 100 leagues long from north to south, 125 leagues from east to west, and has an area of about 6,000 square leagues.

Its capital is Curitiba, and its port and custom-house are at Paranaguá.

The *climate* is moderate, and in general very healthy, except on the low grounds near the coast, where some fevers occur. The wet and dry seasons are not distinctly marked, as rains fall both in winter and summer at intervals.

The *surface* resembles, in its general features, that of São Paulo, the Serra Geral in the east, which runs parallel to the coast, being abrupt in its descent into the low lands near the coast, and falling towards the west into the high plateau which reaches to the Paraná, elevated, here and there, by the low mountains and serras of Agudos, Esperança, Apucarana, and others.

Besides the small rivers on the coast which are of little importance, the province possesses on its western plateau several large rivers, which make their embouchure in the Paraná. Of these the most northern is the Paraná Panema, which, with its tributary the Itarére, forms the northern boundary from the Serra Geral, and, in its course to the Paraná receives the Cinza, the navigable Tibagy, and other smaller streams. South of this, and of the Ivahy, and some others of shorter course, is the Iguassú, which by its confluent the Curitiba, rises near the capital, within 50 miles of the sea, and thus, on its descent to the Paraná, passes through almost the whole breadth of the province, but, owing to its many rapids, giving a difficult passage only to small boats. On the south is the Uruguay, which receives from this province the Timbo, the Chapecó, and others, and by which boats of large size can pass along the whole southern frontier to the rapids of Salto Grande, which interrupts the navigation during low water. These rivers, though for the most part injured by rapids and falls, are capable of being utilised and made invaluable to the commerce and agriculture of this large province.

The mineral wealth still remains undeveloped,

but gold and diamond mines have been worked to some advantage.

The soil is fertile and productive, and fine forests of splendid timber are found, particularly in the north-east; still a very large proportion of the surface consists of great prairies and brushy plains.

The cultivated plants of Europe flourish, and are grown to some extent, but the chief occupations of the inhabitants are cattle, horse, mule, and swine rearing, and the collection and preparation of the maté, which grows native in the country, and of which about 400,000 *arrobas*, value about 1,350,000$, are exported, the fine to La Plata, and the coarse to Chile.

The principal exports are maté, rice, timber, cattle, beef, bacon, &c. Value, in 1862-3, of the foreign exports, 1,073,887$, and of the foreign direct imports, 303,648$.

The *population* is about 105,000, of whom 20,000 are slaves.

The *representation* is one senator and one deputy to the Imperial Assembly, and 20 deputies to the Provincial Chambers.

The *military force* consists of 120 police, 248 soldiers, and about 8,000 national guards.

Public education is provided in one lyceum and 48 primary schools. There are, besides, about 45 private schools.

The provincial *revenue* is about 350,000$, and the Imperial about 200,000$.

STEAM NAVIGATION.

Communication is kept up from Paranaguá twice a month with Rio de Janeiro and Santa Catharina, and the intervening ports, by a line of steamers.

TOPOGRAPHY.

The city of *Curitiba*, the capital of the province, is situated on the high land of the Cubitão, about 30 leagues from the sea. It is paved, and is well laid out on a large scale, but is at present a small place with little trade.

Paranaguá, situated in south latitude, 25° 35′, west longitude, 48° 22′, has the port and customhouse for the foreign commerce of the province. In 1862-3 it exported 1,074,000$, of which 1,031,589$ was maté.

PROVINCE OF SÃO PEDRO DO SUL.

HISTORY.

This province remained almost unknown until about 1680, when it was traversed by the Paulists in the search for gold fields, and it was not until 1737, that a settlement was made by inhabitants of the Azores, at the place where now exists the city of S. Pedro. In 1738 the province was made part of the captaincy of Stª. Catharina, and, in 1745, came a second influx of Azoreans to augment the colony. From the first, the settlers had to defend themselves against the indigenes, the Minuanos, the Tapes, and the Bugres; and, in 1763, the town was captured by the Spanish, who carried off most of the inhabitants. The Spaniards kept possession until 1776, when they were driven off by an expedition under João Henrique Bohom. In 1760, the province was separated from Stª. Catharina, being made a captaincy, under General Ignacio Elroy de Madureira. In 1775, during the government of General José Marcellino de Figueiredo, Porto dos Cazaes, whose name was then changed to Porto Alegre, was made the capital of the province, in place of the fortified town of Viamão, which had grown up after the Spanish invasion in the south. This governor, by his energetic administration, gave a great impulse to the organisation of the settlements, and to the domestication of the Indian tribes. In 1807, the territory of São Pedro was made a captaincy-general, under D. Diogo de Souza, and, in 1822, became a province of the empire, the first president being the Viscount de San Leopoldo, appointed in November, 1823.

Since its first settlement, the possession of this province by the Portuguese was disputed by the Spaniards, causing many wars, during the last of which the Brazilians received a severe defeat at Itusayngo, which led to the peace of 1828 with the Banda Oriental do Uruguay. In September, 1833, broke out the disastrous civil war, which desolated, for more than nine years, the many flourishing settlements and cattle stations of the province. In 1834, the town of Pelotas started a steamboat to ply between that town and S. Pedro, which was the first in Brazil.

GEOGRAPHY, ETC.

This, the most southern province of the empire, is situated between 27° 12' and 33° 43' south latitude, and 49° 36' and 57° 22' west longitude. It is bounded on the south-east by the South Atlantic Ocean; on the north and north-east, by the rivers Pelotas and Mampituba; on the north-west by the Uruguay; and on the south by the Banda Oriental, the boundary line running along the Quarahy, the Serra de St^a. Anna, the Jaguarão, and down the eastern shore of Lake Mirim, to the mouth of the little river Chuy, which empties into the ocean. From east to west, the length is 128 leagues, from north to south, 120 leagues, and its area is estimated at 9,000 square leagues, of which fully two-thirds is arable land. The capital is Porto Alegre.

The *climate* of this province is temperate, and, more than that of any other in Brazil, resembles the climate of the British Isles, the summers being rarely very hot, and the winters as rarely falling below freezing point. The usual heat of the summer months, December, January, and February, in the hottest part of the day, varies from 75° to 80° Fahrenheit, only reaching 90° when a pampero is coming on. In the winter months, May, June, and July, the cold ranges between 24° and 40° in the elevated regions in the interior, sometimes falling to 18°. The seasons are in general regular, and free from extremes hurtful to the labours of the agriculturist; and, in the wet season, which continues from the beginning of August to the end of September, the rains do not fall daily nor cause great inundations. The climate is mild, healthy, and invigorating; the inhabitants rosy and robust, and represented by those best acquainted with them, to be sober, generous, hospitable, and sincere.

The Serra Geral of Brazil enters in the north-east corner, and, after proceeding westward two-thirds across the province, turns, and runs south into Uruguay, meeting, not far from that State, the Serra de Stª. Anna, which forms in part the southern boundary of São Pedro do

Sul, and reaches westward, almost to the Uruguay. West of the lakes Patos and Mirim, the Serra Geral sends out some spurs, which, running eastward, break off in various directions, and are lost in the plains and low hills of the open country near the lakes.

The Serra Geral naturally divides the province into two great watersheds, that of the Uruguay, and its great tributary the Pelotas, and that of the Jacuhy and the smaller rivers emptying into the lakes Patos and Mirim. The great river Uruguay rises in Brazilian territory, forms the boundary between this province and the Argentine Confederation for about 100 leagues, nearly all of which are navigable, and, after a further course of 150 leagues between Uruguay and the Argentine State of Entre Rios, flows into the Rio Plata not far from Buenos Ayres. This river has a width varying from 400 yards to even four miles, and, for 250 leagues from its mouth, has a general depth of from five to eight fathoms. Vessels of six feet draught can ascend in the lowest stage of water as high as Salto Grande (in about latitude 31° 8′, longitude 57° 52′), where the rapids interrupt the navigation; vessels of light draught being, however, able to pass over in high water. Of the many Brazilian tributaries of the Uruguay, the most important of those in this province, are — the Pelotas, Uruguaypuita, Ijuhyguassu, Ijuhymirim, Piratinim and Itabuican, all scarcely navigable ; the Butuhy, navigable for a short distance ; the large river Ibicuhy, more than 70 leagues long, and navigable by its northern fork up to the district of S. Pedro ; and the Quarahy, which separates Brazil from Uruguay. On the eastern watershed, the chief rivers which empty into Lake Mirim, leaving unnoticed the rivers of Uruguay, which have only their outlets in this lake, are the Jaguarão, rising near the Serra de Asseguá, with a course of 50 leagues, and in part separating the province from Uruguay, and various small streams, such as the Arroio Grande, Charqueiro, and Palma, some of them admitting small vessels over their bars, but navigable only for a short distance. Emptying into the long Strait of S. Conçalo, joining Lakes Mirim and Patos, are the Piratinim, which, rising in the hills of the Asperezas, has a course of 30 leagues, but is navigable only for a short distance, owing to its shoals ; the Pavão, Fragata, Santa Barbara, and Pelotas, all short, and of which the Pelotas alone is navigable for most of its length. The chief streams flowing into Lake Patos are the S. Lourenço and Feitoria, unimportant streams, the Camaquam, 50 leagues long, receiving many feeders, yet little navigable, owing to sandbars and falls, the important Jacuhy, taking its rise in the serras of Batuvy, receiving the Vaccacahy, Cambahy, St^a. Barbara, Butucarahy Pardo, and Taquary, and joining near Porto Alegre with the navigable Cahy, the Sinos, and the Caravalahy, flows, as the majestic Guahyba, into the lake, and is navigable by steamers and rowboats, to S. Gabriel, a distance of 80 leagues, and by sailing vessels to Cachoeira, 42 leagues from Porto Alegre.

The Lakes Mirim and Patos are formed by the waters of the numerous rivers which disembogue in them, and they have a united length of about 80 leagues available for vessels of some size. Lake Mirim, 41 leagues long, has a width in places of almost eight leagues, a depth in the channel of nine to ten fathoms, and is navigable throughout its extent by vessels of large size as far as the channel of S.

SÃO PEDRO DO SUL. 243

Conçalo, which is injured by sandbars and accumulations of sand and weeds, easily removable at little cost. Lake Patos has a length of 36 leagues, an extreme width of 14 leagues, a depth in the channel of $4\frac{1}{2}$ to 8 fathoms, and in places 20 fathoms. The channel of Cangassú, however, is shallow, in summer admitting only vessels drawing about nine feet, but would be easily improved by the construction of a short canal close to the isle of Cangassú. The bay of Pelotas, which, under the name of Rio Grande do Sul, forms the outlet of these lakes to the sea, is about 12 leagues long, and three wide. The entrance is dangerous, on account of many flats, the bar at its mouth, and the frequent shifting of the channel, which have necessitated the establishment of a combined system of buoys and signals to guide the vessels entering. The depth of water also varies from time to time, but seldom admits vessels drawing more than 10 or 11 feet water, and then only when the sea is not rough. Inside, however, there is abundance of water, and vessels can bring up and anchor almost anywhere.

The coast is altogether low, sandy, faced

with sand-banks, which stretch far into the sea, and covered with a fine white sand, only dotted here and there with a scanty vegetation. The land on the western sides of the lakes is, however, of a very different character, that lying west of Lake Mirim being undulating and gradually rising to the middle of the province, and as gradually falling to the Uruguay; and that west of Lake Patos and the northern lakes commencing, at a short distance from their shores, to rise slowly into the mountains of the Serra Geral, and on the north and west, falling to the Pelotas and the Uruguay. In this region, lying north and west of the Serra Geral, and north of the Serra de Sta. Anna, the territory in general is basaltic, and in the north-west of the province are found some desert lands. In the east division, the soil of the great alluvial plains, rising from the lakes, is usually a rich loam impregnated with lime and saline substances. The plains generally throughout the province are arable, and, except in the north, only dotted here and there with groves of trees. Being also free from large roots that might obstruct the plough, they are in the most favourable condition possible for the requirements of agriculturists, the grazier, and the shepherd.

In the soil exist many kinds of useful clays and ochres, and a large deposit of a very valuable kaolin, suitable for the manufacture of porcelain. Its quarries furnish basalt, porphyry, granite, marbles of various colours, and a fine white marble for sculptors; and, besides, are found many varieties of cornelian, topazes, and diverse coloured rock-crystal. It is rich with gold, silver, and lead. Copper has been found in many places, and rich veins lie at Caçapava, and in the hills along the courses of the Ibicuhy and Quarahy, at the latter being particularly abundant and accessible. Iron is almost everywhere, but in especial importance at Caçapava, Rio Pardo, and S. Jeronymo (at which places beds of coal exist), Itaquy, Cruz Alta, S. Leopoldo, and Porto Alegre. Coal of a somewhat inferior quality, in large beds, has been discovered near the surface in many parts, particularly those of Arroio dos Ratos (worked a little), Arroio Candista, on the Jaguarão, and in the basin of the Jacury, where a very large deposit exists, reported to be of excellent quality.

The fruits of Europe flourish almost everywhere, and the grapes, pears, apples, and peaches are of superior quality. Among the vegetables used in medicine and the arts, and growing wild in the province, are ipecacuanha, sarsaparilla, turbith, camomile, indigo, &c.; and the timber, though not in abundance, is valuable for construction. The soil produces everything grown in temperate climes, and before the appearance of rust in 1811, wheat yielded eightyfold, and even a hundredfold. Previous to this, the export of wheat amounted to about 460,000 *alqueiras*, but afterwards, from 1811 to 1820, fell to 180 to 200,000 *alqueiras* per annum. Many farmers, therefore, abandoned its culture, turning their attention to grazing and utilising the wild horses and cattle with which the province swarmed, domesticating them and selling them to the beef-packer and the hide-merchant. So rapid became the development of this trade, that in 1835 the products of the herds formed almost the whole export of the province, and amounted to upwards of 8,000,000$. In this year, however, the civil war broke out, which for nine years devastated the country, and which, being followed by a pestilence among the

SÃO PEDRO DO SUL.

cattle, almost exterminated the herds of the province. But these losses were soon retrieved, and grazing still continues to form the main dependence of the Rio Grandian. The exports consist chiefly of dried beef, hides, and other products of the herd, farinha de mandioca, beans, maize, wheat, maté, tobacco, wool, lumber, and logs, and the varied products of the quarries. In 1861-62 the value of the exports was—

Coastwise 9,346,929$
Foreign 7,982,351$
─────────
17,329,280$

The number of cattle slaughtered in the province was in 1863, 560,000 head of steers, in the first nine months of 1864, 517,881.

The *population*, according to the official returns of 1863, was 392,725, of whom 315,306 were free, 77,416 slaves, and 1,000 Indians. Since 1859 the increase has been 49 per cent. of the free, and $9\frac{1}{2}$ of the slave population.

The *representation* is effected by three senators and six deputies for the Imperial Assembly, and by 30 deputies to the Provincial Chamber.

The *military* force consists of 42,991 national guards, namely, 25,741 cavalry, 16,674 and 576 artillerists; of these about 1,200 are on active service in garrison and police duties. The police force is about 400 men.

Public *instruction* is provided for by two lyceums and 168 primary schools. There are also one episcopal seminary and 25 private schools.

The *provincial revenue* is about 900,000$ annually, the Imperial about 3,000,000$.

STEAM NAVIGATION.

This province was the first in the empire to avail itself of the advantages of steam, the enterprising inhabitants of Pelotas, in 1834, running a steamboat between that town and São Pedro. At present about 20 steamers are employed in the rivers, lakes, ports, and at the bar, and communication is kept up with the northern ports four times a month by the steamers of the Companhia Brazileira de Paquetes.

TOPOGRAPHY.

The city of *Porto Alegre*, the capital of the province, is situated on the east side of the Guahibá, about seven leagues from its outlet into Lake Patos. It is well laid out and built, and has a population of about 25,000 inhabitants. In it are the old palace of the governors, the Provincial Chamber, an arsenal of war, an hospital, and an elegant theatre. The port is good, and, from the situation of the city near the mouths of several navigable streams which empty into the Guahibá, it is well placed for commerce. In it is a custom-house for the foreign trade. Its export trade is small, but is rapidly increasing, having amounted in 1857-8 to 57,665$, and in 1862-3 to 205,237$, chiefly maté.

São Pedro do Rio Grande, the ancient capital, is situated on the south-east side of the channel of the Rio Grande, on a sandy plain. Its port is good, and it carries on a considerable commerce with foreign countries, its foreign exports amounting, in 1862-3, to 4,033,000$. The entrance of the bar of the Rio Grande is very dangerous, from the shifting of the channel and varying of the depth, sometimes with certain winds diminishing to only seven feet. South latitude, 32° 7' 15", west longitude, 52° 4' 25".

S. José do Norte, a few leagues to the north-east of S. Pedro, is situated on the peninsula, separating Lake Patos from the sea. Its foreign exports amounted, in 1862-3, to 1,834,000$. South latitude, 32° 0' 0", west longitude, 52° 2' 0".

Uruguayana, on the Uruguay, is a port for foreign commerce, chiefly with the Spanish Republics. In 1862-3 it exported 168,000$, but in 1861-2, 417,000$. Its principal export is maté.

PROVINCE OF ST^A. CATHARINA.

HISTORY, ETC.

THE first settlement in this territory was made, in 1651, by Francisco Dias Velho Monteiro, on the island of St^a. Catharina, but the mainland remained unsettled and unknown, except to roving bands of Paulists in search of Indians for slaves, until about the end of the seventeenth century, when a body of the Paulists fixed themselves at a place in the interior which, in 1749, was made a district of São Paulo, with the name of Villa dos Lages. About 1720, D. Joao V. caused colonies of Azoreans to be located on the mainland and on the island, he making this last also a place for the transportation of criminals. In 1738, the island was separated from the captaincy of São Vincente, and made a distinct government, subject to Rio de Janeiro. In 1777, the Spaniards took possession of it, and retained it until 1778, when, by treaty, it was delivered up to the Portuguese. In 1791, the district of Villa dos Lages was separated from São Paulo and added to St^a. Catharina. In 1813, the present limits were established; and, in 1824, the district was made a province of the empire, the first president being João Rodrigo de Carvalho. In 1839, the mainland was taken possession of by the revolutionists of São Pedro do Sul, who kept it for some time.

GEOGRAPHY, ETC.

This province is situated between 25° 55' and 29° 25' south latitude, and 48° 43' and 51° 41' west longitude from Greenwich. It is bounded on the east by the ocean; on the north and north-west by Paraná, being separated therefrom by the river Sahy, by an offshoot of the Serra Geral, and by the river Timbo; and on the south-west by São Pedro do Sul, the rivers Pelotas and Mampituba forming the dividing line. The estimated area is 2,200 square leagues. Its capital is Desterro, situated on the island of St^a. Catharina.

The *climate* of the province, and especially of the island, is mild and agreeable, but in the high lands, and the elevated regions of the interior, the winter is more severe than on the sea-coast. The wet season sets in about the beginning of August, and continues to the end of September. The dry season is not as regular as in some other provinces, and is frequently interrupted by storms and heavy rains. The climate is genial and healthy, save catarrhs, and, in some isolated districts, cases of periodic fevers, especially in the neighbourhood of the lakes.

The surface is but little broken, except in the island, but the Serra Geral, which stretches south throughout the whole length of the province, divides it into two distinct watersheds; the western one being drained by the Pelotas and its tributaries, and the eastern by the numerous small rivers which empty into the sea. None of these are of great importance as a means of trade with the interior, even the largest, the Araranguá, Itajay, and Itajaymirim, having a free navigation of but six to eight leagues, while the others, the chief of which are the Sahy, Beguassú, Cubatao, Tubarão, and Mampituba, though navigated more or less principally with boats, owe most of their usefulness to the influx of the sea. For these reasons the cultivated lands are chiefly collected near the sea-coast, and round the lakes and streams affording communication by water.

Coal is the chief mineral found, geologists having reported the existence of a large bed in the south-east of this province, supposed to be 20 to 30 miles wide, and 300 miles long, and to extend into the province of S. Pedro do Sul. Hitherto the miners do not seem to have found anything likely to supersede English coal for steam purposes. There are several mineral and hot springs, some of which are in repute for the cure of syphilis and elephantiasis.

The soil is very fertile, and from its forests are procured useful timber for building and furniture, and also dye-woods.

The chief products of the agriculture are European cereals, cotton, cane, mandioca, flax, rice, maize, beans. These they export, together with dried beef, tallow, &c., mostly to the northern provinces, and farinha de mandioca and lumber to Rio Plata. Its direct foreign trade is small, and chiefly with the Hanse cities and Rio Plata. It amounted, in 1862-3, to 107,368$ exported, and 291,647$ imported.

The *population* amounts to about 120,000, of whom 15,000 are slaves.

The *representation* is one senator and one deputy to the Imperial Assembly, and 20 deputies to the Provincial Chamber.

The *military force* consists of about 100 soldiers, a body of police, and about 9,000 national guards.

Public instruction is furnished in one lyceum and 47 primary schools.

The provincial *revenue* is about 200,000$, and the Imperial 150,00$.

STEAM NAVIGATION.

There is communication twice a month with Rio de Janeiro, S. José do Norte, and Rio Grande do Sul, from S. Francisco and Desterro, and with Montevidéo once a month, by the Companhia Brazileira de Paquetes ; and by the Companhia Ferreira twice a month, with Rio de Janeiro, from Desterro, touching at S. Francisco, Paranaguá, Iguape, Santos, San Sebastião, and Ubatuba.

TOPOGRAPHY.

Desterro, the capital and fort for foreign commerce, is situated in south latitude 27° 35′, and west longitude 48° 32′ on the west side of the island of St^a. Catharina. It is a small but strongly fortified place, of about 7,000 inhabitants.

The island of St^a. Catharina is nine leagues long by one or two wide.

S. Francisco is situated in south latitude 26° 15′, and west longitude 48° 31′, on the western shore of the fertile island of S. Francisco, which is six leagues long by three in width. It is advantageously placed for trade.

PROVINCE OF MINAS GERAES.

HISTORY.

THE first discoverer of this province was Sebastião Fernandes Tourinho, who, in 1573, ascending the Rio Doce, forced his way across the Serra das Esmeraldas, and descended the Jequitinhonha, bringing with him to Bahia specimens of the riches he had discovered. His example was followed by other adventurers in search of gold or slaves, but it was not until the end of the sixteenth and beginning of the seventeenth century that the great discoveries of gold at Ouro Preto and elsewhere, attracted general immigration from Portugal and from São Paulo and other provinces. Disputes soon broke out between the Paulists and the others, for the possession of the mines, and several battles were fought between the parties, but, in 1709, peace was restored by the governor of

Rio, and Minas, being created into a district, was made subject to the governor of São Paulo, under which jurisdiction it remained until 1720, when it was separated and made a province, receiving its first governor, Lourenço d'Almeida. In 1727, the gold mines of Aracuahi were discovered, and in 1729, the first diamonds of Brazil were found at Diamantina, then part of the province of Bahia. After the Independence of Brazil, the Visconde de Cahete was the first president appointed.

The *climate*, owing to the great elevation of the general surface, is moderate and healthy, except in the low lands, liable to overflow, along the S. Francisco and other large rivers, where intermittent fevers prevail, especially after the going down of the floods. The wet and dry seasons of this province are the reverse of those of Pernambuco and the other northern provinces, the summer being the time of the greatest rains.

It lies between 14° 30′ and 22° 32′ south latitude, and 39° 58′ and 52° 3′ west longitude. It is bounded on the north by Bahia, the chief limits being formed by the Serra do Grão Mogul, the Rio Verde Grande, and the Carunhanha;

on the west by Goyaz, the Chapada da St^a. Maria, the Serra dos Chrystaes, and the Parnahiba, dividing them; on the south by São Paulo and Rio de Janeiro, the Rio Grande Serra de Lopo, Serra da Mantiqueira, and the Parahyba, separating them; and on the east by Espirito Santo, the Serras dos Pico, dos Arrepiades, and Aimorés being the boundary. It is 150 leagues from north to south, and 220 from east to west, and has an area of 20,000 square leagues.

The city of Ouro Preto is the capital.

The surface is most diversified and broken, the province being not only traversed by the great system of mountain and high land which stretches from the Serra da Mantiqueira in this province, in a north-westerly direction across Minas Geraes, Goyaz and Mato Grosso forming the dividing summit between the great rivers of the north and the south, but also by several offshoots, which ramify in various courses, and divide it into a multitude of plateaux, and of valleys and defiles, usually narrow and tortuous on the eastern side of the province, but larger and more level, proceeding westward. Some of the loftiest summits reach 5,500 feet altitude, and the plateau of Barbacena is at an elevation of upwards of 3,500 feet above the level of the sea.

This province gives origin to several large rivers, whose courses, and those of many of their numberless tributaries, though rapid and embarrassed by ledges and falls, are capable of being turned to essential service to the commerce and development of the interior of this rich and flourishing district of Brazil. These are—the Doce, rising near Ouro Preto, navigable for some distance in this province, but interrupted by the Escadinhas as it enters Espirito Santo, below which its course is free to the sea; the Jequitinhonha, or Belmonte, having birth near Serro, navigable from the S. Gonçalo and the ocean to the rapids of Salto Grande in the Serra dos Aimorés; the S. Francisco, which, starting near Ouro Preto, flowing northward through Minas Geraes and emptying into the ocean between Alagoas and Sergipe, is navigable by its confluent the Velhas from Sabara to the fall of Paulo Alfonso in Alagoas, and from thence to the sea; and the Parnahiba and Grande navigable along the north-western and southern frontiers.

The mineral wealth of this province is exceedingly great. Besides gold, of which it has already produced about 550 tons, and diamonds, now yielding annually about £200,000, it possesses rubies, emeralds, and other precious stones; silver, platinum, copper, iron, lead, mercury, antimony, bismuth, alum, sulphur, crystal, limestone, granite, millstones, amianthus, saltpetre, and lignite; and fossils are found of many extinct animals and vegetables. The gold and diamond mines are still worked at a profit. In Minas Geraes were found the famous crown diamond of Portugal, and the large diamond, the Estrella do Sul, exhibited at the late industrial exhibitions.

The soil is in general very fertile, covered with large forests of excellent timber in some parts, and in others furnishing fine pastoral valleys for grazing. Besides dyewoods and balsams it produces ipecacuanha, jalap, liquorice, indigo, European cereals and fruits, maize, cotton, sugar, coffee, tobacco, maté, &c., and great herds, droves and flocks of horses, mules, cattle, swine, and sheep are reared, making one of the principal occupations of the inhabitants.

The chief articles of export are gold, diamonds, cotton, tobacco, coffee, maté, bacon, lard, cheese, cattle, horses, mules, and cotton, chiefly to Rio de Janeiro and Bahia.

The *population* is about 1,350,000, of whom 150,000 are slaves. The representation is 10 senators and 20 deputies to the Imperial Assembly, and 40 deputies to the Provincial Chamber.

The *military force* consists of about 600 police, 400 soldiers, and 75,000 national guards.

Public education is afforded in 384 primary schools, 60 secondary schools, two lyceums, and two ecclesiastic seminaries.

The provincial *revenue* is about 1,200,000$ and the Imperial about 620,000$.

MEANS OF COMMUNICATION.

Besides the rivers rising in this province, which afford much aid to its trade, there is an excellent road to Rio de Janeiro, and the railroads from Rio de Janeiro and Santos will, when finished into the interior of this province, be of inestimable benefit for the development of the resources of this fertile and healthy district of Brazil.

TOPOGRAPHY.

Ouro Preto, the capital of the province, is situated on the serra of the same name, about 83 leagues to the north of Rio Janeiro. It is unpleasantly situated among steep mountains, and in a cold and cloudy climate. It is badly built, and has no buildings worthy of note. In it are the Government Palace, the Chamber, several churches, 14 fountains, a library, a botanic garden, and the lyceum. It carries on a considerable trade with Rio de Janeiro and the interior.

S. Joãs del Rei is a well-paved town, and is the *entrepôt* of a large commerce.

PROVINCE OF ESPIRITO SANTO.

HISTORY.

THIS province formed the grant made by John III. to Vasco Fernando Coutinho, who established the first settlement at Espirito Santo and Victoria, which, however, had to struggle with the Indians for many years. In the end of the seventeenth century, a descendant of Coutinho sold the grant to Francisco Gil d'Aranjo, and, in 1717, it was again purchased, for the same sum of 40,000 *cruzados*, by John V., and added to the crown domains. For two centuries after the first settlement, the Jesuits civilised and protected the Indians of the province; and, in 1750, the Indian population numbered upwards of 40,000, but after the expulsion of this order they either died of intemperance or returned to savage life. The district was governed by *capitães móres*, subject to the Viceroy, until 1809, when it was created a province.

GEOGRAPHY, ETC.

It lies between 17° 57′ and 21° 24′ south latitude, and 39° 17′ and 42° 7′ west longitude from Greenwich. It is bounded on the north by Bahia, the Mucury being the boundary; on the west by Minas Geraes, the serras dos Aimorés, dos Arrepiados, and do Pico, and the river Preto dividing them; on the south by Rio Janeiro, the Itabapoana being the separating river; and on the east by the Atlantic. It has a sea-coast of 90 leagues, an average width of 24 leagues, and a superficial area of 1,400 square leagues. Its capital is Victoria.

The climate is moderate and damp, the heat of summer being tempered by the breezes, and it is very healthy, except along the courses of the rivers Doce and S. Matheus, where there is experienced much sickness in some localities. The seasons are not so determined as in the northern provinces, rain falling generally. The surface is in general hilly, and in the west and south becomes somewhat mountainous.

It is watered by a great number of rivers which in general flow from the mountains on the western boundary, and are navigable by boats for some distance. The chief rivers, however, which flow through the province are the Mucury, on the northern limit, which rises in Minas Geraes, and is navigated by steamboats to St². Clara; the S. Matheus, navigated to the city of S. Matheus; and the large river Doce, coming from Minas Geraes, which, though injured by rocks, will be ere long an important channel of commerce. The mouths of many of the rivers also furnish small but deep ports.

The soil of this province is in general fertile, productive, and covered with timber; but the best districts are those at the north and south, along the courses of the S. Matheus and Itapemirim. The population is chiefly gathered within a stripe along the sea-coast, with the exception of the unhealthy low lands of the Rio Doce, but in the west the lands of the interior are beginning to be settled by immigrants from Minas Geraes. The principal products of cultivation are coffee, maize, sugar, beans, mandioca, rice, &c., which are almost entirely exported to Rio de Janeiro, through which place its foreign commerce is carried on. Coffee is the chief article of export, and its cultivation is rapidly increasing.

The *population* is about 55,000, of which about 10,000 are slaves.

The *representation* is one senator and one deputy to the Imperial Assembly, and 20 deputies to the Provincial chamber.

The *military force* consists of 173 soldiers, 50 police, and 6,000 national. guards.

Public education is provided in one lyceum, two Latin schools, and 51 primary schools.

The provincial *revenue* is about 130,000$ and the Imperial about 70,000$.

Steam navigation is kept up by two lines of steamers, one trading from Rio de Janeiro to S. Matheus, touching likewise at Itapemirim, Itabapoana, Guarapary, and Victoria in this province, and one from Rio de Janeiro to Caravellas in Bahia, touching at Victoria.

TOPOGRAPHY.

Victoria, the capital, is situated in 20° 18′ 30″ south lat., and 40° 12′ 30″ west long., on the east side of the island, and has a population of

6,000. Its port is small but good. It carries on no foreign trade.

S. Matheus has about 2,500 inhabitants, and carries on the chief trade in mandioca of the province.

Itapemirim is the shipping port of a fine sugar district. Near this town are a large grotto, and a granite rock forming a natural pyramid.

PROVINCE OF PARÁ.

HISTORY, ETC.

The first coloniser of this province was Francisco Caldeira, who established himself in Belem, in 1616, the territory forming part of the united government of Pará, Maranhão, and Ceará, from 1624 to 1652, when the separate government of Grao Pará was made independent of Maranhão, with Rega Barreto as governor. In 1654 it was reunited to that province, until 1754, when it was definitely raised to a captaincy, but remained with that province under the government of a captain-general, until 1774, in which year the captain-generalship of Grao Pará was formed of the captaincies of Pará and Rio Negro, which remained united until 1850, when the province of Amazonas was separated from Grao Pará, and the present limit of the province of Pará established.

GEOGRAPHY, ETC.

Pará, the most northern maritime province of Brazil, is bounded on the north-east by the Atlantic, on the north by French Guiana; on the west by Amazonas, the river Neamunda forming, in part, the dividing line; on the south by Maranhão and Goyaz, the chief separating lines being made by the rivers Gurupy, Araguaya, Vertentes, Fresco, Atoary, Frez Barros, Tapajoz, and Oreguatus. It lies between 4° 15′ north latitude, and 9° 54′ south latitude, and 45° 54′ and 58° 59′ west longitude. Its superficial extent is estimated at 39,000 square leagues. Its capital is Belem or Pará, on the south side of the river Pará.

The *climate*, like that of all the valley of the Amazonas, is humid and very warm during the day, the nights and mornings, however, being quite cool. During the summer it rains almost every afternoon, and in winter at all hours of the day. The climate is not healthy for strangers who expose themselves to the heat of the sun in the low grounds near the rivers, which, being subject to overflow during several months of the year in the wet season, dysentery and intermittent fevers are prevalent, and yellow fever since 1849, epidemic in various parts of the province. Sufferers from elephantiasis are also found along the rivers, owing, as it is asserted, to the habitual use of the food *(piraracu)* found in great abundance in them.

Mountains form but a small feature in the configuration, this province generally being flat; but rising, in its more northern extreme, into hills and mountainous elevations, and towards Mato Grosso and Goyaz into the continuous plateau which limits the navigation of the rivers flowing thence. The rivers, however, which drain the vast plains are very numerous, and many others of great importance flow through the province to discharge their waters into the ocean. Of these the greatest are the Amazonas, the longest river in the world, which, rising in Perú, after flowing through Pará in an easterly direction for 800 miles, enters the ocean at the equator, navigated by steamboats, 2,500 miles from the sea; the Tapajoz, which, flowing for about 350 miles through the south-west of the province, empties into the Amazonas, but whose navigation is interrupted by falls, not far from Mato Grosso; the Xingú, also a large river tributary to the Amazonas; and the Tocantins, which, taking its course from Goyaz to the Amazonas through Pará, forms the channel of communication by which Goyaz carries on its trade with the ocean. The Amazonas is deep and free from impediments to the navigation of vessels of even great size, and is destined to be the channel of a commerce exceeding even that of the Mississippi. So gradual is the elevation of its bed, that sailing vessels can ascend nearly to the foot of the Andes, and the tide of the ocean affects the river 400 miles above its mouth. From this arises the great bore, or as the natives call it, the Pororoca, which occurs at spring tides, when the flood, with three or four immense waves, attains its full height in two or three minutes.

The Amazonas, about 200 miles from its embouchure, divides, forming a number of islands of great fertility, which are used as grazing stations for large herds of cattle. One of these islands, called Marajo, is nearly 180 miles long and 450 in circumference.

Little has been done in the examination of

the mineral resources of the province, yet it has been ascertained that gold, quicksilver, iron, diamonds, and coal exist. Its soil is exceedingly rich, and, favoured by the equability of the climate, which limits the time of seeding to no special season, produces three crops in the year. The surface is generally covered with splendid forests of excellent timber, and with trees and plants whose products are valuable in arts, medicine, and commerce, such as india-rubber, cocoa, castanhas de Pará, or Para nuts, sarsaparilla urucu, oil of capaiva, tapioca, rice, millet, cotton, sugar cane, indigo, vanilla, ginger, jalap, ipecacuanha, cassia, cloves, pepper, &c., &c., with an innumerable variety of fruits and flowers. But, until lately, the scantiness of the population and this overflowing abundance of its spontaneous resources, prevented the development of its agriculture, by the indolence, which the ease of procuring their livelihood induced among the peasantry. Great numbers of cattle are raised in this province, and wide tracts of land are devoted to this business, in which are largely engaged the Messrs. James and Ambrose Campbell, the greatest land-owners in the province, who inherit from their mother, a descendant of one of the most distinguished families in the empire, three large estates near Pará, and one-fourth of the great island of Marajo. These gentlemen are zealous in the improvement and cultivation of their immense property, and derive great profits from the lucrative trade in which they are engaged, furnishing the beef market of Pará, and even shipping cattle to Cayenne and Demerara.

The chief exports are gum elastic, Brazil nuts, cocoa, sarsaparilla, oil of capaiva, and other medicinal substances, tapioca, timber, isinglass, hides, deer skins, &c.

The *population* of the province is about 250,000, of which about 39,000 are slaves, and 4,000 native Indians called Tapuas, to whom the government affords great facility of education, employing persons to teach them in their own language.

The *representation* is one senator and three deputies to the Imperial Assembly, and thirty deputies to the Provincial Chamber.

The *military force* consists of 700 soldiers, 300 policemen, and about 23,000 national guards.

For *public instruction* there exist two ecclesiastical schools, one in Belem and one in Obidos, one normal school in Pará, and about 80 primary schools throughout the province. Besides these there are many private schools.

The provincial *revenue* is about 700,000$, and the Imperial 1,400,000$.

Steam navigation is progressing with rapid strides; communication being kept up with the maritime provinces of the empire, and also with Amazonas, through the river Amazonas and its tributaries; the Amazon steamship company, who hold the exclusive right of their steam navigation, maintaining nine vessels, which trade between Belem and Chaves, Itacuan and Soure, once a month to each; between Belem and Manáos, twice a month; between Manáos and Tabatinga on the frontier of Perú, once a month; and between Belem and Cametá, twice a month. This line of steamers has done much for the development of the trade of the province, as will be seen from the following statistics. The steamers commenced running in 1853:—

IMPORTATION.

Years.	1st Line.	2nd Line.		3rd Line.	Total.
		Amazonas.	Peru.		
1853	60,000$000	500$000	300$000	...	60,800$000
1854	120,000$000	800$000	700$000	...	121,500$000
1855	500,000$000	16,000$000	17,000$000	70,000$000	603,000$000
1856	650,000$000	20,000$000	42,000$000	125,000$000	837,000$000
1857	700,000$000	55,000$000	50,000$000	130,000$000	935,000$000
1858	900,000$000	70,000$000	93,000$000	160,000$000	1,223,000$000
1859	1,120,000$000	80,000$000	179,000$000	140,000$000	1,519,000$000
1860	2,200,000$000	200,000$000	300,000$000	200,000$000	2,900,000$000
1861	2,100,000$000	195,000$000	285,000$000	142,000$000	2,722,000$000
1862	1,750,000$000	150,000$000	200,000$000	150,000$000	2,250,000$000
	10,100,000$000	787,300$000	1,167,000$000	1,117,000$000	13,171,300$000
	1,868,510$800	130,237$310	164,574$380	138,685$630	2,302,008$620

EXPORTATION.

Years.	1st Line.	2nd Line.		3rd Line.	Total.
		Peru.	Amazonas.		
1853	152,070$300	2,560$000	1,226$000	...	155,856$300
1854	376,040$700	149,814$000	1,500$000	...	527,354$700
1855	442,461$200	129,045$000	3,900$000	46,500$000	621,906$200
1856	730,324$400	361,676$000	3,800$000	91,000$000	1,186,800$400
1857	946,932$300	427,832$000	29,500$000	89,000$000	1,493,264$300
1858	866,592$300	269,862$000	46,495$080	179,660$500	1,362,609$880
1859	984,681$700	...	379,845$500	127,899$200	1,492,426$400
1860	1,547,605$000	245,124$900	70,630$000	295,346$000	2,158,705$900
1861	1,338,878$220	154,083$200	29,931$300	178,679$500	1,701,572$220
1862	1,304,450$800	...	259,344$600	198,716$500	1,762,511$900
	8,690,036$920	1,739,997$100	826,172$480	1,206,801$700	12,463,008$200
	1,903,912$400	369,587$800	192,460$400	271,088$360	2,837,088$360

TOPOGRAPHY.

There are seven cities in the province Belém, Cametá, Santarem, Bragança, Obidos, Vigna, and Macapá, and three colonies, one of which, established by a liberal and enterprising Bahian, Senr. José do Ode Almeida, in front of the capital, on the opposite side of the Guajará, is prospering, benefiting alike the promoter and the emigrants.

Belém, or Pará, the capital of the province, and its port for foreign trade, is situated on the east side of the river Guajará, which flows into the river or estuary of Pará. Its population is about 25,000. It is a well laid out town, macadamised roads, and possesses some fine buildings, such as the Palace of the Government, the best in the provinces, and the Bishop's Palace. There are 12 squares and 13 chapels in the city; but squares and chapels are alike devoid of elegance. The roads, however, about Belém, are most beautifully lined with fine trees, and form as perfect avenues as the eye could rest upon. One of especial beauty leads to the small chapel of Nossa Senora de Nazareth, at which, during the month of November, a great festival takes place, lasting for fourteen days, and visited nightly by thousands.

The port of Belém is large and safe, but is only frequented by small vessels of from 150 to 300 tons burden. It is favourably placed for commerce, as it forms a depôt for the export and import trade of the provinces of Pará, Amazonas, Mato Grosso, and Goyaz. A fine road, 100 leagues long, from this town to Santa Theresa in Goyaz has been made, by which the cattle of Goyaz can come to Belém. Belém lies in 1° 28' south latitude, and 48° 28' west longitude. Atalaia Point is in south latitude 0° 34', west longitude 47° 17' 9".

Obidos is situated on the north side of the river Amazonas, about 600 miles from Belém. Here the Government has some well-mounted fortifications, which are taken charge of by a government military colony, located close by. Macapá more to the north, is also noted for its fortifications and the good discipline maintained.

RECEIPTS at the Custom House of Pará (Belém).

Years.	Value in Milreis.	Years.	Value in Milreis.
1842–43	319,140$000	1853–54	1,388,650$000
1843–44	379,220$000	1854–55	1,310,070$000
1844–45	419,790$000	1855–56	987,690$000
1845–46	455,550$000	1856–57	1,269,680$000
1846–47	526,900$000	1857–58	1,230,310$000
1847–48	417,360$000	1858–59	1,286,070$000
1848–49	409,820$000	1859–60	1,496,160$000
1849–50	519,550$000	1860–61	1,921,240$000
1850–51	810,230$000	1861–62	1,488,870$000
1851–52	800,700$000	1862–63	1,358,993$000
1852–53	841,560$000		

FOREIGN TRADE of Parú (Belém).

Direct Imports.   Exports.

Years.	Value in Milreis.	Years.	Value in Milreis.
1852–53	2,866,239$000	1852–53	2,605,287$000
1853–54	4,932,976$000	1853–54	5,294,831$000
1854–55	4,298,971$000	1854–55	3,854,847$000
1855–56	2,912,364$000	1855–56	3,567,059$000
1856–57	3,616,720$000	1856–57	4,055,965$000
1857–58	3,688,601$000	1857–58	3,549,631$000
1858–59	3,946,364$000	1858–59	3,917,104$000
1859–60	4,709,896$000	1859–60	5,912,860$000
1860–61	5,660,147$000	1860–61	5,341,304$000
1861–62	3,668,055$000	1861–62	4,604,851$000
1862–63	4,471,314$000	1862–63	5,573,769$000

SHIPS which Sailed from the Port of Belém in 1863–64.

Number.	Nationality.	Tons Burden.
65	Brazilian	30,461
36	English	7,996
23	Portuguese	6,791
19	French	5,717
12	American	2,450
4	Danish	656
3	Hanoverian	507
2	Hamburg	428
1	Dutch	265
1	Swedish	255
166		55,526

PRINCIPAL ARTICLES Exported

To what Countries.	Ships.	Tons.	Caout-chouc.	Cocoa.
			Arrobas.	Arrobas.
England	24	5,618	117,391	3,758
United States	36	7,508	83,054	2,874
France	19	5,655	4,949	224,775
Portugal	19	5,761	3,382	14,272
Hamburg	6	1,126	1,683	18,100
Italy	1	265	...	4,100
Imperial Ports	61	29,593	18	89
Total	166	55,526	211,477	267,968

Oil of Capaiva.	Deer Skins.	Honey.	Uruçu.	Isinglass.	Sarsaparilla.
Pounds.	Pounds.	Pounds.	Arrobas.	Arrobas.	Arrobas.
34,816	...	6,400	2,154	1,667	15
65,144	107,611	121,477	1,604	...	...
9,041	...	...	...	...	120
30,870	...	34,137	1,134	66	2,342
...	...	...	359	...	...
...	...	...	40	...	...
5,443	...	...	...	...	1,456
145,314	107,611	162,014	5,291	1,733	3,933

from Belém in 1863-64.

Brazil Nuts.	Goyaz Dry Hides.	Pará Dry Hides.	Salt Hides.	Rice in Husk.	Rice Hulled.
Alq^e.	Number.	Number.	Pounds.	Arrobas	Arrobas.
24,848	1,258	...	...	...	...
32,064	6,000	635	523,03	69,776	...
137	9,426	104	...	...	...
7,966	15,751	4,215	905,331	27,363	76
7,420	2,886	...	...	...	...
34	6,385	...	...	...	...
74	...	...	...	18,561	41
72,543	41,706	4,954	957,634	115,700	117

Cotton.	Sugar.	Piassaba.	Cumuru.	Chile Hats.	Quina.	Total Value of Exports.
Arrs.	Arrs.	Arrs.	Pounds.	Number	Arrs.	Milreis.
427	...	6,247	3,435	...	457	2,014,144$740
3,825	404	...	6,256	...	...	1,781,263$735
...	...	451	535	...	1,000	1,212,065$129
379	23,188	2,989	2,768	...	100	451,908$235
...	...	1,872	...	...	...	151,995$876
...	...	...	...	...	...	37,295$800
...	...	262	...	61,485	...	389,823$739
4,631	23,592	11,825	13,264	61,485	1,557	6,038,497$254

PROVINCE OF CEARÁ.

HISTORY.

The first settlement within the limits of this province was made by Martim Soares Moreno, it remaining dependent on Maranhão. It was afterwards united to the province of Pernambuco, so remaining until 1799, when, by charter of the 17th of January, it was created a province. In 1822, the first president, Senor Pedro José Barros, was appointed.

GEOGRAPHY.

It lies between 2° 35' and 7° 9' south latitude, and 36° 41' and 40° 67' west longitude. It is bounded on the north and north-east by the ocean, on the west by Piauhy, on the south by Pernambuco, and on the east by Parahyba and Rio Grande do Norte.

It has a sea-coast of upwards of 120 leagues and an area of 4,500 square leagues. Its capital is Fortaleza. Its *climate* is warm and humid, close to the shore; but in the interior it is dry and subject to drought. The wet season of February to June forms the winter of the province, but is very irregular in the interior. The heat is great in the low lands, near the coast, but the nights and mornings are cool and agreeable, while in the mountains and elevated regions the climate is excellent and in general healthy.

The surface is very unequal. Near the coast the lands are low, but rise gradually to the chain of the Serra Ibiapaba, 2,500 feet high, which, commencing near to Granja, surrounds it like an amphitheatre nearly on three sides. This general configuration is, however, disturbed toward the middle of the maritime half of the province by the hills and plateaux which lie between the Aracurú and Jaguaribe, and from which flow the minor streams that empty into the ocean between them.

The Jaguaribe is the most important stream in the province, as, with a course of 120 leagues, it traverses it throughout its breadth, but it is shallow and interrupted by sand-banks, especially near its mouth. The Aracurú and Curú are the only others worthy of note, and many of the smaller rivers are completely dried up during the dry season.

The minerals found are gold, silver, iron, copper, lead, plumbago, alum, salt, saltpetre, crystal, &c.

The soil is of varied quality. The high grounds, slopes, and low lands of the coast are in general very fertile, but along the river courses it is frequently sandy, and in the interior the dryness of the seasons renders it unproductive.

Large prairies covered with excellent pasturage exist in the interior, on which are reared great numbers of horses and cattle, but fine forests of good timber cover some localities, and near the coast are found large quantities of the valuable palm tree, the Carnaúba. Balsams, gums, resins, and medicinal substances, and vegetable tallow are in abundance. The chief products of cultivation are cotton, coffee, sugar, tobacco, castor oil, farina de mandioca, starch, maize, rice, beans, fruits, &c. The principal articles exported are cotton, coffee, sugar, tobacco, cattle and hides. The total value of the exports, both foreign and coasting, is about

3,000,000$, and of the whole production of the province, exclusive of cattle and horses, about 7,000,000$. The number of horned cattle in the province is about 450,000, and of horses and mules about 50,000.

The foreign exports of Ceará amount to about 2,300,000$, and the direct foreign imports to 1,300,000$.

The *population* of Ceará is estimated at about 486,000, of which about 30,000 are slaves.

The *representation* is made by four senators and eight deputies to the General Assembly, and thirty-two deputies to the Provincial Chamber.

The *military force* consists of about 36 regulars, 250 policemen, and 40,000 national guards.

Public education is provided for by 111 primary schools, and by one Lyceum in Fortaleza.

The *provincial revenue* is about 400,000$ annually and the Imperial about 700,000$.

STEAM NAVIGATION.

Steam communication is maintained twice a month with the chief ports north and south, by the mail steamers of the Companhia Brazileira de Paquetes, which call at the port of Ceará; and by other steamers, with Maranhão, Pernambuco, and the intervening minor ports, and which also keep up intercourse with the ports of Aracaty, Acaracú, Mundahú, Granja, and Amarração.

TOPOGRAPHY.

Fortaleza, or Ceará, the capital of the province, is situated in south latitude 3° 31', and west longitude 37° 41', in a little inlet two leagues from the mouth of the Ceará. It is the port for the foreign trade of the province, and has about 20,000 inhabitants. It is well laid out and built on a plain, and its streets are wide, and carefully paved. It contains several handsome buildings, among which are the president's palace, the hospital, the fine cathedral, &c. One of its seven squares is well planted, and the city contains besides a fountain and three water-reservoirs. The lighthouse is on the Point of Mucuripe. The port is formed by a short reef which, however, is of little service in protecting it from the Atlantic swell, and in consequence, when the winds blow strongly from the sea, the embarkation and disembarkation of goods and passengers become difficult and even dangerous. The foreign exports of 1862-3 amounted to 2,283,936$, and the direct foreign imports to 1,298,129$.

Aracaty, eight miles up the Jaguaribe, is, next to Fortaleza, the most important city for its commerce and industry. It is the depôt of the whole valley of the Jaguaribe, and manufactures and exports large quantities of candles, leather, hats, and mats.

Aracarú, *Granja*, *Mundahú*, and *Amarracão* are the chief ports besides. Granja possesses the best port of the province.

PROVINCE OF PIAUHY.

HISTORY.

THIS province was first discovered in 1674, by Domingos Affonso Mafrense and Domingos Jorge, two adventurous explorers who established there about fifty large estates for the rearing of cattle, which estates are now the property of the Government, but owing to mismanagement, yield but little revenue. This province was formerly subject to the Captain-General of Bahia, but in 1718 was made a captaincy, remaining, however, subordinate to Maranhão until 1811, when it was separated entirely.

GEOGRAPHY.

It lies between 2° 32' and 11° 17' south latitude, and 38° 38' and 45° 59' west longitude.

It is bounded on the north by the Atlantic, on the west and north-west by Maranhão, from which the river Parnahiba separates it, on the south by Goyaz, the Serra dos Coroádos being the division : on the south-east, by Bahia and Pernambuco, and on the east by Ceará, the Serras dos Dois Irmãos, da Borborema and Ibiapaba forming their dividing boundaries. Its greatest length is from north to south-west 188 leagues, its breadth very unequal, and its area about 11,000 square leagues. It has only five leagues of sea-coast. The city of Teresina is its capital, Parnahiba its port.

The *climate*, like that of all the northern provinces, is warm and humid in the low grounds near the rivers and lakes. In the interior, away from the large rivers, great droughts occur during the dry season, which usually continues from May to September. Along the low lands, bordering on the rivers and lakes, intermittent fevers are common, but otherwise the climate is not unhealthy, especially on the open plains.

The surface of the whole province is, in its general features, one vast plain, broken up here and there by hills and low mountains, which stretch from the right bank of the Parnahiba to the continuous serras which form the natural boundary on the south and east. This immense tract is drained by the noble river Parnahiba, and all the tributaries which it receives on its right, many of the smaller streams of which, however, during the dry season, either dry up entirely, or dwindle into the merest threads, while many others are only navigable during the season of high waters. The Parnahiba itself, however, is an important stream, not only from its length, but from its navigation, giving free access to steamboats and small vessels up to the confluence of the Urussuhy, 150 leagues, and during the wet season, 260 leagues, and by its tributaries, a communication by means of barges and canoes to most parts of the interior of the province, though particularly to the south. There are many of these minor rivers useful only during high waters.

The chief minerals found are copperas, alum-slate, iron, and stone of various kinds. Saltpetre and potash are exceedingly abundant throughout the province, and impregnate the soil to such an extent as to injure the water in some districts. The soil itself is fertile, but the droughts which prevail during the dry season confine the cultivation very much to the borders of the rivers and lakes which do not dry up, and the rest of the province is abandoned to the rearing of cattle and horses, for which the fine plains seem peculiarly adapted, and which forms the principal occupation of the people. Before 1759 the Jesuits possessed in this province 54 cattle fazendas, containing 3,379 square leagues of land, valued at 240,000$, on which they had 600 slaves, and about 1,500 Indians, and from which they derived a yearly revenue of about 214,000$. On the expulsion of the Jesuits from Brazil, these cattle fazendas were taken possession of by the Crown, and of them there now remain in the hands of the Government 26, with an area of $314\frac{2}{3}$ square leagues, which are stocked with upwards of 50,000 head of horned cattle, horses, mules, &c., but which, owing to bad management, yield but a trifling income, some of them even proving a loss. On these fazendas the Government has several hundred slaves who are virtually valueless under the system carried out, and ought either to be set free or disposed of to others who could make their employment profitable.

The principal objects of cultivation are cotton, rice, tobacco, and articles for home consumption. The chief exports consist of cotton, cattle, horns, hides, hair, leather, tatagiba, tobacco, and isinglass.

The exports to foreign countries amounted in 1862-3 to 223,101$, and the direct foreign imports to 213,720$. A large proportion of the trade of the province is carried on through the ports of the adjoining provinces, and therefore the true value of the total exports is unknown.

The *population* is about 175,000, including 10,000 slaves.

The *representation* is one senator and three deputies to the General Assembly, and twenty-four deputies to the Provincial Chamber.

The *military force* consists of about 400 soldiers, 250 police, and 20,000 national guards.

Public education is provided for by one normal school and 36 primary schools; and there is an institution for the teaching of trades to boys.

The provincial *revenue* is about 190,000$, and the Imperial about 150,000$.

Steam navigation exists on the Parnahiba, and between the town of Parnahiba and Maranhão.

TOPOGRAPHY.

The chief towns are Teresina, the capital; Parnahiba, the foreign shipping port of the province; and Oeiras, the former capital.

Teresina, since 1852 the capital of the province, is situated in south latitude 5° 40', west longitude 41° 59', near the east side of the river Parnahiba, has a population of about 9,000, and, in spite of the unhealthiness of its location, is progressing rapidly.

Oeiras, the former capital, is situated on the Canindé, about the middle of the province. Placed in an unproductive district, it is rapidly decaying.

Parnahiba, in south latitude 2° 53', west longitude 41° 38', is situated on the Iguarassú branch of the Parnahiba, about 4 leagues from the ocean. It is the commercial port of the province, and in it is the custom-house. It is very subject to intermittent fevers, owing to its unhealthy site, but is, nevertheless, growing rapidly, and is the most populous town of the province.

PROVINCE OF RIO GRANDE DO NORTE.

HISTORY.

THIS province, deriving its name from the Rio Potengi, which was called by the first discoverers Rio Grande, formed part with Maranhão of the grant to Senr. João de Barros, but was not colonised until 1599, when Jeronymo d'Albuquerque, acting under orders of the Governor-General of Brazil, commenced the foundation of the town of Natal. About 1635, the town and country fell into the hands of the Dutch, who remained possessors until 1654. It remained subject to the Governor of Pernambuco until 1818, when it was made a distinct province.

GEOGRAPHY.

It is bounded on the west by Ceará and Parahyba, from which the Serra of Apodi separates it; on the south by Parahyba; and on the north-east by the ocean. It has about 75 leagues of coast, and an area of 1,500 leagues. It lies between 4° 43′ and 6° 39′ south latitude, and 34° 53′ and 37° 24′ west longitude. Its capital is Natal.

The *climate* is hot, particularly in the low lands, where the days and nights are of almost equal temperature, but in the high lands of the interior the air is pure and dry, and the climate in general very healthy. In the plains of the western part of the province the droughts are great and destructive, that of 1845-6 having destroyed almost all the cattle of the province.

Mountains are but a small feature, the only ones of importance being the range on the western boundary, and the Serra Borborema, between the forks of the Piranhas, and some smaller ones near Natal.

The surface rises from the sea-coast, where it is low and sandy, particularly in the north, to the elevated plains, which, at some distance in the interior, stretch on to the mountains in the south, and on the western boundary, the slope to the seaward being drained by innumerable rivers of no great length, and the great plains on the north and west and the broken lands of the south by the more important rivers Apodi and Piranhas. Besides these two rivers, the chief ones are the Aguamaré, Cearámirim, Cunhahu, Guajahi, Potengi, Serido, and Trary, which are navigated chiefly with large canoes and barges at high stage of water. The ports also are small and shallow, and unfitted for the development of a large and important export trade. Metals have been found, hitherto but in small quantities, also crystal, amianthus, various kinds of building stone, and particularly salt.

The soil near the shore is sandy and covered with cocoa-nut trees, but the province possesses a fine soil, though its productiveness is injured by the droughts. Many forests of fine building timber exist, and gums, resins, balsams, Brazil wood, medicinal roots, wild honey, cochineal, and wax, are found in abundance. The chief articles of cultivation are cotton, sugar, and articles of food, and in the interior are reared large herds of horses and cattle. The chief exports are cotton, sugar, cattle, and hides, salt, Brazil wood, and Carnaúba tallow, and fibre. The foreign trade is principally carried on through Pernambuco, owing to the want of good ports.

The foreign exports of 1862-3 were 472,609$, and the direct foreign imports 3,726$.

The *population* is about 210,000, including 20,000 slaves.

The *representation* is one senator and two deputies to the Imperial Assembly, and 22 deputies to the Provincial Chamber.

The *military force* is about 100 police, and 20,000 national guards.

Public education is provided for by 48 primary schools, five advanced schools, and one lyceum.

The provincial *revenue* is about 80,000$, and the imperial 80,000$.

Steam navigation exists between Natal and Pernambuco on the south, and Fortaleza on the north, touching at various intermediate ports, including the port of Assú.

TOPOGRAPHY.

Natal, the city and capital of the province, is situated in south latitude 5° 45' and west longitude 35° 13' 15" on the south side of the river Potengi, or Rio Grande do Norte, about one league from the coast. Its port is a kind of bay between the city and the Fort of Reis Magos, and would be one of the most valuable in Brazil were the banks of sand formed by the river Potengi removed, so as to allow the entrance of larger vessels into that river. Natal is the foreign shipping port of the province, but carries on but a small direct foreign trade, amounting, in 1862-3, to only 472,609$ exported, and 3,726$ imported.

The ports of *Assú* and *Macáu* are the two other chief ports. Macáu exports a large quantity of salt. The reef which surrounds nearly the whole coast shelters a number of other small ports and inlets, from which is carried on a coasting trade with Natal and other places.

PROVINCE OF SAO PAULO.

HISTORY.

This province formed part of the grant made in 1535 to Martim Affonso de Souza and his brother Pedro Lopes de Souza, which was known as the captaincy of S. Vincente, from its capital S. Vincente, founded in 1531 by Martim Affonso de Souza, until 1710, when João V., having purchased the districts of Minas Geraes and S. Paulo, formed them into a captaincy-general with the town of S. Paulo as capital. In 1748, when the captaincies of Goyaz and Mato Grosso were dismembered from this captaincy-general, it was abolished and the government of S. Paulo subordinated to that of Rio de Janeiro, but in 1765, S. Paulo was removed from under this jurisdiction, and again given a captain-general. The first president after the Independence of Brazil was the Visconde de Congonhas.

The Paulists, descended from the European

colonists and the aborigines with whom they intermarried, were bold enterprising adventurers, who scoured the interior of Brazil, in the search for gold and slaves, thinking no hardship or toil too great to be endured, and thus caused the early settlement of many of the internal provinces. They were also reckless, bloodthirsty men, grasping at gain at any cost of life to themselves or others, and became for very many years, in despite of reiterated orders from the kings, the terror of the Indians of the interior, and of the Jesuit Missions on the Paraguay, sacking and destroying their villages, and carrying off their inhabitants into slavery.

GEOGRAPHY.

It lies between 20° and 25° 0′ south latitude, and 44° 18′ and 53° 23′ west longitude. It is bounded on the north by Minas, the Serra da Mantiqueira, Serra do Lopo, and the Rio Grande separating them on the west by Goyas and Mato Grosso, and Paraná dividing them; on the south by Paraná, the Paraná Panema and its tributary the Itarére forming the great part of the boundary; and on the south-east by the ocean. It is about 95 leagues from north to south, 170 from east to west, and has an area of about 11,000 square leagues.

The capital of the province is São Paulo, but its custom-house and port for foreign commerce are at Santos.

The climate of the interior in general is temperate and agreeable to Europeans and is very healthy, except in the low lands near the coast, where it is hot and humid in summer and liable to fevers. Goître is found in the coldest parts, and in some localities elephantiasis is not uncommon among the negroes and poorest classes.

The greater part of the province is elevated, but not mountainous, except in the south-east, where the Serra Geral, or Serra do Mar, runs, under different names, nearly parallel with the sea, throughout the province, dividing it into its two great watersheds, and descending almost abruptly into the low lands along the sea-coast; but forming on the north-west the elevated plateau that stretches on to the Paraná and Parnahiba.

The rivers on the sea-coast are all small, the Iguape being the only one of any pretensions; but on the north-western slope flow a number of important rivers, which receive many tributaries and empty into the Paraná. Of these the most northern is the Grande, which takes its rise in the Minas Geraes, and forms for 90 leagues the boundary between Minas Geraes and São Paulo. South of the Grande is the Tieté, which, originating in the Serra do Mar, near to the city of São Paulo, and flowing westward through nearly the whole breadth of the province, was the channel by which the Paulists in former years carried on their intercourse with the interior provinces of Mato Grosso and Goyaz, and with the Spanish settlements on the Paraná and Paraguay. South of this river, and, like it, having its head waters from the Serra Geral, flows the Paraná Panema, which empties into the Paraná, forming, with its tributary the Itaréré, nine-tenths of the southern boundary. These, with their tributaries, and the minor streams which flow into the Paraná, offer, together with the Paraná, facilities for a most extended intercourse, were the falls and rapids which injure their navigation removed or improved. In the Paraná, however, exist the two great falls of the Urubú Punga and Sete quedas (seven falls), the former about south latitude 20° 32′ and the latter at the Serra do Maracajú, which form complete barriers to the passage of vessels.

There are several islands along the coast, the most important of which are, Ilha dos Porcos, S. Sebastião, S. Amaro, S. Vincente, Cananéa, and Ilha do mar Pequeno.

The mineral wealth of São Paulo is great, the gold mines alone having produced, up to the end of the last century, nearly 70 tons of gold. Iron abounds in all parts, and particularly in the metalliferous mountains of Ipanema (where there is a Government foundry), and Araassoiva, and copper, silver, precious stones, anthracite, and bituminous schist.

The soil is rich and very productive, and, besides native timber of excellent quality, produces all European plants, but the great products of agriculture are coffee, sugar, tobacco, tea, cotton, and breadstuffs. Coffee, though suffering since 1861 from the coffee-blight, has had especial development, even to the supersedure in some localities of the culture of sugar-cane.

Great numbers of horned cattle, horses, mules, and swine are reared, and form important items in the trade of the province. The chief

x

articles of export are coffee, sugar, rice, tea, spirits, timber, bacon, cattle, horses, mules, hides, &c.; amounting in 1861-2 to 16,529,310$. In 1862-3, the value of the foreign exports was 8,412,972$; and of the direct foreign imports, 2,018,804$.

The *population* is about 800,000, of whom 60,000 are slaves.

The *representation* is four senators and nine deputies to the imperial assembly, and thirty-six deputies to the provincial chamber.

The *military force* consists of the police, 552 men, the garrison corps, 127 men, a cavalry company of about fifty men, and about 40,000 national guards.

Public education is supplied in three seminaries, one normal and 211 primary schools. Besides these there are about 120 private schools, 11 schools for preparing law students, the Faculdade de Direito (Inns of Law), the Episcopal seminary, and some church schools.

The provincial *revenue* is about 1,200,000$, and the imperial about 1,600,000$.

MEANS OF COMMUNICATION.

Besides the aid derived from the rivers flowing west, and roads of communication with all the provinces surrounding, this province has a railway from Santos to Jundiahy, intended to connect Santos with Minas Geraes.

Starting from Santos the road runs to the Cubatão river over a swampy country, unpopulated, and without any present apparent powers of production, except rice and reptiles, at first upon a road and bridge constructed by the government to connect Santos with *terra firma*. Four miles from Cubatão the land becomes more elevated at Mugy, a large "campo" purchased by Mr. Sharpe, where he has a private residence. This must eventually become a most valuable property, it being the only land available for agriculture between Santos and the foot of the serra. Here you have the mountain gorge before you whose ascent of 2,600 feet of perpendicular height, gives the S. Paulo railway so emphatic a character.

Passing over the Mugy river you arrive quickly at the foot of the gorge formed by the two out-jutting spurs of the buttress-like mountain, and the black defiant ravine is suggestive of anything but a railway course. Here the line climbs boldly up the side of the Mugy spur, at a usual ascent of one in ten, crossing mountain torrents, leaping gloomy chasms, cutting through solid rocks, holding hard on to every foot gained, until it attains a resting-place upon the table land, 2,600 feet high, after five miles of gigantic excavations, removing 1,100,000 cubic yards of granite rock and earth.

Here we must give a slight idea of how this daring plan is utilized, which was at one time laughed at as an engineering impossibility, and which even yet stands pre-eminent among similar works.

This entire and almost straight ascent of upwards of five miles is divided into four "lifts" of about a mile and a quarter each, having a level platform of some 400 feet in length between them. On these lifts, as in general on all the line, the track is single, except at the upper half, where it is doubled to admit of the ascending and descending trains passing each other. At the upper end of each platform is placed a powerful stationary engine of 200 horse-power, whose two cylinders are 26 inches diameter and 5 feet stroke, calculated to haul up 50 tons at the rate of ten miles an hour, which are supplied by five Cornish boilers, three of which suffice for the duty.

A steel wire rope, tested to a strength far exceeding the requirements which will ever be made upon it, passes over a friction-wheel on each side of the fly-wheel drum upon which it is wrapped round, and, one end being attached to an ascending and the other to a descending train, it is intended to make the "lift" partially self-acting, as it now wholly is at one of the inclines which is not supplied with its stationary engine, the weight of the descending train drawing up the ascending one. Powerful breaks that will stop a train instantly are supplied to guard against a breaking down of any part of the machinery, or a rupture of the rope. From this short description our readers can form an idea of the mechanical contrivances for effecting the ascent.

Throughout these wonderful inclines the most majestic and wild scenery is observed along the slightly winding way. On the third lift occurs a ravine still more gloomy than the rest, which is called the Bôca do Inferno (Mouth of Hell); that, having a width of 900 feet, is crossed by an iron viaduct, which lies on rows of iron columns resting on stone piers 200 feet below in the centre of the line.

The system pursued in railway making in the United States should be followed here. Whenever a part of the line is ready for traffic let the public have the immediate benefit of it, at the same time that the contractor is not relieved from his twelve months' responsibility for keeping up its condition.

We are firmly convinced that the greater part of the premium held out to the contractors for the completion of the line before the stipulated time has been expended, for the engineer of the contractors, Mr. Henderson, spares neither money nor men in carrying out the works to Jundiahy, and on many portions of the line they are working with torch-lights at night. He is now completing a line which, for solidity and permanency, may compete with any one in Europe, and it is exceedingly pleasant to find such rare frankness as he exhibits in showing to every one that seeks it his plans, the cost of construction, and his practical and theoretic ideas thereon.

The benefits that will be derived by the country from this railway must be enormous, and the sooner it is used the better for all. We see from the statistics of the toll bridge of Cubatão that the great number of 513,542 mules crossed it, paying a toll of 115,043$900, during the past year, and, in addition to a great mass of other articles up and down, 26,178 tons of coffee passed over in the same period. All this great amount of produce must travel by the railway once it is opened, and so great will be the advantages of its speedy opening, and the saving of interest and guarantee upon the £1,800,000 it will cost, that we cannot doubt the Government will not permit any delay in carrying out this object of its construction. We feel sure that when once in operation the shareholders will have no need to call upon the Government for any portion of the 7 per cent. guarantee, and we trust that they will feel encouraged to carry on the line at least to Campinas, which is the finest coffee-growing district in the province.

The cultivation of cotton also promises to become a main source of wealth to the province, and of traffic to the railway. This year an enormous increase has taken place in its production, the season's crop amounting to 9,600,000*l.*, and, what is of great importance, the fazendeiros have acquired the conviction that its culture brings a certain and remunerative return; a result mainly due to the untiring exertions of Messrs. Aubertin and Hutchings. No one can speak of the progress of this great staple in the province without associating with its relation the names of these two English gentlemen.

Recognising at once the great capacity of S. Paulo for its growth, and the enormous benefits to the province and the company they represent, which its cultivation would induce, they took advantage of a position bringing them into daily and intimate relations with the authorities, and with the most influential and spirited inhabitants of the province, to point out and impress upon them the great advantages of this crop as a staple of S. Paulo. Instructions, and useful and encouraging information, have been disseminated amongst them through the varied and valuable writings of Mr. Aubertin. Seed of the best qualities, procured by Mr. Hutchings through the Manchester Cotton Association, has been distributed to the planters.

Success has followed their endeavours; and their goodwill and friendly desire to promote the prosperity of the province are fully acknowledged by the Paulenses, amongst whom they are deservedly popular. Indeed the Railway Company and the contractors have been unusually fortunate in the selection of all their officials, and we rejoice to find such men, and such charming and cultivated ladies as their wives, brought in contact with the hospitable but somewhat proud and Asiatic Paulense fazendeiro.

The Paulense is sociable and intelligent, and, when men of suavity, talent, and literary powers, such as we find among the officials of the railway, throw themselves heart and soul into the promotion of industrial progress and good feeling, we may safely expect that the results will not be diminutive, whether socially, commercially, or politically.

Steam Navigation is kept up between Santos and Rio de Janeiro and the ports north and south by the steam packet companies and by other steamers which call at Santos.

PROVINCE OF ALAGOAS.

HISTORY.

The territory of this province formed part of the grant made to Duarte Coelho Pereira, the donatorio of Pernambuco, and, during the Dutch invasion, it shared the same fate as that province. After the expulsion of the Dutch it remained a district of Pernambuco; but, in 1817, was erected into a separate province with the town of Alagoas as capital, which town was, in 1839, superseded by Maccio, the present capital.

GEOGRAPHY.

This province lies between 8° 50′ and 10° 15′ south latitude and 35° 6′ and 37° 49′ west longitude. It is bounded on the north and west by Pernambuco, the dividing line being formed by the rivers Persinunga, Una, Jacuipy and Taquará, the serra Pellada, and by the Moxoto, a tributary of the S. Francisco; on the south by the province of Sergipe, being separated therefrom by the S. Francisco, and on the east by the Atlantic. It has a sea-coast extension of 56 leagues, and a superficies of 1,200 square leagues.

The climate in the low part of the province is very humid in consequence of the numerous lakes, but is healthy away from these and from the borders of the river of S. Francisco, where some intermittent fevers occur during the wet season.

No mountains of any great elevation are found in the province except at the extreme north-east end. Near the coast the lands are low and sandy, but towards the interior, rising into fertile hills and high lands.

It is intersected by many rivers, which have in general an easterly course, and by a number of lakes which run north and south, communicating with one another and the rivers by shallow channels. These rivers are of little importance, only admitting boats for a short distance, except the large river of S. Francisco, on the southern boundary, which is navigable to Piranhas, 38 leagues from the sea. 18 leagues above this place is the great Brazilian cataract Paulo Affonso, where the river descends 150 feet.

The lakes are navigable to some extent, and afford means of transport by small craft, but might at a slight expense be made available for steamboats of little draught, thus diminishing the enormous cost of carriage of the staples of the interior, sometimes amounting to one-half their value.

The mineral wealth does not seem to be great, though gold, amianthus, and other valuable substances have been found, and also anthracite, bituminous schist, granite, sandstone, and ochres.

The lands away from the sea-coast are extremely fertile, and are covered with splendid forests of excellent timber, except where cleared for cultivation. Among some of the richest and most productive localities of the province are the district of Atalaia and the domains of Sinimbu, whose owners are endeavouring to introduce new and improved modes of husbandry, which, it is to be hoped, will be the initiative to further much-needed improvements throughout the province, not only as regards agriculture, but in the equally important object of facilitating and cheapening the transmission of the products of the country, and of the articles of importation required in the interior.

Brazil wood and various gums, resins, oils, and a coarse native silk, are found in abundance. Almost everything will grow, but the chief articles of culture are cotton, sugar, and tobacco, which, with timber, constitute the principal articles of export.

The foreign exports of 1862-3 amounted to 4,765,460$, and the direct foreign imports to 103,753$.

A large coasting trade in foreign and native goods is carried on with Pernambuco and Bahia.

The *population* is about 250,000, including about 45,000 slaves.

The *representation* is made by two senators and five deputies to the Imperial Assembly, and by 30 deputies to the Provincial Chamber.

The *military force* consists of 128 regulars, 152 national guards on duty, and 149 police, in all, 429 men on duty, and about 25,000 national guards in reserve.

Public education is provided for by 84 primary schools.

The provincial *revenue* is about 400,000$, and the Imperial about 470,000$.

Steam navigation, though calculated to be of great benefit to the province, has been neglected hitherto, but of late a company has been established to place small steamers on the chief lakes.

The mail steamers from Para to Rio de Janeiro, call at Maceió, and keep up a half-monthly communication with the chief northern and southern ports of the empire. Further intercourse is maintained with Bahia and the intervening ports by a Bahian line; and with Pernambuco, from Penedo, by a Pernambuco line, which proceeds between Aracajú, in Sergipe, and Pernambuco, touching at various ports.

TOPOGRAPHY.

Maceió, the capital of the province, is situated in 9° 39′ 18″ south latitude, and 35° 41′ 24″ west longitude, on an eminence facing the sea, and is almost concealed from view by the luxuriant vegetation in which it is embowered. It contains about 3,000 houses, and a population of

18,000. It possesses a fine cathedral, an elegant Palace of the Assembly, an office for the inspection of cotton, a lighthouse, and three landing stages for goods. Until 1839, Maceió, though the shipping port, had no custom-house, this being located at Alagoas, then the capital of the province. In consequence, great delay took place in the loading and discharge of vessels. In the above year, however, the illustrious statesman, Senr. Cansançao de Sinimbu, who is a native of the province, proposed and carried the law changing the capital to Maceió, despite the strong opposition of the land-owners of the old city, and thus essentially benefited the commerce of the province.

The harbour of Maceió is an open roadstead, protected in some degree by the reef outside from the force of the ocean waves, but exposed to storms from all quarters, the lands in the neighbourhood having but little elevation. The water deepens slowly from the low sandy beach, and vessels have to lie off at some distance and discharge into barges, receiving cargo in the same manner, the expense of which is very great. Maceió is the only port open to the foreign trade. Both the import and export commerce is carried on through the merchants of Bahia and Pernambuco.

In 1862-3 the direct foreign imports amounted to 103,732$
,, the foreign imports coastwise amounted to 1,518,684
,, the national imports coastwise amounted to 272,962
,, the national exports coastwise amounted to 507,985
,, the national exports abroad amounted to 4,766,306

Total, 7,169,669$

The city of *Alagôas*, until 1839 the capital of the province, is situated on the south side of the lake Mandaú, in the centre of a very fertile district. Its population is about 8,000.

The city of *Penedos* is built on the north side of the S. Francisco, eight leagues from the sea. From its situation it is destined to be an important commercial point, especially after the finishing of the railroads from Bahia and Pernambuco to the S. Francisco.

PROVINCE OF RIO DE JANEIRO.

HISTORY.

This province was conferred as a gift on Martim Affonso de Souza, who built, in 1552, a small fort near the Sugarloaf in the Bay of Rio Janeiro. Having, however, neglected its further colonisation, some French Huguenots, under the command of Admiral Villegaignon, established in 1556 a strong fortress in this bay, on an island which still bears his name. The French settlers were well received by the neighbouring Indians, the Tamoyes, who were at enmity with the Portuguese, but their friendly relations caused alarm to D. João III., and he ordered the expulsion of these colonists, which was effected by the Governor of Bahia, Mem de Sã, in 1567, after which a colony of Portuguese was placed at Beira da Misericordia. In 1572 D. Sebastião divided Brazil, making two capitals, that of St. Sebastião do Rio de Janeiro in the southern half, and that of Bahia in the northern division. Four years afterwards this order was rescinded, and Bahia became as formerly the capital of Brazil. In 1711 Rio Janeiro was again taken by a French squadron under Duguay Trouin, who exacted as ransom 610,000 cruzados, and 500 boxes of sugar, besides large contributions of cattle and other things from individuals. Despite of these and other struggles the province prospered, and in 1763 the Vice-royalty was removed from Bahia to Rio Janeiro. In 1808 the royal family of Portugal, forced to leave in consequence of the French invasion, came to Rio, and thus gave a strong impulse to the enrichment and growth of the city, which remained the capital of the province until 1834, when Netherohy was selected. The first president of the province of Rio Janeiro was the Viscount of Itaborahy.

GEOGRAPHY.

The territorial limits extend from 21° 35′ to 23° 25′ south latitude, and from 40° 58′ to 45° 7′ west longitude. It is bounded on the north by Espirito Santo, from which it is separated by the river Itabapuana; on the north and north-west by Minas Geraes, separated therefrom by the rivers Preto and Parahyba and by the mountains of Mantigueira, on the south-west by the province of S. Paulo, and on the south and south-east by the Atlantic Ocean. The whole province contains about 2,400 square leagues.

The capital is Nitherohy, but its foreign port is Rio de Janeiro.

CLIMATE.

The climate is in general temperate and very agreeable, but varies greatly according to locality and elevation. The high districts are very healthy, but in low marshy places there are often cases of intermittent fever during the months of December, January, and February.

The province is very mountainous, and is intersected by numerous rivers. The coast has got some good ports, but all produce must go to Rio de Janeiro for foreign export. The principal ports are Angra dos Reis, St. João da Barra, Mangaratiba Cabo Frio, Macahe, and Rio de Janeiro. The chief rivers are the Macahe,

Itabapuana, and Parahyba. The last receives many small rivulets, runs through Campos, and empties into the ocean at St. João da Barra. It is navigable as far as St. Fideles, and small steamers run every day between that place and St. João da Barra. The chief mountains are the Macau, Santa Anna, Manga Larga, and the Orgãos (organs), this last running from east to west.

The largest island on the coast is Ilha Grande, four leagues in breadth, which is very productive, and is situated about 16 leagues from the mouth of the Bay of Rio Janeiro.

The island of Marambaya, about nine leagues westward of Rio, is about seven leagues in length. At the east end of the shore of Marambaya is the great point of Guaratiba, where begins the range of mountains that surrounds the Bay of Rio de Janeiro. From this you may see the Gavéa at a distance of six leagues to the E.N.E., which mountain is remarkable for its size, and is unlike any other about the entrance of the harbour, when approaching from the south.

The island of Sebastião is about four leagues long in its greatest extent, and its mountains are as elevated as those of the continent, from which it is separated by the Gullet or Strait, which forms a most useful roadstead for vessels, being so protected by the high lands that the water is as smooth as a pond. A late survey has, however, discovered many submerged rocks not laid down in any existing chart. There are a few more small islands in the Bay of Angra dos Reis.

The Ilha da Raza, on which is placed a lighthouse, is close to the entrance to the Bay of Rio, and may be seen at a distance of many leagues, and in the bay itself are the islands of Paquetá, Governador, and some others.

The most important capes are Ponta Negra, St. Thomé, and Cabo Frio.

AGRICULTURE.

This province produces almost all kinds of tropical and temperate plants. Among them are coffee, cotton, sugar-cane, mandioca, tobacco, ipecacuanha, rice, cacáo, potatoes, and most of the vegetables cultivated in Europe. Among the fruits are mango, banana, guaiba, pine-apple, cajú, orange, bread-fruit, tamarinds, sweet and sour lemons, &c. *Coffee* is the greatest staple of the province, and is the most lucrative to the planter. It was first introduced in 1770 from Pará and Maranham, by the Chancellor João Alberto Castello-Branco. A celebrated Portuguese writer, Monsenhor Pizarro, says, the cultivation of this plant was prohibited in Brazil, under the penalty of death, during the reign of D. Manoel, but that this outrageous law was repealed after his death. Since that time the culture of this important staple has yearly augmented, as the statistics of the exports of coffee from this province will show. The decrease which has taken place since 1860 was caused by partial failure in the yield.

The statistics of the export include not only the production of this province, but also a part of that from some others, the proportion respectively being about—

79 per cent. for the province of Rio de Janeiro.
8 ,, ,, ,, Minas Geraes.
11 ,, ,, ,, St. Paulo.
2 ,, ,, ,, Espirito Santo.

The value of the coffee of the province exported to foreign countries was, in 1860, 5,660,522*l*.; 1862, 3,675,744*l*.; 1863 3,506,133*l*.

COFFEE.—Exports from the province of Rio de Janeiro.

Years.	Arrobas.	Average Price.	Value.
1817–18	318,032	...	...
1818–19	371,345	...	...
1819–20	269,574	...	...
1820–21	539,000	...	...
1826–27	1,304,450	...	...
1827–28	1,754,500	...	...
1828–29	1,845,735	...	...
1829–30	1,875,535	...	...
1830–31	1,958,925	...	...
1831–32	2,241,245	...	...
1832–33	2,394,550	...	...
1833–34	2,808,460	...	..
1834–35	2,803,795	...	...
1835–36	3,237,190	...	...
1836–37	3,579,465	...	...
1837–38	3,285,025	...	...
1838–39	3,833,480	...	...
1839–40	4,446,620	...	...
1840–41	4,982,221	3$519	17,544,647$
1841–42	5,482,731	3$286	18,002,288$
1842–43	5,843,476	2$902	16,929,581$
1843–44	6,206,841	2$878	17,780,749$
1844–45	6,052,771	2$811	17,087,477$
1845–46	6,720,221	3$028	20,446,846$
1846–47	7,598,864	2$761	21,028,910$
1847–48	9,201,355	2$632	24,237,026$
1848–49	8,258,046	2$502	20,735,398$
1849–50	5,706,833	3$866	22,059,518$
1853–54	8,063,033	4$071	32,828,328$
1854–55	11,900,790	3$737	44,471,628$
1858–59	9,972,347	4$539	45,269,413$
1859–60	8,573,063	5$986	51,319,178$
1860–61	13,054,061	5$508	71,908,314$
1861–62	8,162,191	5$896	48,124,558$
1862–63	6,891,872	6$576	45,324,110$

Sugar comes next to coffee in importance as a product of this province. According to the testimony of different writers, the sugar-cane readily acclimated, and its culture was easily carried on, and yielded large profits to the cultivator.

The number of sugar houses in this province was:—

In	1661 at above		100
,,	1711	,,	136
,,	1852	,,	792
,,	1860	,,	980

The export to foreign countries has not increased during the last fifteen years, but that to the other provinces and the home consumption have greatly augmented. The production has not kept pace with the increase in some other articles, the cultivation of sugar-cane being comparatively neglected for that of coffee. The annual yield of sugar is estimated at about 21,424 tons, worth, in 1862, about £430,000.

SUGAR of the Province of Rio de Janeiro.—Total Exports, Foreign and Coastwise.

Years.	Arrobas.	Years.	Arrobas.
1711–12	353,500	1837–38	894,138
1827–28	1,173,000	1838–39	1,002,538
1828–29	1,146,264	1839–40	996,284
1829–30	1,200,764	1840–41	673,832
1830–31	1,302,924	1841–42	600,000
1831–32	1,100,200	1842–43	600,000
1832–33	832,250	1843–44	600,000
1833–34	856,694	1844–45	600,000
1834–35	901,930	1845–46	600,000
1835–36	1,149,990	1854–55	507,935
1836–37	1,087,440		

SUGAR.—Exports to Foreign Countries.

Years.	Arrobas.	Value in Milreis.
1846–47	359,067	...
1847–48	383,026	...
1848–49	230,752	...
1849–50	448,527	880,237$
1850–51	579,043	...
1851–52	625,205	...
1853–54	448,437	893,174
1854–55	383,014	1,058,795
1858–59	636,250	1,842,757
1859–60	171,599	629,896
1860–61	127,043	486,504
1861–62	671,106	1,777,213
1862–63	448,785	1,177,556

The *population* is estimated at about 850,000, including 200,000 slaves.

The *representation*, including that of the municipality of Rio de Janeiro, is six senators and twelve deputies to the Imperial assembly, and 45 provincial deputies to the provincial chamber.

The *military force* consists of about 400 police, 2,000 soldiers, and 43,000 national guards.

Public instruction is given in one normal school, four secondary for languages, and 164 primary schools, including four German at Petropolis. Besides these are 47 private colleges, and above 200 private primary schools.

The provincial revenue is about 3,700,000$.

MEANS OF COMMUNICATION.

Besides many bridle and carriage roads running in all directions, this province has some short canals, namely, those of Magé, Itaguahy, Nogueira, and that from Campos to Macahé.

The railroads are, the Pedro Segundo, intended to join Rio de Janeiro with Minas Geraes and S. Paulo, of which 147 miles are finished, the Mauá, from Mauá to the Serra da Estrella, and the Cantigallo; all these lines have been constructed with native capital, and, though not lucrative, are of vast importance to the agriculture of the province.

Steam navigation has made rapid progress, and a continuous connection is kept up between the various ports of the province and with the city of Rio Janeiro and other places.

Nitherohy, situated on the opposite side of the bay from Rio de Janeiro, consists chiefly of a very nice town called Praia Grande, which has been, since 1834, the legal capital of the province. It contains some well-built houses mostly the residences of persons in business in Rio. Its commerce is entirely dependent on Rio, which deprives it of all importance as a commercial place. In it reside the president of the province and other provincial authorities.

PETROPOLIS.

To get to this far-famed place you take the steamer from Rio to Mauá, there the railway to Fragosa, whence you proceed in carriages up a most beautifully constructed macadamised road, the engineering of which is a masterpiece of its kind. This road is cut zig-zag up the side of a mountain, and, while ascending, you not unfrequently see a zone of clouds hanging about the middle, while the loftier peaks are glittering in the sunshine long after the sun has set on the plains below.

Two or three days spent in viewing the scenery around Petropolis will be well bestowed; but the village itself has little to recommend it, with the exception of the emperor's palace, where he spends the four summer months, and which, though devoid of pretension, is a very delightful residence. The houses, or Swiss cottages, which surround the village are elevated, one above the other here and there, seeming like bird-cages perched in rocky niches, displaying, in striking contrast with the mountains on which they stand, the littleness of the works of man in presence of those of the Creator. Returning to Rio the scene which expands before you in the blue distance is exquisite.

Campos, situated on the navigable river Parahyba, is the most northern town of the province, and, in consequence of the district around being well suited to the growth of sugar-cane, it is a very thriving place. The town contains 25,000 inhabitants. All its foreign trade has to be carried on through Rio. From this place comes the greater part of the rosewood shipped from Rio, as also the sugar.

PROVINCE OF BAHIA.

HISTORY.

THIS province justly claims the title of Primogenita de Cabral, as Porto Seguro in this province was the first land visited by Cabral, on the 21st of April, 1500. The territory of Bahia was granted to Francisco Pereira Coutinho, but this gentleman, while attempting to colonize it, unfortunately fell a victim to the savages, and his son afterwards sold it to the King of Portugal, who, in 1548, sent out a colony under charge of Thomé de Souza, appointing him Governor-General of Brazil. This person founded, in 1549, the city of St. Salvador, making it the seat of the Vice-royalty, which pre-eminence it enjoyed until 1763, when Rio de Janeiro became the seat of the Vice-royalty, and Bahia a captain-generalship. In 1624 the province was invaded by the Dutch, and the city taken possession of by them; but they were driven out the next year, notwithstanding which, their occupation of the northern province for many years, and a threatening aspect, retarded the progress of Bahia.

The independence of Brazil was strongly opposed here by the Portuguese General, Madeira; who was not expelled until the year 1823, on the 2nd of July, which day, in consequence, is considered their day of independence, in celebrating which party feeling often excites animosity against the Portuguese.

The districts of *Porto Seguro* and *Ilheos* were incorporated with the province of Bahia in 1759, and still remain so. The districts bordering on the river S. Francisco, comprising the villages of Pilão Arcado, Compo Largo, and Carinhanha, were separated from Pernambuco and joined to Minas Geraes in 1824, but subsequently, in 1827, were annexed to Bahia.

Bahia is not only the oldest province in the empire, but is also one of the most important. From Bahia also come most of the poets and illustrious men of the empire, and many of the ministerial portfolios are entrusted to Bahians.

By a bull of the 1st of March, 1555, Bahia was created the first bishoprick in Brazil, but the

Bishop, while on a voyage to Portugal, was shipwrecked on the coast near the mouth of the S. Francisco, and, together with others, was devoured by the cannibal Indians, the Cahetes.

GEOGRAPHY.

The province is situated between 9° 42' and 18° 12' south latitude, and 37° 9' and 46° 9' west longitude. It is bounded on the north by Sergipe and Pernambuco, being separated from the former by the river Real and from the latter by the S. Francisco, on the west by Minas Geraes and Goyaz, the Serra dos Aimores dividing it from the first, and the Serra da Tabatinga and Chapada da St. Maria, from the last; on the south by Espirito Santo, the boundary being the Mucury, and on the east by the Atlantic ocean. Its extent from north to south is 160 leagues, from east to west 180 leagues, and its estimated area is 14,000 square leagues.

The capital and port, open to foreign commerce, is S. Salvador da Bahia.

The *climate* varies according to the locality and height of the land. For about 20 leagues from the coast the surface is very uneven, and there rains fall frequently and abundantly. In that district it is hot and very humid, but further in the interior on the wide level plateaux of the different mountains, where droughts are common, it is dry, and, though warm, genial and healthy. Along the low lands bordering on the S. Francisco, intermittent fevers of a dangerous kind prevail.

The *surface* is in general considerably elevated, and even mountainous, particularly in those parts that border on the provinces of Minas Geraes and Goyaz, but on the coast the ground is low and without great elevations. In the middle are vast table-lands, subject to droughts, and extensive valleys along the large rivers, these valleys and the maritime portion of the province being the most productive and best cultivated.

The mountains scattered in the interior are almost unknown, but seem to form part of the two Cordilleras of Brazil which run north and south, one near the coast, and the other further in the interior.

Of the rivers, which this province possesses, the principal ones are: — the S. Francisco, which, taking its rise in Minas Geraes, empties into the sea between Sergipe and Alagoas, and is navigable throughout nearly its whole length, except for 50 miles from the great fall of Paulo Alfonso; the Itapicurú, which, coming from the district of Jacobina, has a course of 150 leagues; the Sergi-mirim and Paraguassú 100 leagues long, both emptying into the Bay of Bahia; the Pardo and the Contas; the Jequitinhonha, which has its origin in Minas Geraes and disembogues below Belmonte; and the Mucury, also rising in Minas Geraes, is navigated by small steamers to St^a. Clara.

This province abounds in mineral riches. The gold mines of Chapada Gentio and Sincora while worked were very lucrative, and the diamonds found in those localities and at the Lençōes were once the wonder of Europe. The silver mines discovered by Roberto Dias are now unknown, and the gold mines all abandoned for agricultural pursuits, which are found more profitable, but which in the gold-hunting days were neglected by an improvident population to such an extent that food rose to enormous prices. The country abounds also with iron, copper, coal, and other minerals, but all are unused for lack of labour and enterprise.

A highly inflammable bituminous earth is found in a part of the province, whole districts abounding with it. It may be obtained with great facility, but it is never used, though, as it is reported to contain 40 per cent. of volatile matter and 55 per cent. of carbon, it would be valuable for the production of gas or as fuel for steam purposes.

The province has numerous forests, producing several valuable kinds of wood, such as lignum vitæ, rosewood, satinwood, and many suitable for naval construction and house-building. Some of the hard woods are unsurpassed for durability and toughness. A kind of cedar is in great request for making the insides of drawers and wardrobes, and also for cigar boxes and similar light work. This fertile province also yields balsams, gums, numerous medicinal roots, cotton, sugar-cane, coffee, tobacco, tapioca, and all fruits of tropical climes are found here, and although not cultivated or looked after, produce largely. Among the fruits are the mango, pine-apple, orange, fig, lemon, and saputí. Vegetables for table use can be readily grown, but in consequence of the scarcity of labour are very dear. Yams are very good and very plentiful. Poultry, except ducks and geese, is abundant. Cattle are raised in sufficient numbers for the consumption of the province, but the meat is lean, flabby, and tasteless. Mutton, lamb, and veal are almost impossible to procure.

The productive industry of Bahia is mainly devoted to agriculture, and to the obtaining of their much-prized gums, roots, and dye-woods, of which, including the Páo de Brazil, large amounts are exported. But the chief riches of the province are derived from the cultivation of cotton, sugar-cane, tobacco, and coffee, of all which the exports are very great, and so remunerative that manufactures are almost of no importance.

Sugar commands the first place among these products. In 1711 there were only 146 sugar-mills in the province, exporting 14,500 boxes of sugar, weighing 507,500 arrobas, and value 1,070,206$. In 1852, there were more than 800 large sugar-mills, besides about 400 smaller ones, used chiefly for the manufacture of rum, but many of which likewise made sugar.

The Average Production of Sugar in the Province was—

		Arrobas.
During the 10 Years ending ...	1816	725,125
,, 10 ,, ...	1826	1,321,180
,, 10 ,, ...	1836	1,277,452
,, 10 ,, ...	1846	1,563,559

The Average Export to Foreign Countries was—

		Arrobas.
During the 3 Years ending ...	1842	1,315,559
,, 3 ,, ...	1849	2,333,865
,, 3 ,, ...	1856	2,481,051
,, 3 ,, ...	1860	1,474,663
,, 2 ,, ...	1862	2,953,174

TOBACCO.

Next in importance to sugar comes the growth and manufacture of the tobacco of the province, which is of a superior quality, and has always been one of the chief staples of Bahia since the commencement of its culture in 1600.

The Exportation of Tobacco to Foreign Countries was—

	Years.	Arrobas.	Average Price.	Value.
The average of 10 years ending	1711	200,000	1$516	303,100$
Ditto	1816	620,494	1$340	830,874$
Ditto	1826	473,629	1$445	680,864$
Ditto	1836	258,519	2$190	565,147$
Ditto for the year	1846	180,560	3$160	569,272$
Ditto	1849	280,946	2$196	617,063$
Ditto	1853	611,145	2$877	1,757,065$
Ditto	1855	802,896	2$325	1,862,000$
Ditto	1856	1,536,507	2$185	3,282,000$
Ditto	1858	493,791	5$177	2,420,916$
Ditto	1860	249,170	6$176	1,538,986$
Ditto	1862	1,036,598	5$183	5,372,666$

COFFEE.—Though in 1810 this Province only exported 3,893 arrobas to Foreign Countries, its exports had increased—

	Arrobas.	Average Price.	Value.
In 1830 to	45,882	2$100	96,247$
In 1840 to	52,365	3$509	179,702$
In 1849 to	85,876	3$145	269,856$
In 1858 to	233,904	3$989	933,168$
In 1860 to	198,604	5$099	1,011,074$
In 1862 to	286,167	6$160	1,762,940$

The produce of the whole crop of—

	Arrobas.		
1854 was	147,577	Exported to Rio	16,214
1855 „	226,631	„	28,217
1856 „	255,458	„	50,680

COTTON.

Previous to the outbreak of the civil war in the United States of North America, this staple received but little attention, and its statistics anterior to that event show none of the great development of production observable in other products of this province.

However, since then, the great increase in the value of cotton has stimulated the Bahianos to extend and improve its culture, and they have eagerly purchased improved seed, and cotton gins for the better separating the fibre from the seed.

The Exportation to Foreign Ports was—

		Arrobas.
In the Year 1854	...	24,343
„ 1855	...	50,216
„ 1856	...	62,844
„ 1858	...	9,361
„ 1859	...	9,279
„ 1860	...	1,160
„ 1861	...	18,493
„ 1862	..	45,814

CACÁO.

The culture of cacáo was first begun in 1780, plants being brought from Pará, where it is indigenous, to the districts of Valença, Camamú, and Ilhéos. Since then its culture has steadily increased, and the quantities exported were:—

Years.	Arrobas.	Average Price.	Value.
In 1830	1,788	2$600	4,618$
„ 1840	7,244	2$980	21,810$
„ 1845	13,332	3$180	42,508$
„ 1849	20,261	2$260	45,653$
„ 1854	27,378	2$155	59,000$
„ 1855	34,764	3$380	114,000$
„ 1856	31,582	4$890	153,000$

The *population* is estimated at 1,200,000, including 250,000 slaves.

The *representation* is 7 senators and 14 deputies to the Imperial Assembly, and 42 deputies to the Provincial Chamber.

The *military force* consists of 1,700 men in garrisons, 700 police, and about 110,000 national guards.

Public instruction is given in one lyceum, one normal school, and 181 primary schools.

Besides these are one medical school, an orphan school, and a number of private establishments.

The provincial *revenue* is about 1,400,000$ and the Imperial about 6,700,000$.

STEAM NAVIGATION.

Besides communication kept up from the city of Bahia twice a month with the chief northern and southern ports, by the mail steamers of the Companhia Brazileira de Paquetes, and with Pernambuco, Maceió, and Rio de Janeiro by the English and French mail steamers, there are various steamers plying between Bahia and Cachoeira on the Paraguassú, Nazareth, S. Amaro, Valença, Caravelas, and Maceió, calling at the intermediate ports; and between Caravelas and Rio de Janeiro.

A *railroad* $77\frac{1}{4}$ miles long runs to Alagoinhas, to the north of the capital, intended finally to be prolonged to the S. Francisco to connect with the Pernambuco and S. Francisco railway partly completed.

TOPOGRAPHY.

S. Salvador, usually called *Bahia*, the capital

of the province, has a population of 180,000, and is the only port open to foreign trade. It is situated in 13° 0′ 55″ south latitude, and 38° 31′ 44″ west longitude from Greenwich, as determined by observations taken at the lighthouse on Fort Antonio, a small antique fort built on a sandy beach inside. This fort is commanded by another, Fort Cabo, and by the circular battery of S. Diogo. At the extremity of the city is Fort Gamboa, and beyond that another mounting 30 guns defends the arsenal. There are two more small forts near the entrance, and one at Montserrat, but the principal defence is the Fort do Mar, which was built in 1600, on a rocky bank in the inner bay, about a quarter of a mile from the shore. First commenced by the Portuguese, it was enlarged by the Dutch during their possession of the city, and has since then received further additions. It is of a circular form of about 285 feet diameter, the original tower having been raised, and an extensive lower battery built around it. It mounts about 60 guns of heavy calibre, none of which are less than 24-pounders.

This is the place of deposit of the gunpowder

and other ammunition, and being so near the city an explosion would be exceedingly destructive to it.

The fort is paved with flags carefully cemented, so as to conduct all the water falling on their surfaces through a grate into a large reservoir, capable of containing sufficient water to supply the garrison for six months.

The officers and commandant reside in the fort, and there are, besides, some apartments for prisoners of state, which, however, are vacant. The fort also defends the Arsenal of Marine.

The view of the bay is beautiful, the hills being diversified with trees of the freshest verdure, and may be compared with the richest scenery in Europe. The crests of the surrounding hills and islands are crowned with groves of mango, cedar, and other trees, while the slopes to the right are occupied with well laid-out gardens. This bay receives the waters of several rivers, and forms an extensive gulf, with an entrance of two and a quarter leagues broad, and with a circumference of about forty leagues. Here, sheltered from every wind, and surrounded by a country exuberantly rich, fleets may ride safe at anchor in a gulf which seems as if formed by nature to be the emporium of the world and to receive its shipping, while the town itself, seen picturesquely crowning the high bluff that circles round the eastern side of the bay, seems a fitting mistress of the lovely scene.

But, unfortunately, a cursory view of that part of the town which is built on the narrow ribbon of low flat ground lying at the foot of the hill, much of it close, filthy, and dilapidated, is apt to give an impression to the traveller which a better acquaintance with the city can alone remove; but even in this many of the houses and shops are well-constructed buildings, and the Rua Novo do Commercio is a well-built street, mostly occupied with merchants' offices. This lower town is the chief seat of trade, but, from its plan and situation, being deprived of the land and sea-breezes, those inestimable blessings in a tropical clime, few of the business men reside in it. The lower town consists principally of a street running parallel with the beach for a distance of three miles, and leading to the terminus of the S. Francisco railway, which is called the Calçado. Near this is the church of the Bom Fim, a splendid edifice richly ornamented, and where an annual *festa* is celebrated, which is attended by the whole population of the city. At Calçado is a very good hotel kept by an Englishman, a great accommodation to the stranger, who had previously either to throw himself on the hospitality of the citizens or to take rooms and furnish them. Not far from Bom Fim, located on a small bay eastward of Montserrat, is Tapagife, where all kinds of ship-repairs may be made, and where the water is smooth as a pond. At the other end of the lower town, and near the Rua Novo do Commercio, is the new Custom House, which, though erected at great cost, is inadequate to the growing commerce of the city, which is second only to that of Rio. Close to the Custom House is the Marine Hospital, a well-constructed building, whose internal arrangements are kept in a high state of efficiency. There, also, is the beautiful church of the Conceição, whose marble front was imported at an enormous cost.

The traveller wishing to ascend the steep bluff, 100 feet high, to the upper town, can take the Ladeira da Conceição, but will no doubt avail himself of a cadeira, or sedan-chair carried by the negroes. On the top of the bluff begins the upper town, from which a most lovely view of the bay and surrounding scenery may be obtained.

As in all Catholic countries, the churches are distinguished above all other edifices, and the cathedral is a large handsome building, richly gilt and embellished with gaudily-dressed saints.

In the palace are the public offices, the provincial treasury, the supreme court or Relação, the house of assembly, and the palace of the president of the province, which last was fast falling into decay until the distinguished administration of Mr. Sinimbu, who repaired and renovated it, and whose refined taste, seconded by the wise judgment of his accomplished wife, a lady of English origin, who superintended its internal arrangements, has made it truly a palace.

The theatre is also a fine building, but the company being usually third-rate, the music is in general the only tolerable part of the performance.

There are many large and elegant mansions, beautifully fitted up, to be found in the suburbs; the neighbourhood of Victoria is the chief locality in which the handsome and prettily situated residences of the foreign merchants are found. Here, in the Campo Grande, are the two trees to which the African negroes in Bahia pay superstitious adoration, and to which they make frequent offerings of fruits and vegetables.

The Passeio Publico, or public walk, leads to the suburb of Victoria, and its centre is adorned with the monument erected in honour of Dom John. The walks are very fine, and well shaded with mango and other trees.

In the bay and in front of Victoria was fought that celebrated engagement between the Spanish admiral, D. Antonio Oquendo and the Dutch admiral, Adrian Patryd, in which the latter, finding himself overpowered by superior force, threw himself into the sea, exclaiming, "the ocean is the only tomb worthy of a Batavian admiral."

The foreign exportation of 1862-3 amounted to	18,029,367$
" importation of 1862-3 amounted to	17,137,541
	35,166,908

PROVINCE OF AMAZONAS.

HISTORY.

THIS district, at first known as Rio Negro, was founded July 11th, 1757, under the governorship of Joaquim de Mello Povoas, the first capital being at Barcellos, now a small village. In 1774, the captaincies of Rio Negro and Pará were formed into the captain-generalship of Grão Pará, and remained united until 1850, when the present province of Amazonas received a distinct organization.

GEOGRAPHY.

This immense province stretches between 4° 23' north latitude and 10° south latitude, and between 56° 59' and 75° 3' west longitude. It is bounded on the north by Guiana, Venezuela, and New Granada, being divided from these by the range of mountains which, under various names, runs along the northern boundary of

Brazil; on the west by Equador and Peru, the Japurá, for part of its length, and the Javari, from south latitude 10°, forming most of the dividing line; on the south by Peru, Bolivia, and the province of Mato Grosso, the tenth degree of south latitude being the divisional line from the two first, and the rivers Madeira and Machado that from Mato Grosso.

Its length from east to west is 330 leagues, from north to south 280 leagues, and its estimated area 64,000 leagues. Its capital is Manaos.

The *climate* is humid, and is very hot during the day, but cool in the night. The heat is also mitigated by the rains, which fall irregularly at all seasons, and very heavily during the months of July and November. The climate is unhealthy for persons who have to expose themselves to the heat of the sun and to the damp air of the night, and agues and dysenteries are frequent, particularly in the lands lying near the rivers, which are liable to overflow in the wet season. With care, however, it is not unfavourable to longevity.

The only mountains of importance in this province are those which form its northern boundary, but which, though making a united chain of great length, are only of moderate height. The surface thus is almost only one immense plain, watered by a splendid system of rivers, among which the Amazonas flows pre-eminent.

This enormous river takes its rise in the Andes, within 100 miles of the Pacific, and after a course of 1,800 miles through Peru, enters the western confines of Amazonas—already a first-class stream—and flows for upwards of 1,200 miles to Pará, through which it passes to disembogue in the ocean, after a course of 3,950 miles, 2,100 of which are in Brazilian territory, and navigable for even sailing vessels of great size. It receives in this province a multitude of tributaries, most of which are unexplored, but probably are all more or less navigable. Among the largest and best-known are, the Javary, on the confines of Peru; the deep Içá; the valuable Japurá, 1,000 miles long, 350 of which are in Brazil; the winding Purús, navigable, in high water, to the boundary of Brazil, 720 leagues, by steamboats of four to five feet draught; the important Negro, which, at their confluence, almost rivals the Amazonas; and the Madeira, navigable from its mouth 250 leagues to the plateau of Mato Grosso, from which it comes, after seventeen falls in 200 miles.

Besides the rivers there are a number of bayous connecting the rivers with one another, in various parts of their courses, and a great many lakes into which the water-courses expand, such as the Uaicurupa, the Ariticurituba, &c.

The surface of the country is almost one vast plain, the only elevations of importance being in the extreme north, where the land rises into the boundary chain of low mountains, and in the south-east, where the plateau that stretches from Maranhão in the east across the Madeira in the west breaks away between that river and the Purús. The mineral resources are unknown, for but a small portion of the province has been explored or even traversed; still some indications of crystals and silver have been discovered, but remain unexamined.

The vast extent of level ground is of unexceeded fertility, and is mostly covered with immense forests, in which are found many kinds of timber suitable for furniture and for the construction of ships and houses, dye-woods, and trees and other plants producing gums, oils, resins, sarsaparilla, ipecacuanha, oil of capaiva, cotton, cocoa, and a host of other substances, procurable with little expenditure of labour. But above all in importance to the industry of the province is the *gum-elastic*, which is the juice of a tree growing in the greatest abundance in this province, and which employs one-half of the population in its collection, to the neglect of agriculture.

The *population* of the province is about 70,000, exclusive of a large number of Indians, many tribes of whom lead a savage and independent life, while others cultivate the ground and collect gum-elastic, sarsaparilla, &c.

The *representation* consists of one senator and one deputy to the Imperial Assembly, and twenty deputies to the Provincial Chamber.

The *military force* is composed of the garrisons of various posts, and about 2,700 national guards.

For *public instruction* there are two normal schools and twenty-five primary schools.

The provincial *revenue* is about 60,000$.

Steam navigation is kept up with Belém in Pará and Tabatinga on the frontier of Peru by the Amazon Navigation Company, which despatches a vessel from Manáos twice a month to

Belém, and between Manáos and Tabatinga once a month. It is also contemplated to extend the benefits of steam communication to several other of the large rivers. This company has a monopoly of the steam navigation. Small sailing vessels also carry on the trade along the river, and even ascend the Amazonas as far as Tabatinga. Should the free navigation of this river be conceded, as is expected, to all nations, it may become the channel of an enormous trade, not only with Brazil, but with the Republics of Bolivia, Peru, and those on the north, which would enrich not only these states, but, in a much greater degree, Brazil, through which the great trade with those places must of necessity pass.

TOPOGRAPHY.

Manáos, the capital of the province, is situated on the left bank of the Rio Negro, a few miles from its embouchure into the Amazonas. The population is about 5,000, and the town contains about 350 houses and the governmental buildings, which are allowed to remain in a very dilapidated condition.

This place serves as a depôt for the trade of the province, shipping to Belém the produce of the surrounding country, and receiving the European goods for destribution.

Steam communication is held twice a month with Belém, and once a month with Tabatinga on the Peruvian frontier, whence steamboats proceed to Nauta, the head of ship navigation, and about 2,500 miles from the ocean.

PROVINCE OF SERGIPE.

HISTORY.

This province was first colonised in 1592, by orders of the Governor of Bahia, in order to expel the French, who had made it a depôt for a considerable smuggling trade which they carried on through the Indians. The colony was first located at Aracaju, but afterwards removed to a more healthy place, called S. Christovão.

From this the Dutch dispossessed them, and it was not until the capitulation of Pernambuco, in 1654, that it fell into the hands of the Portuguese. It remained subject to Bahia until 1824, when it was organised as a distinct province, with S. Christovão as capital, but in March, 1855, Aracajú was made the capital of the province.

GEOGRAPHY, &c.

It lies between 10° 20′ and 11° 34′ south latitude, and 36° 11′ and 38° 25′ west longitude.

It is bounded on the north by Alagôas, the river S. Francisco separating them ; on the west and south-west by Bahia, the rivers Real and Hingo forming in part the boundaries ; and on the east by the Atlantic. Its coast extent, from the Real to the S. Francisco is 30 leagues, from east to west 40 leagues, and its area about 1,200 square leagues. The capital is Aracajú.

The *climate* of the eastern part is similar to that of Alagôas, but in interior districts it is more subject to droughts. On the borders of the rivers and in the marshy places, it is very unhealthy, and fevers are common.

The chief rivers are :—the navigable S. Francisco, on the northern boundary, and the Sergipe, Vasa-barris, and others, navigable by steamers for a short distance from their mouths, and for a greater distance by boats.

Metals are not in abundance, but in the interior have been found some diamonds, carboniferous and bituminous schist, with supposed beds of coal, marble, lime, chalk, crystal, amianthus, saltpetre, carbonate and nitrate of soda, iron, gold, precious stones, and on the banks of the S. Francisco, colossal fossil bones.

The country is generally level, but is very unequal both in appearance and productiveness. For about a league or two from the sea the land is sandy and barren. For ten leagues further inland it becomes rich and well cultivated; at sixteen it is extremely fertile, but at about twenty-five leagues from the shore it turns in general poor and dry, and fit only for the rearing of cattle. The forests are scanty, but contain valuable timber and dye-woods. Ipecacuanha, quina, cacáo, vanilla, &c., grow spontaneously. The chief productions of their agriculture, besides articles of food, are sugar and cotton; and those exported, cotton, sugar, spirits, and edibles.

The foreign exports of 1862-3, chiefly sugar, amounted to 1,106,000$, and the direct foreign imports to 59,780$.

A considerable part of the commerce, especially in foreign goods, is carried on through Bahia.

The *population* is about 250,000, including 50,000 slaves.

The *representation* is two senators and four deputies to the Imperial Assembly, and twenty-four deputies to the Provincial Chamber.

The *military force* is about 200 police and 20,000 national guards.

Public education is provided for by about 80 primary schools.

The provincial *revenue* about 550,000$, the Imperial about 190,000$.

Steam navigation is much neglected, but a small steamer is employed in trading between the mouths of the various rivers and Aracajú, and communication is kept up between Vazabarris and Aracajú, Rio S. Francisco and Maceió to the north, and Villa Real and Bahia to the south, by a Bahian company, and by a Pernambucan line from Aracajú to Pernambuco and the intervening ports.

TOPOGRAPHY.

Aracajú, the capital of the province and port for foreign commerce, is situated in 10° 52′ south latitude, and 36° 49′ west longitude, at the mouth of the river Sergipe. It is unhealthily situated, but has rapidly prospered since its foundation in 1855, owing to its favourable situation for commerce.

Foreign exports in 1862-3, amounted to 1,106,380$.

Larangeiras, situated at the head of the navigation of the Sergipe, in the centre of a flourishing agricultural district, is an important town, but is disadvantageously situated in the midst of ponds, which render it unhealthy.

S. Christovão, the former capital, 5 leagues from Aracajú, is small and declining.

PROVINCE OF PARAHYBA.

HISTORY.

The first settlement of this territory was made in 1582 on a small island called Camboa, near to the present situation of the capital of the province. In 1634 it fell into the hands of the Dutch, when they possessed themselves of the adjoining province of Pernambuco. On their expulsion in 1654 it was made subordinate to the Captain-general of Pernambuco, but was afterwards declared a separate province.

GEOGRAPHY.

It lies between 6° 15′ and 7° 50′ south latitude, and 34° 36′ and 37° 52′ west longitude.

It is bounded on the north by Rio Grande, on the west by Ceará, on the south by Pernambuco, and on the east by the Atlantic ocean. It contains about 1,500 square leagues of surface.

The *climate* is warm and dry, but the heat is

tempered on the coast by the sea-breeze, and the climate may be looked on as healthy. The rainy season commences about March and ends about July, but the interior is liable to droughts which often do great injury. The face of the country is very unequal, it being traversed by spurs of the Borborêma Cordilheira forming extensive valleys which are usually sandy and only fit for grazing, for which the herbage of the country is well adapted, being very succulent. The land of many parts of this province, as in those adjoining, suffer at times from want of water. Half the province is covered with virgin forests which furnish building timber and dyewoods, also gums, balsams, and resins. Along the rivers there are large tracts of fine land suitable for sugar, cotton, tobacco, mandioca and other tropical products. On the sandy lands along the coast cocoa-nut trees grow in great numbers.

There is iron in the province, but the mines are unexplored. The productions of most importance are cotton, sugar, and tobacco, also Brazil wood and other dyes. Of these cotton and sugar make up nearly the whole of the value exported to foreign countries.

Cotton has been for some years gradually superseding the growth of sugar-cane, as being better fitted to contend with the droughts that injure many parts of the province. The great advance in the price of cotton has had its due effect on the production in this province.

In 1838 there was exported 118,618 arrobas
„ 1858 „ „ 156,151 „
„ 1862 „ „ 201,899 „

In 1813 the value of cotton exported was 100,000$; in 1815, 256,680$; in 1816, 456,550$; in 1861, 2062,360$. The sudden increase in 1815 and 1816 over 1813 was caused by the establishment in 1814 of the house of McClacan and Co., in Parahyba.

The exports of sugar were :—

In 1838 ... 68,286 arrobas
„ 1858 ... 800,075 „
„ 1862 ... 620,270 „

Formerly the trade with foreign countries was entirely carried on through Pernambuco, and even now a large share of this trade takes that direction, the merchants of Pernambuco making heavy advances to the planters. Pernambuco is also the mart in which the dealers of Parahyba make their chief purchases of imported goods. On this account the custom-house returns of Parahyba do not give full information of the real exports and imports of this province.

The *population* is about 260,000, including about 5,000 slaves.

The *representation* is two senators and five deputies to the Imperial assembly, and thirty deputies to the provincial chamber.

The *military force* is about 400 soldiers and police and about 21,000 national guards.

Public instruction is given in one lyceum and 59 primary schools.

The provincial *revenue* is about 550,000$ and the imperial about 350,000$.

STEAM NAVIGATION.

The city of Parahyba is placed in bi-monthly communication with the chief ports, north and south, by the mail steamers of the Companhia Brazileira de Paquetes, and with Pernambuco and Fortaleza and intervening ports by the steamers of a Pernambuco company.

TOPOGRAPHY.

The most important places are the cities of Parahyba, Mamanguape, Aréa, and Souza..

Parahyba, the capital and the only port of

the province free to foreign commerce, is situated in 6° 57' south and 34° 50' west, about three leagues from the mouth of the river of same name. It has a population of about 16,000 persons, and is the richest and most commercial, as well as most populous city in the province. The port is also the best, but vessels of more than 12 or 13 feet draught cannot well enter. It is defended by the fort of Cadebello, once famous during the Dutch invasion, but now somewhat ruinous. The view at the entrance of the river is very fine, the dense virgin forests lining it to the water's edge. The city is divided into two parts, the high city and the low city, in which last the commerce of the place is chiefly carried on. The streets of Parahyba are mostly well paved, but there are few edifices worthy of notice except the palace of the president and four churches. The only important public work is the large wooden bridge near the city.

Area, the second city of the province, is in the centre of a rich agricultural district.

Souza is situated in the interior, on the river Peixe, and is important as a great locality for grazing stations.

EMIGRATION.

The attention of emigrants has not hitherto been directed to Brazil, although this country possesses many advantages over others to which a continuous stream of emigration is pouring.

In the main, the chief reason for this is, undoubtedly, the want of precise knowledge of the country, as the books hitherto published have been devoted more especially to those striking characteristics in the geology, vegetation, animal life, and peculiarities of the country generally, which were of a nature to interest and amuse the reading public, but which served little purpose towards affording the *emigrant* the *practical* information which he needs.

Another reason is, the most erroneous idea which prevails respecting the Brazilian climate —that it is unhealthy. Far from this; it can rank with the healthiest and most *enjoyable* climates of the world, and its ill-repute has had origin chiefly from the sanitary conditions of certain regions best known, and therefore judged characteristic of Brazil, and from the occasional existence of yellow fever in certain ports, just as in New York not many years ago before proper sewage existed, and as still in New Orleans and some other ports.

Another is the language—of course a drawback and a material one at first—but the experience furnished by the emigration to the River Plate has shown conclusively that the Spanish language (almost identical with Portuguese) offers little difficulty, and that a command of it is obtained in a very short time, particularly by the Irish.

Another is, the want of information on the localities to which the emigrant should proceed, the means of access, the prices and terms on which lands are sold, the inducements offered by Government or companies, and various other detailed information necessary to guide the emigrant in his course. These it is our purpose to supply as far as possible within the narrow limits within which we wish to bound our present observations.

Brazil contains about 1,900,000,000 acres of land, upon which is a population of about 8,000,000. This, however, is not equally distributed.

In the whole of the immense valley of the Amazonas in the north, comprising one-third of the whole extent of Brazil, there is a population of only 100,000. In the interior a similar disproportion exists, and nine-tenths of the free population, and almost all the slaves, are gathered into the strip of low land along the sea-coast where sugar, cotton, and tobacco are cultivated, and particularly into the province of Rio de Janeiro and the other coffee-growing districts around it, the remainder of the country being abandoned to solitude, to the working of such gold washings as still repay the rude processes used, and to the rearing of cattle and horses.

The level valley of the Amazon, and the low land along the coast, constitute the hot region of Brazil, but though lying within the tropics the climate, owing, in a great measure, to the prevailing winds being from the sea, is so modified as to permit of white labour being used. In point of fact this is the main dependence in the sugar and cotton districts in the northern, and therefore warmest provinces, the superior profits of the coffee-culture having caused the withdrawal of the bulk of the slaves to the more wealthy coffee region, so that the proportion borne by the slave to the white population in the northern and most southern provinces does not exceed one slave to ten freemen.

South of the valley of the Amazon and east of the low land of the coast, is a vast elevated region buttressed up as it were on hills and mountains.

This high land rises somewhat rapidly in the north; towards the east lifts itself abruptly out of the low land; in the middle attains its greatest elevation among the mountains of Minas Geraes, which turn into great plains and low swells as they recede westward into Goyaz and Mato Grosso; and in the south falls, and approaches nearer to the sea until the high land and the mountains on the seacoast die away into the low mountains, hills, and plains of the province of Rio Grande do Sul.

Two important effects result from this elevation of the interior, of which the first is that, though many large navigable rivers enter this high land, falls occur where their descent is made into the low land, which prevent continuous navigation from and to the sea, and thus it is only in the south-western part of Mato Grosso and in the southern province of Rio Grande do Sul (otherwise S. Pedro do Sul) that a free interior communication with the sea exists—with Mato Grosso by the Paraguay through the Paraná, and with Rio Grande do Sul by the Uruguay, this and the Parana joining near Buenos Ayres to form the river Plate.

The other effect is, that the elevation of the land added to the direction of the wind diminishes the temperature so much as to render even the most northern part moderate in its heat, while in the southern half slight frosts occur in winter, and the climate is moderate and pleasant, though somewhat warmer in the summer than in England, the summer range of temperature being between 65°F. and 80°, and at times, but rarely, reaching 90°F.

The climate, therefore, of all this vast region fits it for the residence of Europeans, and all the crops usually cultivated in Europe may be grown on it, including tobacco, cotton, Indian

EMIGRATION. 375

corn (maize) and wheat, besides tea, mandioca, coffee in the warmer parts, and a host of other tropical plants, while it is likewise well suited to the rearing of cattle, horses, mules, goats, and sheep.

In the northern half, however, the seasons are too regularly divided into the wet and dry, and great droughts are so common and injurious as to unfit a large proportion of it for an agricultural region without resort to irrigation; and, as in Buenos Ayres, at times the cattle even die from want of water in localities.

In the southern half the seasons are not injuriously regular, and rains fall more or less throughout the year; this region, therefore, is well fitted in all respects for both agriculture and grazing.

The great valley of the Amazon (including the provinces of Pará and Amazonas) is suitable to the cultivator of sugar, tobacco, cotton, cocoa, and a thousand other natives of warm countries; and from this valley comes the gum-elastic and a great deal of the sarsaparilla of commerce. Cattle also can be raised, but not sheep, as the climate is too damp and warm for these last.

Along the sea-coast low land the cultivated products are similar, and coffee is raised upon its cooler and drier slopes. The same remarks apply respecting sheep, and both regions are covered with timber, unless where it has been cleared for the cultivation of the land.

On the northern half of the interior, highland sheep and cattle thrive, and must be the main dependence, particularly sheep, which require less water comparatively than cattle. In the southern half lies, therefore, the best field for such emigrants as do not purpose to cultivate sugar-cane and perennial tropical plants. In this interior country, and particularly in the province of Rio Grande do Sul, the mountains and the banks of streams are timbered, but plains form a feature and afford excellent pasture and agricultural land, similar to the prairies of the United States, and the River Plate.

The great drawback in Brazil is the scarcity of roads for vehicles, and, indeed, of good roads of any kind. This want was not so much felt, as the lands in cultivation lie usually at no great distance from the sea, but the disadvantages arising from their absence have been so strongly impressed upon the Government and people in the present war, by the difficulties encountered in forwarding troops and supplies overland, that we believe a great change is commencing in this respect, and that many good roads will be established between all the main points at least, thus opening up vast tracts of splendid country to settlements; still, our advice would be to wool-raisers, not to withdraw far from roads, and to agriculturists, to settle only in their vicinity, since ready access to a market is the greatest advantage they can have, particularly in a country where transport of produce is high.

Besides the rivers, there are five railways which go towards the interior. The northernmost, belonging chiefly to an English company, starts from the port of Pernambuco, and runs for miles through a sugar and cotton raising country. The next, also in most part belonging to an English company, runs from the port of Bahia, through a country where sugar, cotton, and tobacco are the main productions. The third, originating at the port of Rio de Janeiro, the capital of the empire, opens out a fine coffee region, but has only a portion yet finished. The fourth starts from the vicinity of Rio, and, in connection with the splendid carriage road made by the União and Industria Company, develops an excellent coffee and agricultural district, and forms communication with the interior pastoral and agricultural province of Minas Geraes, whence is derived a large proportion of the food and exports of Rio. The fifth will be completed this year, and runs from the port of Santos in the province of S. Paulo, on to the high interior plains of that province, and will open out a large extent of coffee, agricultural and pastoral country. Another railway, projected by an English company, will start from the port of Rio Grande do Sul, and traverse perhaps the finest part of that splendid province, (Rio Grande or S. Pedro do Sul) to the vast coal-beds on the Candiota branch of the River Jaguar o, and the Government is pushing on the construction of a road bringing the interior of the province of Paraná in ready communication with its seaports.

The great tides of emigration to the Americas has been to the United States in North America, and Buenos Ayres in South America, yet Brazil possesses inherent advantages over both, especially for emigrants with enterprise and some capital.

As compared with the northern United States, the climate is incomparably more genial, and therefore life is easier both to the agriculturist and the grazier. In the one, frosts are rare and slight, pasture continues in the winter, and thus the labour of the farmer may be spread, as in England, over the whole year, and the grazier need not hoard by vast supplies of winter provender for his stock. In the other the soil is frost-bound for five to seven months, during which the plough is useless and the farmer's labour is crowded into six months of sweltering weather; the pasture is killed or covered up with snow, and the wintering of their animals dissipates the stores which the farmer and the grazier (necessarily a farmer also) gathered with so much toil and cost, and which, to feed out, required so much additional cost and labour.

In Brazil less expense is necessary in houses, clothes, bed-clothes, firing, shelter for cattle, &c. Coffee, sugar, and beef, are very cheap; food is more easily grown, the preservation of vegetables is not endangered and made difficult by intense frosts, and not only can all that is grown in the United States be raised in Brazil, but the mildness of the winter allows of the cultivation of many valuable tropical plants, and gives great advantages in the cultivation of such commercial staples as cotton, coffee, and tobacco.

Other advantages exist in the small cost at which the emigrant can obtain his working beasts, horses and cattle being worth only from £1 to £2 (five to ten dollars). In taxation there is a manifest advantage in Brazil over the United States, for in the States from the first, the emigrant must pay one per cent. at least, each year, upon the value of all his land, horses, cattle, &c.—*all* his property—whether he has earned anything as yet or not; while in Brazil the tax is levied only on the *increase* of his stock and on his *surplus* produce (as export duty), and therefore during his first struggles as settler, these are not aggravated by the heavy direct taxation which falls so embarrassingly in the States upon this most critical and expensive period of a settler's life.

It is a knowledge of the advantages which a mild climate offers to a settler which has of late years drawn a rapidly increasing emigration to the great treeless plains of Buenos Ayres, where stone, and wood for fencing and firing are almost unknown, and which makes the settlers content to burn thistles and dung for cooking purposes and brick-making, and endure the chilliness of winter without a fire. Brazil, however, in the great expanse of country which we have indicated as the best field for emigration, possesses the advantages of a still more genial climate than Buenos Ayres, and is without its disadvantages; for stone is abundant, and timber sufficient for house and farming purposes is found upon the streams; and this Brazilian region is free from those periodic storms of wind and sleet which cause so much damage and loss to graziers, and also from the excessive droughts which render Buenos Ayres unfit for agriculture and at times destroy cattle by thousands.

The government of Brazil has been for a long time most desirous of drawing emigration to this country, and some years ago undertook to do this by the establishment of assisted colonies, and by encouragement and aid given to the provinces, and to companies and individuals to establish others. The colonies, however, have not been so successful as the sacrifices made by the government should have warranted; for though some have done moderately well, others have stood still, and several have decayed.

Several influences and circumstances have operated towards this result. One is, that a large proportion of the emigrants introduced consisted of the floating scum of Continental Europe, pennyless and worthless. They were located on heavy timber land, where the ground had to be cleared before any crops could be sown. The crops cultivated were such as required to be manufactured in some degree before being ready for market, and therefore required a certain amount of capital and skill, which the poor class of emigrants could not supply; the want of roads discouraging the growth of the more bulky crops for sale; the absence of a ready sale at home for the articles produced, owing to the want of capital and enterprise, and the diminutive quantity of production; the excessive rates of transport and freight to the place of export, that too greatly reduced the value of the products at the farm. Add to these, the inexperience, incapacity, or mismanagement on the part of the directors of the colonies, and, in the case of the private colonies, too often a want of due regard to the requirements and interests of the colonists, who were made subjects of speculation by the owners or their managers, and it cannot be a matter of surprise that so few of the colonies have succeeded, even to a moderate extent.

In our opinion, the greatest error was in locating such emigrants in a timbered country, for timber land means bad roads and wearying, excessive labour; and the mere clearing of a few acres for a crop burdened the colonist with an amount of debt which, in an open country, would have supplied him with the implements and stock necessary to a successful start. Timber land also precludes the rearing of sheep, and, to a great degree, of any stock, except hogs, which, however, though valuable to the established farmer, are only an embarrassment and an injury in a new settlement, since their presence necessitates more costly fencing.

Our advice, then, to emigrants is to avoid the timbered land, unless where proximity to an important town, or other considerations, overbalance the disadvantages. In the United States, these disadvantages are so well appreciated, that it is a common saying that it is better to settle on prairie land fifteen miles from timber, than to make a farm by clearing timber; and, as alone the mere hauling of the fence of forty acres for this distance would require the uninterrupted labour of one man with a two-horse waggon for at least four months, the disadvantages of a cleared farm must be great and obvious in the eyes of the experienced American. The prairies also form natural roads, requiring but trifling labour, and, from their exposure to the winds and sun, dry up rapidly after rains, while the roads in timber countries are expensive to clear, and usually remain mere mudholes, unless when covered with poles, planks, or stone. Add to these the greater healthiness of the prairies, and their superiority in ease of cultivation, abundance of natural pasture without resort to clearing, and other things which will suggest themselves to the farmer, and we think we have fully established our proposition, that prairie land is most suited to emigrants in general.

We say, therefore, to the emigrant with small means as well as to the emigrant with capital who wishes to employ it in grazing, to procure prairie land proportioned to his means, with timber enough to make his buildings and pens, and fence at least ten acres, and let his available funds be at once invested in sheep, be they sufficient for but ten ewes or for a thousand, keeping no more of other stock than are absolutely needful. Ten acres of land should supply him with all the food his family requires, fatten some hogs if he prefer their flesh to beef or mutton, and supply him with some grain and provender for occasions, while to his wool-shearing he could ere long look for his luxuries, and to the increase of his sheep for wealth. When not too far from roads and market, cotton and tobacco might be raised; if nearer towns, maize, beans, mandioca, potatoes, onions, &c., and if in their proximity, vegetables and fruits would be found profitable productions.

Away from the district around Rio de Janeiro, cattle and horse raising is not profitable, nor is it suitable to the emigrant, still, the rearing of *improved breeds* of horses and mules would be remunerative, though mares are usually valued only for their hides and tallow.

It must be borne in mind that where the condition of the roads, or where the distance from the seaport makes transport costly or difficult, only such articles as are valuable in proportion to their weight and bulk are profitable to the farmer, and therefore wool-raising is best fitted to the circumstances of an interior settlement. But while he might depend upon his wool for his main income, the settler ought not to follow the lazy practice of the Buenos Ayrean, and even of the Brazilian graziers, who live on beef or mutton, guiltless of any variation of their meat with such things as bread, vegetables, milk and butter, purely from too great indolence to cultivate a plot of ground, or milk a cow, among the hundreds they may have around them.

Foreigners arriving in this country without a passport are allowed to land unless suspected of being malefactors. A certificate from their respective legation or consulate will stand substitute for that document in case of need.

Those who are provided with passports can reside wherever they please, and travel all over the empire by obtaining a "visto" on it, which is granted gratis by the police authority, when passing from one to another province.

Foreigners going abroad are bound, like the

Brazilians themselves, to advertise for three successive days their intended departure, in the interest of their creditors. The formality in question is only enforced upon unknown people or exceptional individuals. A bond in the latter case, with liability to a fine before the police, is often admitted as a substitute for the advertisement. All known people of good repute are practically exempt from this formality.

The expense of a passport to go abroad amounts to about 12*s*. (three dollars.)

A foreigner residing in the empire for two years, having an establishment, or known to be of good conduct, or if married to a Brazilian woman, can travel freely in the interior of the country, being provided with a certificate from the police authority proving any one of the said circumstances.

The residence in this country is not dependent upon any permit from a public authority.

Foreigners are only bound, like all Brazilians, by municipal law, and, for statistical purposes, to produce a list of the persons composing their families, on the occasion of occupying a house. Even this formality is seldom practised.

Foreigners enjoy all the civil rights of Brazilians; they can acquire and possess all sorts of property, and dispose of it in every way; exercise all branches of trade, commerce, and industry, wholesale and retail. All employments not considered public ones are accessible to them. Brokers, auctioneers, and dispatchers in the custom-houses are considered public employments, being in the gift of Government. Yet foreigners are allowed to clear goods at custom-houses, when their own or consigned to them.

Naturalised Brazilians enjoy all the rights of natives, except that they cannot become Deputies or Ministers of State. All other public employments and situations are open to them.

Two years' residence and good conduct are the only conditions required by law for the naturalisation of foreigners; but the Parliament is daily dispensing with the former condition in all applications from acceptable individuals.

Colonists arriving in this country enjoy special facilities for their settlement. An agency office for colonisation was established here last year, where all information upon lands to be sold, and other particulars, can be easily obtained.

EMIGRATION. 389

A steady monarchical representative government, now 42 years old, guaranteeing individual liberty by an *Habeas Corpus* law exactly such as exists in England; general religious toleration; unfettered liberty of the press; trial by jury; free right of association and petition; no hereditary aristocracy or titles; no distinction of castes; perfect equality before the law; are the principal political features of the Brazilian nation.

Ships bringing emigrants enjoy certain advantages ; and the extended commerce with the great seaports of Europe and the United States enable the emigrants to reach Rio de Janeiro with facility from London, Liverpool, Glasgow, Southampton, Newcastle, Newport, Cardiff, Swansea, Sunderland, etc., in the United Kingdom; Bremen, Hamburg, Havre, Bordeaux, Marseilles, and the chief ports of the continent of Europe both in the north and south. From the United States a brisk intercourse is maintained through New York and Baltimore, Boston, Philadelphia, and probably soon again from New Orleans and other Southern ports. At Rio de Janeiro is a Government lodging-house for emigrants, where board is supplied at moderate rates. An officer is deputed to go on board each vessel and furnish information to the emigrants; and at the lodging-house, and the office of the Official Agent any required elucidation can likewise be obtained. Luggage, and agricultural implements, can be imported free of duty; and if the emigrant elect to proceed to one of the Government colonies he will be furnished with free passage to its nearest seaport. At these colonies, and at other places, he will find tracts of land divided into townships (territorios) of two leagues square, or 43,056 acres, subdivided into various tracts, the lowest being a quarter section of 62,500 square braças or 75 acres, the price for which is generally one real the square braça, equal to one shilling and eleven pence, or 47 cents the acre) cash, or payable by instalments within five years, with 6 per cent. per annum interest. The title-deeds are given on marking off the tract and payment of its price, and convey full rights of ownership except as to minerals, and to a few provisions for the general good of the locality as to roads and water.

As regards localities open and suitable for

settlement, besides tracts of lands which in some districts individuals are willing to sell, in some cases even at less than the Government prices, there are public lands in the provinces of S. Pedro (Rio Grande do Sul), Santa Catharina, Paraná, S. Paulo, and Espirito Santo, already surveyed in or near the colonies there, and within easy access to ports in communication with Rio by steam.

S. Pedro, which is commonly known as Rio Grande do Sul, is chiefly a pastoral province, and immense herds of horned cattle and horses are reared upon its fine plains. The Government colonies, in a great measure composed of German immigrants, are, however, mostly located in the timber land on the rivers flowing into Lake Patos, near Porto Alegre, the capital. Grazing settlements are forming outside the timber on the plains. The colonies have thriven, and many of the older settlers are well to do, even rich. They raise, besides minor articles, beans, maize, mandioca, and export large quantities of mandioca, flour, and rum. A large number of the poorer settlers are employed in logging. Wheat grows well, but very little is used from a want of local demand, and from not being able to compete with American and other foreign flour, owing to the absence of good mills, and to the extortionate rates of freight due to a monopoly which it is expected will be destroyed at the next Parliament.

In the province of Santa Catharina are large extents of Government timber lands of great richness, lying between the D. Francisca and Blumenau colonies, and communicating with the sea-coast by the Itajahy-Grande, Itajahy-Pequeno, Itapocú, and the S. Francisco, which flows through the colony of D. Francisca.

To the south, and almost contiguous to the district of the Itajahy colony, which adjoins to the Blumenau colony, is a surveyed township of four square leagues in the valley of the Tijucas Grandes, which can easily be put in communication with the main Lages road by which the cattle and working animals are brought from the interior. It is likewise not difficult to effect direct communication with the seaboard, and thence with Desterro, the capital.

In the south of the province, in the Municipality of Laguna, are lands drained by the Tuberão and its affluents, whose port and market is the city of Laguna, situated on the

Bay of Laguna. These lands extend to the north boundary of the province of Rio Grande do Sul, and the settlements forming will in a little time be in communication with the Rio Grande colonies of Tres Torquilhos and Torres.

S. Catharina lies against the sea-coast, and, therefore, with its many rivers, its genial climate and fine land, offers many advantages to settlers.

In the province of Paraná the Government holds a very large quantity of land. In the district of Assunguy, where is the Government colony of Assunguy, there are three townships surveyed, platted and laid off in sections and colonial lots. These are settling up, and therefore five other contiguous townships have been surveyed and are ready for subdivision. Next to these, in the direction of the province of S. Paulo, and towards Cananéa and Iguape, two important ports of S. Paulo, there is a great extent of Government timber land and prairie, well adapted for a great immigration. All this immense region communicates on one side with the city of Coritiba, the capital of Paraná, and thence by the Graciosa road with the ports of Antonina and Paranaguá, situated on the Bay of Paranaguá, and a road could be run direct to the latter port; on the other side are the village of Castro and other important ones of the interior, whence come the supplies of cattle; and on another side with the province of S. Paulo, running down to the coast of Cananéa and to the Ribeira de Iguape, whose waters take their rise in the districts of Assunguy.

From the city of Coritiba to the Serra do Mar in a south-easterly direction, there are excellent timber and prairie lands which end in that serra and come on the truck road constructing to the port of the D. Francisca colony situated upon the river D. Francisca.

In the letters of that intelligent American gentleman, Dr. Blue, will be found a faithful, interesting, and practical account of the district of the Assunguy, and the prospects of immigrants there. Emigrants from the United States and Great Britain will find there a rapidly increasing settlement of Americans, a few of whom have resided there for many years, and thus can have the advantage of settling near persons speaking their own language and able to give most useful information to the new comer.

In the province of S. Paulo may be mentioned as applicable to the purposes of immigrants the two municipalities of Cananéa and Iguape, already referred to, in each of which exists a surveyed township divided into lots. In that of Cananéa is commenced a colony of the same name, which, though but a short time in existence, promises well. It communicates with the sea by a tolerable road of short length. In the township of Iguape a settlement is about to be made, a number of Brazilians having the intention of moving to it.

To the east-north-east and north-east of these townships lie other fertile Government lands touching on the villages of Xiririca, Juquiá and others, and cut by the rivers Ribeira de Iguape, Juquiá, S. Lourenço, &c.

Besides these Government lands situated in the provinces to the south of Rio de Janeiro there are others in the provinces of the north.

In the province of Espirito Santo, one day's steam to the north, and connected with Rio de Janeiro by lines of steamers touching at various ports, are public lands of superior quality near the coast, and cut by rivers navigable for some distance, and having for natural markets various towns called at by steamers. Those to the north and south of the province are the best.

At the south, in the Municipality of Itapemerim, is the Rio Novo colony, and beside it, but nearer to the coast, is a township to which could be added the lands to the north of the Benevente, whose margins are very fertile, and those which lie along the Municipality of Guaraparg, where runs the Guaraparg, which is navigable for several leagues from the sea.

Towards the top of the serra, starting from the port of Guarapary in the direction of the old Aldeamento do Imperial Affonsino and of the province of Minas Geraes, there extends to the north-west a strip of more than 60 miles wide, leaving the colony of Rio Novo to the south and that of Santa Isabel to the north. These lands are advantageously situated, and are fit for cotton, coffee, &c.

In the north of the province are other lands which, going in the direction of the Santa Leopoldina colony, with a general northerly course by the Santa Theresa road, extend to the province of Minas Geraes, near Porto de Souza, and to the projected colony of Guandú, where is a surveyed tract of 50 lots, and much other public land in their vicinity.

This point is likewise acccessible by the fine river Doce, which only needs some improvement at its bar, or the establishment of proper assistance to cross it, to become capable of a useful navigation. Along the banks of this river is likewise a large quantity of fertile public land, and the Government possesses, besides, at a little distance from it, several domains purchased from Dr. Franca e Leite, and known as Francilvania, Rio Prete and Limão, which have been surveyed and marked off.

A little to the south of the Doce there are pretty fertile public lands in the municipality of Santa Cruz, communicating with the sea by the Santa Cruz, and which, by means of some easily-made canals between the lakes, could be brought into water-communication with the Doce.

More to the north, in the municipality of S. Matheos, and cut by the S. Matheos, there are good lands near the boundary of the province of Bahia; which province, also, can furnish, in this direction, public lands of very fertile quality, and abounding in good building timber.

In the municipality of Caravellas, in Bahia, running up the valley of the Mucury into Minas Geraes, the Government possesses, likewise, a quantity of land.

Besides the locations which we have cursorily mentioned as open and suitable for emigration, the Government has tracts of smaller dimensions in all these provinces. The emigrant, therefore, has an opportunity of selecting from a vast variety of tracts and situations, healthy, well watered, and at no great distance from the sea, and possessed of a temperate climate and a rich soil, permitting the growth of almost every remunerative staple and luxury that may be desired. Industrious farmers, and persons who will turn their attention to agriculture or grazing, will do well and enjoy life in southern Brazil; and any number of such need not fear to bring themselves and their families to the fertile and grateful woods and plains of this country.

THE END.

London: Murray and Co., 13, Paternoster Row

TO MERCHANTS, CAPTAINS, AND SHIPPERS

These UNIQUE PREPARATIONS are universally held in high esteem. From their general use in all civilized countries, and their consequent great demand, they well merit the attention of MERCHANTS and CAPTAINS.

ROWLAND'S MACASSAR OIL,

This *elegant* and *fragrant* Oil is universally in high repute for its unparalleled success during the last sixty years in promoting the *growth, restoring, preserving, and beautifying the human hair.*

ROWLAND'S KALYDOR,

AN ORIENTAL BOTANICAL PREPARATION FOR IMPROVING AND BEAUTIFYING THE COMPLEXION AND SKIN.

Eradicating Cutaneous Visitations, and rendering the skin soft, clear, and blooming.

ROWLAND'S ODONTO; or, Pearl Dentifrice.

Compound of *oriental Ingredients*, is of inestimable value in Preserving and Beautifying the Teeth, Strengthening the Gums, and in giving a *pleasing Fragrance to the Breath.*

A. ROWLAND & Sons, 20, Hatton Garden, London.

BY ROYAL  COMMAND.

METALLIC PEN MAKER TO THE QUEEN.
JOSEPH GILLOTT

Respectfully directs the attention of the Commercial Public, and of all who use Steel Pens, to the incomparable excellence of his productions, which, for QUALITY of MATERIAL, EASY ACTION, and GREAT DURABILITY, will ensure universal preference. They can be obtained, retail, of every dealer in the world; wholesale, at the Works, Graham Street, Birmingham; 91, John Street, New York; and at 37, Gracechurch Street, London, E.C.

VICTORIA WORKS, BIRMINGHAM.

The "Excelsior" (Prize Medal) Family
SEWING & EMBROIDERING MACHINE,

With all the Latest Improvements. Is the Simplest, Cheapest, and Best. Easy to operate, simple to learn, and not liable to derangement; Sews from two ordinary reels, requires no re-winding and the seam, if cut at every inch will not rip. It is eminently adapted for Family Sewing. It will Hem, Fell, Stitch, Gather, Quilt, Braid, and Embroider in a very superior manner, and with wonderful rapidity.— Price, from Six Guineas.

WHIGHT and MANN,
143, HOLBORN BARS, LONDON, E.C.

Manufactory: Gipping Works, Ipswich.

CHLORODYNE.
DISCOVERED BY DR. J. COLLIS BROWNE,

Admitted by the Profession to be the most valuable Medicine ever introduced.

Vice-Chancellor Sir W. PAGE WOOD stated in Court that Dr. J. COLLIS BROWNE was undoubtedly the Inventor. Consequently all other compounds under the name of Chlorodyne MUST BE SPURIOUS.

EARL RUSSELL communicated to the College of Physicians and J. T. Davenport that Chlorodyne was the only Medicine of any use in Cholera.

COUGHS, COLDS, ASTHMA, BRONCHITIS, NEURALGIA, ETC.,
ARE IMMEDIATELY RELIEVED.

The immense demand enables the Proprietors to reduce the price: it is now sold in bottles, 1s. 1½d., 2s. 9d., 4s. 6d., and 11s.

CAUTION.—None genuine without the words "DR. J. COLLIS BROWNE'S CHLORODYNE" on the Government Stamp. Overwhelming Medical Testimony accompanies each bottle.

SOLE MANUFACTURER:

J. T. Davenport, 33, Great Russell Street, Bloomsbury, London.

www.ingramcontent.com/pod-product-compliance
Lightning Source LLC
Chambersburg PA
CBHW030604300426
44111CB00009B/1100